Study Guide
with
PowerPoint® Lecture Outlines

for

Henslin

Sociology
A Down-to-Earth Approach

Ninth Edition

prepared by

Shelly Dutchin
Western Wisconsin Technical College

Dan Cavanaugh

PEARSON

Boston   New York   San Francisco
Mexico City   Montreal   Toronto   London   Madrid   Munich   Paris
Hong Kong   Singapore   Tokyo   Cape Town   Sydney

ISBN-13: 978-0-205-57040-9
ISBN-10:   0-205-57040-2

Printed in the United States of America

10 9 8 7 6 5 4 3 2 1   11 10 09 08 07

Contents

CHAPTER 1
THE SOCIOLOGICAL PERSPECTIVE

CHAPTER SUMMARY

- Sociology offers a perspective that stresses the social contexts in which people live and how these contexts influence people's lives. For C. Wright Mills, this is the interaction of biography and history.

- Sociology is the scientific study of society and human behavior, and, as such, is one of the social sciences, which study human behavior. In contrast, the natural sciences focus on nature.

- Sociology is different from the other social sciences because sociology focuses primarily on industrialized societies, does not look at only a single social institution, and focuses on factors external to the individual.

- The study of sociology emerged during the upheavals of the Industrial Revolution. Early sociologists such as Auguste Comte, Herbert Spencer, Karl Marx, Emile Durkheim, Max Weber, and Harriet Martineau focused on how the sweeping social changes brought about by the Industrial Revolution affected human behavior.

- Sociologists agree that sociological research should be value free but disagree concerning the proper purposes and uses of social research. Some believe its purpose should be only to advance understanding of human behavior; others feel that its goal should be to reform harmful social arrangements.

- Weber believed that sociologists must try to see the world from another's perspective in order to understand their behavior (*Verstehen*); Durkheim stressed the importance of uncovering the objective social conditions that influence behavior (social facts).

- During the early years of sociology, only a few wealthy women received an advanced education. Harriet Martineau was an Englishwoman who wrote about social life in Great Britain and the United States and published a book entitled *Society in America*.

- At the end of the nineteenth century in North America, departments of sociology began to be established. In the early years, the contributions of women and minorities were largely ignored.

- Pure sociology is research whose only purpose is to make discoveries; applied sociology is the use of sociology to solve social problems in settings ranging from the work place to the family.

- A theory is a general statement about how sets of facts are related to one another. Because no one theory encompasses all of reality, sociologists use three primary theoretical frameworks: (1) symbolic interactionism, which concentrates on the use of symbols and focuses on the micro level; (2) functional analysis, which stresses that society is made up of various parts which, when working properly, contribute to the stability of society and focuses on the macro level; and (3) conflict theory, which emphasizes that social life is based on a competitive struggle to gain control over scarce resources, and also focuses on the macro level.

- A tension between social reform and social analysis has always run through sociology. The American Sociological Association is promoting public sociology to make politicians more aware of the sociological perspective.

- Globalization is also leaving its mark on sociology and will likely direct sociologists to give greater consideration to global issues.

LEARNING OBJECTIVES

1. Explain the sociological perspective: what it is, what it offers, and why C. Wright Mills referred to it as "the intersection of biography (the individual) and history (the social factors that influence the individual)." (4)
2. Know what is meant by social location and how it helps people define themselves and others define them. (4)
3. Understand how sociology is applicable to the growing global world. (5)
4. Identify, understand, and make distinctions between the natural sciences and the social sciences. (5)
5. Understand how sociology views and studies human behavior and how its particular areas of focus are different from the other social sciences. (6-7)
6. Identify and explain the goals of science. (7)
7. Discuss the social changes and social conditions which fostered the development of sociology as a distinct academic discipline in the middle of the nineteenth century. (8-9)
8. Identify and critique the sociological contributions of the following mid- to late-nineteenth and early twentieth century European sociologists: Auguste Comte, Herbert Spencer, Karl Marx, Emile Durkheim, and Max Weber. (10-13)
9. Understand how and why levels of social integration may affect rates of suicide and how Emile Durkheim's nineteenth century study of suicide helped demonstrate how social forces affect people's behaviors. (12-13)
10. Explain the role of values in social research as prescribed by Max Weber, and the ensuing controversies over whether sociological research can be and/or should be value free.(14)
11. Distinguish between "*Verstehen*," as envisioned by Max Weber, and "social facts," as defined by Emile Durkheim; explain how, despite their differences, both can be used together in social research. (15-16)
12. Discuss why there were so few women sociologists in the nineteenth and early twentieth century, and how the contributions of women sociologists, such as Harriet Martineau, during this time were received and evaluated by their male counterparts. (16-17)

13. Trace the history of sociology in North America from the late 1800s to the present time, identifying the specific sociological contributions of the following American sociologists: Jane Addams, W.E.B. Du Bois, Talcott Parsons, and C. Wright Mills. (18-21)

14. Understand the historical tensions and ongoing debates in North American sociology between social reform and social analysis, and how the sociological contributions of Jane Addams, W.E.B. Du Bois, Talcott Parsons, and C. Wright Mills fit into these tensions and debates. (18-21)

15. Discuss the current state of American sociology as it relates to the debate between social reform and social analysis and what role applied sociology plays in this debate. (21-22)

16. Explain what applied sociology is and some of the careers that applied sociologists may have. (22)

17. Discuss how U.S. intelligence officers used network analysis to locate Saddam Hussein. (23)

18. Define what is meant by theory and explain why it is an important part of sociology. (22-23)

19. Identify the three major theoretical perspectives in sociology — symbolic interactionism, functional analysis, and conflict theory — and describe the particular level of analysis, characteristics, viewpoints, and concerns that are associated with each of these. (23-30)

20. Apply each of the three sociological perspectives to a contemporary issue such as the increasing rates of divorce in America. (33-30)

21. Explain the relationship of sociology to the reforming of society and identify the three stages sociology has gone through. (31-32)

22. Explain why the American Sociological Association is promoting public sociology. (32)

23. Describe the current trends that are shaping the future of sociology in the United States, and how globalization, in particular, may expand American sociologys' horizons in the twenty-first century. (33)

KEY TERMS

applied sociology: the use of sociology to solve problems — from the micro level of   family relationships to the macro level of crime and pollution (21)

basic or pure sociology: sociological research whose only purpose is to make discoveries about life in human groups, not to make changes in those groups (21)

bourgeoisie: Karl Marx's term for capitalists; those who own the means to produce wealth (11)

class conflict: Marx's term for the struggle between the capitalist and workers (11)

common sense: those things that "everyone knows" are true (8)

conflict theory: a theoretical framework in which society is viewed as composed of groups competing for scarce resources (29)

functional analysis: a theoretical framework in which society is viewed as composed of various parts, each with a function that, when fulfilled, contributes to society's equilibrium; also known as functionalism and structural functionalism (26)

generalization: a statement that goes beyond the individual case and is applied to a broader group or situation (7)

globalization: the extensive interconnections among nations due to the expansion of capitalism (33)

globalization of capitalism: capitalism (investing to make profits within a rational system) booming the globe's dominant economic system (33)

macro-level analysis: an examination of large-scale patterns of society (30)

micro-level analysis: an examination of small-scale patterns of society (30)

natural sciences: the intellectual and academic disciplines designed to comprehend, explain, and predict events in our natural environment (5)

nonverbal interaction: communication, without words, through gestures, space, silence, and so on (30)

objectivity: total neutrality (14)

patterns: recurring characteristics or events (7)

positivism: the application of the scientific approach to the social world (10)

proletariat: Marx's term for the exploited class, the mass of workers who do not own the means of production (11)

replication: repeating a study in order to check its findings (14)

science: the application of systematic methods to obtain knowledge and the knowledge obtained by those methods (5)

scientific method: the use of objective, systematic observations to test theories (10)

social facts: Durkheim's term for a group's patterns of behavior (15)

social integration: the degree to which members of a group of society feel united by shared values and other social bonds; also known as social cohesion (12)

social interaction: what people do when they are in one another's presence (30)

social location: the group memberships that people have because of their location in history and society (4)

social sciences: the intellectual and academic disciplines designed to understand the social world objectively by means of controlled and repeated observations (6)

society: a term used by sociologists to refer to a group of people who share a culture and a territory (4)

sociological perspective: understanding human behavior by placing it within its broader social context (4)

sociology: the scientific study of society and human behavior (10)

subjective meanings: the meanings that people give to their own behavior (15)

symbolic interactionism: a theoretical perspective in which society is viewed as composed of symbols that people use to establish meaning, develop their views of the world, and communicate with one another (22)

theory: a general statement about how some parts of the world fit together and how they work; an explanation of how two or more facts are related to one another (22)

value free: the view that a sociologist's personal values or biases should not influence social research (14)

values: the standards by which people define what is desirable or undesirable, good or bad, beautiful or ugly (14)

***Verstehen*:** a German word used by Weber that is perhaps best understood as "to have insight into someone's situation" (15)

KEY PEOPLE

Jane Addams: Addams was the founder of Hull House — a settlement house in the immigrant community of Chicago. She invited sociologists from the nearby University of Chicago to visit. In 1931 she was a winner of the Nobel Peace Prize. (18-19)

Ernest Burgess and Harvey Locke: Research by these early sociologists documented a fundamental shift that was occurring in the symbolic meaning of U.S. marriages. They found that marriage was increasingly dependent on mutual affection, understanding, and compatibility. (24)

Auguste Comte: Comte is often credited with being the founder of sociology because he was the first to suggest that the scientific method be applied to the study of the social world. (10)

Charles Horton Cooley: One of the founders of symbolic interactionism, a major theoretical perspective in sociology. (23)

Lewis Coser: Coser pointed out that conflict is likely to develop among people in close relationships because they are connected by a network of responsibilities, power and rewards. (29)

W. E. B. Du Bois: Du Bois was the first African American to earn a doctorate at Harvard University. He was concerned about social injustice, wrote about race relations, and was one of the founders of the National Association for the Advancement of Colored People (NAACP). (18-19)

Emile Durkheim: Durkheim was responsible for getting sociology recognized as a separate discipline. He was interested in studying how individual behavior is shaped by social forces and in finding remedies for social ills. To do so, he conducted rigorous research on suicide in several European countries. (12-13, 15)

Harriet Martineau: An Englishwoman who studied British and U.S. social life, Martineau published *Society in America* decades before either Durkheim or Weber were born. She is known primarily for translating Auguste Comte's ideas into English. (17)

Karl Marx: Marx believed that social development grew out of conflict between social classes; under capitalism, this conflict was between the bourgeoisie — those who own the means to produce wealth — and the proletariat — the mass of workers. His work is associated with the conflict perspective. (11, 29)

George Herbert Mead: Mead was one of the founders of symbolic interactionism, a major theoretical perspective in sociology. (18, 24)

Robert Merton: Merton contributed the terms *manifest* and *latent functions* and *dysfunctions* to the functionalist perspective. (26-27)

C. Wright Mills: Mills suggested that external influences (a person's experiences) become part of his or her thinking and motivations and explain social behavior. He saw the emergence of the power elite composed of top leaders of business, politics and the military as an imminent threat to freedom. (4, 21)

William Ogburn: As early as 1933, Ogburn noted that personality was becoming more important in mate selection; this supported the symbolic interactionists' argument that there was a fundamental shift in the symbolic meaning of U.S. marriages. (24)

Talcott Parsons: Parsons' work dominated sociology in the 1940s and 1950s. He developed abstract models of how the parts of society harmoniously work together. (21)

Albion Small: Small was the founder of the sociology department at the University of Chicago and the *American Journal of Sociology*. (18)

Herbert Spencer: Another early sociologist, Spencer believed that societies evolve from barbarian to civilized forms. He was the first to use the expression "the survival of the fittest". His views became known as *social Darwinism*. (10)

William I. Thomas: Along with Mead and Cooley, Thomas was important in establishing symbolic interactionism as a major theoretical perspective in sociology. (23)

Max Weber: Weber's most important contribution to sociology was his study of the relationship between the emergence of the Protestant belief system and the rise of capitalism. He believed that sociologists should not allow their personal values to affect their social research; objectivity should become the hallmark of sociology. He argued that sociologists should use *Verstehen* — those subjective meanings that people give to their behavior. (13-16)

PRACTICE TEST

1. An approach to understanding human behavior by placing it within its broader social context is known as: (4)
    a. social location.
    b. the sociological perspective.
    c. common sense.
    d. generalization.

2. Sociologists consider occupation, income, education, gender, age, and race as: (4)
    a. insignificant aspects of social life.
    b. constant features of individual well-being.
    c. influential in shaping society.
    d. dimensions of social location.

3. How is sociology different from the other social sciences? (7)
    a   it focuses on a single institution.
    b. it focuses on factors external to the individual.
    c. it focuses primarily on pre-industrial societies.
    d. it focuses on biological factors that influence human behavior.

4. By what year had Europe begun to change from agricultural to factory production? (9)
    a. 1650
    b. 1900
    c. 1850
    d. 1775

5. Who is often referred to as the founder of sociology? (10)
    a. Emile Durkheim
    b. Max Weber
    c. Sigmund Freud
    d. August Comte

6. Karl Marx referred to the controlling class, who own the means to produce wealth, as the: (11)
    a. upper class.
    b. Republicans.
    c. bourgeoisie.
    d. proletariats.

7. How did Marx believe that the workers could gain control of society? (11)
    a. through having a strong leader
    b. by being more involved in the election process
    c. by forming unions
    d. through revolution

8. Emile Durkheim's study of suicide made the key contribution to advancing knowledge about individual behavior by proving that: (12-13)
    a. individual behaviors have the same patterns within a country, but different patterns in comparison to other countries.
    b. strong social bonds always help people, even to the extent of always protecting them from committing suicide.
    c. individuals have free will, hence there are never patterns to their behavior.
    d. human behavior must be studied in the context of the social forces that affect people's lives.

9. Max Weber's insistence that sociology be value free, focuses on: (14)
    a. religious freedom.
    b. sociologists having no individual values of their own.
    c. society's accepting all values without showing favoritism towards a particular value.
    d. objectivity in research.

10. The best way to ensure that sociological studies are objective is through: (14)
    a. honesty.
    b. replication.
    c. subjectivity.
    d. validity.

11. Social facts and *Verstehen*: (15)
    a. have no relationship to each other.
    b. have been disproved.
    c. go hand-in-hand.
    d. were both concepts developed by Durkheim.

12. Harriet Martineau's book, *Society in America:* (17)
    a. contained significant insights about gender inequality which were not seen by most others until the latter part of the 20th century.
    b. establishes that no book on gender inequality was written until after 1950.
    c. was based on her opinions rather than any type of data gathering, such as interviews.
    d. is best seen as an argument against feminism theory.

13. Jane Addams is primarily known for: (18)
    a. translating Comte's ideas into English.
    b. her emphasis on positivism.
    c. working for social justice.
    d. working with the mentally ill.

14. W. E. B. Du Bois is an example of a sociologist who: (18-19)
    a. developed a strong critique against Marxism.
    b. utilized the functionalist perspective in his research.
    c. based all his writings on editorial opinions rather than objective research.
    d. served in the role as both researcher and social activist.

15. In the 1940s the central focus of sociology: (21)
    a. shifted from data gathering to social activism.
    b. shifted from social reform to social theory.
    c. shifted from theories developed in America to theories developed in Europe.
    d. shifted from predicting behavior to explaining behavior.

16. Sociologists who research social problems for government commissions or agencies are: (21)
    a. politically correct.
    b. basic sociologists.
    c. applied sociologists.
    d. pure sociologists.

17 What method did U.S. intelligence agents use to locate Saddam Hussein: (23)
    a. DNA identification.
    b. network analysis.
    c. dramaturgical analysis.
    d. psychological profiling.

18. Which sociologist observed that personality was becoming more important in mate selection? (24)
    a. Karl Marx
    b. William Ogburn
    c. Herbert Spencer
    d. Robert Edgerton

19. Industrialization and urbanization have undermined the traditional purposes of the family, according to theorists using _____ analysis. (26)
    a. conflict
    b. exchange
    c. symbolic interaction
    d. functional

20. Which of the following **is not** a function of the family? (27-28)
    a. economic production
    b. locating a prospective spouse for children
    c. sexual control
    d. recreation

21. Functionalists and conflict theorists focus on what level of patterns in society? (30)
    a. micro level
    b. macro level
    c. primary
    d. secondary

22. According to your text, which theoretical perspective is best for studying human behavior? (31)
    a. the functionalist perspective
    b. the symbolic interactionist perspective
    c. the conflict perspective
    d. a combination of all of the above.

23. The first phase of sociology in the United States was characterized by: (29)
    a. a concern with establishing sociology as a social science.
    b. a focus on establishing sociology as a respectable field of knowledge.
    c. an interest in using sociological knowledge to improve social life and change society.
    d. a broad acceptance of women and racial minorities within the discipline.

24. What was the goal in the second stage of the development of sociology? (31)
    a. making sociology a respected field of knowledge
    b. the importance of conducting social research
    c. making laws based on sociological research
    d. none of the above.

25. What is the American Sociological Association promoting? (32)
    a. globalization
    b. cultural diversity
    c. the use of technology
    d. public sociology

Answer Key

1. B
2. D
3. B
4. C
5. D
6. C
7. D
8. D
9. D
10. B
11. C
12. A
13. C
14. D
15. B
16. C
17. B
18. B
19. D
20. B
21. B
22. D
23. C
24. A
25. D

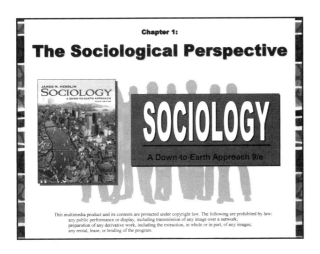

Chapter 1:
The Sociological Perspective

SOCIOLOGY

A Down-to-Earth Approach 9/e

This multimedia product and its contents are protected under copyright law. The following are prohibited by law: any public performance or display, including transmission of any image over a network; preparation of any derivative work, including the extraction, in whole or in part, of any images; any rental, lease, or lending of the program.

Seeing the Broader Social Context

❋ **How Groups Influence People**

❋ **How People are Influenced by Their Society**

   ❋   **People Who Share a Culture**

   ❋   **People Who Share a Territory**

Copyright © Allyn & Bacon 2008   Chapter 1: The Sociological Perspective   2

Social Location - Corners in Life

❋ **Jobs**   ❋ **Gender**

❋ **Income**   ❋ **Age**

❋ **Education**   ❋ **Race/Ethnicity**

Copyright © Allyn & Bacon 2008   Chapter 1: The Sociological Perspective   3

C. Wright Mills - History and Biography

✳ History—Location in Broad

Stream of Events

✳ Biography—Individual's

Specific Experiences

Copyright © Allyn & Bacon 2008   Chapter 1: The Sociological Perspective

The Global Context and the Local

✳ The Global Village

✳ Instant Communication

✳ Sociology Studies both the Global

Network and Our Unique Experiences

Copyright © Allyn & Bacon 2008   Chapter 1: The Sociological Perspective

Sociology and the Other Sciences

✳ The Natural Sciences—Explain and

Predict Events in Natural Environment

✳ The Social Sciences—Examine Human

Relationships

Copyright © Allyn & Bacon 2008   Chapter 1: The Sociological Perspective

Sociology and the Other Sciences

* **Anthropology - Studies Culture**

* **Economics - Studies the Production and Distribution of Goods and Services**

* **Political Science - Studies How People Govern Themselves**

Copyright © Allyn & Bacon 2008   Chapter 1: The Sociological Perspective   7

Sociology and the Other Sciences

* **Psychology - The Study of Processes Within Individuals**

* **Sociology - Similarities to Other Disciplines**

Copyright © Allyn & Bacon 2008   Chapter 1: The Sociological Perspective   8

The Goal of Science

* **Explain Why Something Happens**

* **Make Generalizations**

* **Look for Patterns**

* **Predict What will Happen**

* **Move Beyond Common Sense**

Copyright © Allyn & Bacon 2008   Chapter 1: The Sociological Perspective   9

Risks of Sociology

❋ **Nooks and Crannies People Prefer Hidden**

❋ **People Attempt to Keep Secrets**

❋ **People Feel Threatened by Information**

Copyright © Allyn & Bacon 2008   Chapter 1: The Sociological Perspective   10

Origins of Sociology

❋ **Tradition vs. Science**

❋ **Emerged mid-1800s**

❋ **Grow Out of Social Upheaval**

❋ **Rethinking of Social Life**

❋ **The Success of Natural Sciences**

Copyright © Allyn & Bacon 2008   Chapter 1: The Sociological Perspective   11

Auguste Comte and Positivism

❋ **Applying the Scientific Method to Social World**

❋ **Coined the Term "Sociology"**

❋ **"Armchair Philosophy"**

Copyright © Allyn & Bacon 2008   Chapter 1: The Sociological Perspective   12

Herbert Spencer - Social Darwinism

✳ **Second Founder of Sociology**

✳ **Lower and Higher Forms of Society**

✳ **Coined Phrase "Survival of the Fittest"**

Copyright © Allyn & Bacon 2008   Chapter 1: The Sociological Perspective   13

Karl Marx and Class Conflict

✳ **Engine of Human History is Class Conflict**

✳ **The Bourgeoisie vs. The Proletariat**

✳ **Marxism Not the Same as Communism**

Copyright © Allyn & Bacon 2008   Chapter 1: The Sociological Perspective   14

Durkheim and Social Integration

✳ **Got Sociology Recognized as Separate Discipline**

✳ **Studied How Social Forces Affect Behavior**

✳ **Identified "Social Integration" – Degree to Which People are Tied to Social Group**

Copyright © Allyn & Bacon 2008   Chapter 1: The Sociological Perspective   15

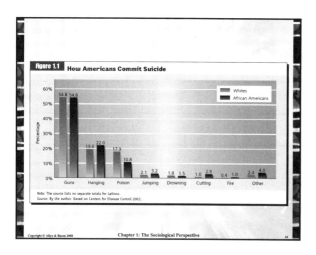

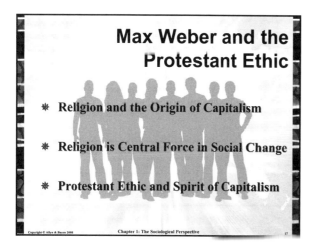

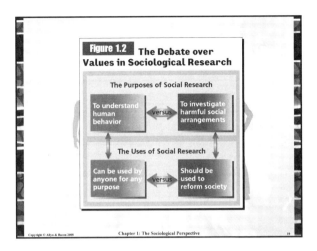

Figure 1.2 The Debate over Values in Sociological Research

The Purposes of Social Research

To understand human behavior ←versus→ To investigate harmful social arrangements

The Uses of Social Research

Can be used by anyone for any purpose ←versus→ Should be used to reform society

Copyright © Allyn & Bacon 2008   Chapter 1: The Sociological Perspective   19

Verstehen and Social Facts

* Weber
  * Verstehen - "To Grasp by Insight"
  * Importance of Subjective Meanings
* Durkheim
  * Stressed Social Facts
  * Explain Social Facts with Other Social Facts
* How Social Facts and Verstehen Fit Together

Copyright © Allyn & Bacon 2008   Chapter 1: The Sociological Perspective   20

Sexism in Early Sociology

* Attitudes of the Time
  * 1800s Sex Roles Rigidly Defined
  * Few People Educated Beyond Basics
* Harriet Martineau
  * Published Society in America Before Durkheim and Weber Were Born
  * Her Work was Ignored

Copyright © Allyn & Bacon 2008   Chapter 1: The Sociological Perspective   21

Sociology in North America

* Early History: Tension Between Social Reform and Sociological Analysis
* Jane Addams and Social Reform
* W. E. B. Du Bois and Race Relations
* Talcott Parsons and C. Wright Mills: Theory vs. Reform
* Continuing Tension and Rise of Applied Sociology

Copyright © Allyn & Bacon 2008　　Chapter 1: The Sociological Perspective　　22

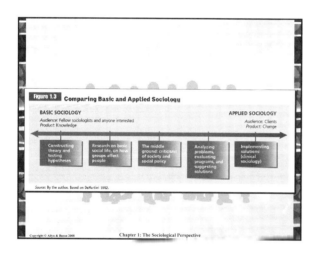

Figure 1.3 Comparing Basic and Applied Sociology

BASIC SOCIOLOGY
Audience: Fellow sociologists and anyone interested
Product: Knowledge

APPLIED SOCIOLOGY
Audience: Clients
Product: Change

Constructing theory and testing hypotheses | Research on basic social life, on how groups affect people | The middle ground: criticism of society and social policy | Analyzing problems, evaluating programs, and suggesting solutions | Implementing solutions (clinical sociology)

Source: By the author. Based on DeMartini 1982.

Copyright © Allyn & Bacon 2008　　Chapter 1: The Sociological Perspective

Theoretical Perspectives

* Symbolic Interactionism - How People Use Symbols in Everyday Life
* Applying Symbolic Interactionism - Changing the Meaning of Symbols Affects Expectations
* Network Analysis and the Capturing of Saddam Hussein

Copyright © Allyn & Bacon 2008　　Chapter 1: The Sociological Perspective　　24

Applying Symbolic Interactionism - Examples

* **Emotional Satisfaction**

* **The Love Symbol**

* **The Meaning of Children**

* **The Meaning of Parenthood**

Chapter 1: The Sociological Perspective 25

Applying Symbolic Interactionism - Examples

* **Marital Roles**

* **Perception of Alternatives**

* **The Meaning of Divorce**

Chapter 1: The Sociological Perspective 26

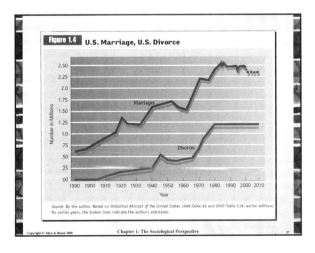

Figure 1.4 U.S. Marriage, U.S. Divorce

Source: By the author. Based on *Statistical Abstract of the United States* 1998:Table 92 and 2007:Table 119; earlier editions for earlier years. the broken lines indicate the author's estimates.

Chapter 1: The Sociological Perspective 27

Applying Symbolic Interactionism - Examples

* **Marital Roles**

* **Perception of Alternatives**

* **The Meaning of Divorce**

* **Changes in the Law**

Copyright © Allyn & Bacon 2008   Chapter 1: The Sociological Perspective   28

_____

_____

_____

_____

_____

_____

_____

Functional Analysis

* **Society is a Whole Unit Made Up of Interrelated Parts that Work Together**

* **Functionalism, Structural Functionalism**

Copyright © Allyn & Bacon 2008   Chapter 1: The Sociological Perspective   29

_____

_____

_____

_____

_____

_____

_____

Robert Merton and Functionalism

* **Functions**
  * Manifest
  * Latent

* **Dysfunctions**

Copyright © Allyn & Bacon 2008   Chapter 1: The Sociological Perspective   30

_____

_____

_____

_____

_____

_____

_____

_____

Applying Functional Analysis

❋ **Economic Production**

❋ **Socialization of Children**

❋ **Care of the Sick and Elderly**

Copyright © Allyn & Bacon 2008   Chapter 1: The Sociological Perspective   31

Applying Functional Analysis

❋ **Recreation**

❋ **Sexual Control**

❋ **Reproduction**

Copyright © Allyn & Bacon 2008   Chapter 1: The Sociological Perspective   32

Applying Functional Analysis

❋ **A Glimpse of the Past - 1800s**

❋ **Changes in the Functions of…**

　＊ **Family**

　＊ **Friends**

Copyright © Allyn & Bacon 2008   Chapter 1: The Sociological Perspective   33

Conflict Theory

* **Karl Marx and Conflict Theory**

* **Conflict Theory Today**

* **Feminists and Conflict Theory**

* **Applying Conflict Theory**

Copyright © Allyn & Bacon 2008   Chapter 1: The Sociological Perspective   34

Lovolo of Analysis

* **Functionalists and Conflict Theorists - Macro Level**

* **Symbolic Interactionists - Micro Level**

Copyright © Allyn & Bacon 2008   Chapter 1: The Sociological Perspective

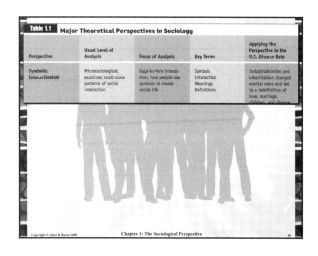

Table 1.1	Major Theoretical Perspectives in Sociology			
Perspective	Usual Level of Analysis	Focus of Analysis	Key Terms	Applying the Perspective to the U.S. Divorce Rate
Symbolic Interactionism	Microsociological: examines small-scale patterns of social interaction	Face-to-face interaction, how people use symbols to create social life	Symbols Interaction Meanings Definitions	Industrialization and urbanization changed marital roles and led to a redefinition of love, marriage, children, and divorce

Copyright © Allyn & Bacon 2008   Chapter 1: The Sociological Perspective   36

Table 1.1 — Major Theoretical Perspectives in Sociology

Perspective	Usual Level of Analysis	Focus of Analysis	Key Terms	Applying the Perspective to the U.S. Divorce Rate
Symbolic Interactionism	Microsociological: examines small-scale patterns of social interaction	Face-to-face interaction, how people use symbols to create social life	Symbols Interaction Meanings Definitions	Industrialization and urbanization changed marital roles and led to a redefinition of love, marriage, children, and divorce.
Functional Analysis (also called functionalism and structural functionalism)	Macrosociological: examines large-scale patterns of society	Relationships among the parts of society; how these parts are functional (have beneficial consequences) or dysfunctional (have negative consequences)	Structure Functions (manifest and latent) Dysfunctions Equilibrium	As social change erodes the traditional functions of the family, family ties weaken, and the divorce rate increases.

Copyright © Allyn & Bacon 2008   Chapter 1: The Sociological Perspective   27

Table 1.1 — Major Theoretical Perspectives in Sociology

Perspective	Usual Level of Analysis	Focus of Analysis	Key Terms	Applying the Perspective to the U.S. Divorce Rate
Symbolic Interactionism	Microsociological: examines small-scale patterns of social interaction	Face-to-face interaction, how people use symbols to create social life	Symbols Interaction Meanings Definitions	Industrialization and urbanization changed marital roles and led to a redefinition of love, marriage, children, and divorce.
Functional Analysis (also called functionalism and structural functionalism)	Macrosociological: examines large-scale patterns of society	Relationships among the parts of society; how these parts are functional (have beneficial consequences) or dysfunctional (have negative consequences)	Structure Functions (manifest and latent) Dysfunctions Equilibrium	As social change erodes the traditional functions of the family, family ties weaken, and the divorce rate increases.
Conflict Theory	Macrosociological: examines large-scale patterns of society	The struggle for scarce resources by groups in a society; how the elites use their power to control the weaker groups	Inequality Power Conflict Competition Exploitation	When men control economic life, the divorce rate is low because women find few alternatives to a bad marriage. The high divorce rate reflects a shift in the balance of power between men and women.

Copyright © Allyn & Bacon 2008   Chapter 1: The Sociological Perspective   28

Trends Shaping the Future

* **Sociology Full Circle: Reform vs. Research - Three Stages**
* **Public Sociology**
* **Diversity of Orientations**
* **Globalization**

Copyright © Allyn & Bacon 2008   Chapter 1: The Sociological Perspective   29

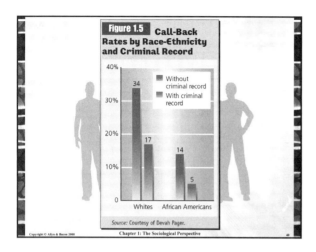

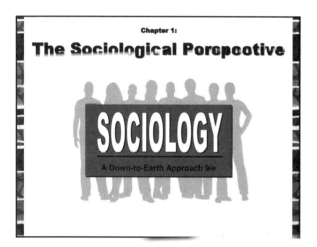

CHAPTER 2
CULTURE

CHAPTER SUMMARY

- Culture is universal; all human groups create a design for living that includes both material and nonmaterial culture. Material culture consists of such things as jewelry, art, buildings and weapons. Non-material culture consists of a groups' way of thinking and doing, and patterns of behavior, including language, gestures, and other forms of interaction.

- Ideal culture, a group's ideal norms and values, exists alongside its real culture, the actual behavior that often falls short of the cultural ideals.

- All people perceive and evaluate the world through the lens of their own culture. People are naturally ethnocentric; that is, they use their own culture as a standard against which to judge other cultures. In comparison, cultural relativism tries to understand other peoples within the framework of their own culture.

- The central component of nonmaterial culture is symbols—anything to which people attach meaning and use to communicate with one another. Included in nonmaterial culture are gestures, language, values, norms, sanctions, folkways, and mores. Language allows culture to exist and human experiences to be cumulative; it provides a social or shared past and future, allows shared perspectives and complex, shared, goal-directed behavior.

- According to the Sapir-Whorf hypothesis, language determines our consciousness and therefore our perception of objects and events.

- All groups have values and norms and use positive and negative sanctions to show approval or disapproval of those who do or don't follow the norms.

- Norms that aren't strictly enforced are known as folkways while those norms that are strongly ingrained are known as taboos.

- A subculture is a group whose values and behaviors set it apart from the general culture; a counterculture holds values that stand in opposition to the dominant culture.

- Although the U.S. is a pluralistic society made up of many groups, each with its own set of values, certain core values dominate. Sociologist Robin Williams has identified 12 core values, and some cluster together to form a larger whole. Core values that contradict one another indicate areas of social tension and are likely points of social change.

- A value cluster of four interrelated core values is emerging along with a fifth value, concern for the environment.

- Cultural universals are values, norms or other cultural traits that are found in all cultures.

- Cultural lag refers to a condition in which a group's nonmaterial culture lags behind its changing technology. Today the technology in travel and communication makes cultural diffusion occur more rapidly around the globe than in the past, resulting in some degree of cultural leveling, a process by which cultures become similar to one another.

LEARNING OBJECTIVES

After reading Chapter 2, you should be able to:

1. Understand what is meant by the term culture. (38)
2. Distinguish between material and nonmaterial culture. (38)
3. Know what is meant by cultural shock, provide examples of situations that may result in cultural shock, and explain how cultural shock forces people to challenge their own cultural assumptions. (39)
4. Define ethnocentrism and cultural relativism, offer examples of both concepts, and list the positive and negative consequences of each. (39-42)
5. List and explain the principles of culture. (40-41)
6. List the components of symbolic culture. (44)
7. Define—and differentiate between—gestures and language. (44-45)
8. Explain why language is the basis of culture, including why it is critical to human life and essential for cultural development. (45-48)
9. Explain the Sapir-Whorf hypothesis and provide examples of how language not only reflects and expresses thinking, perceptions, and experiences, but also shapes and influences them. (48)
10. Define values, norms, sanctions, folkways, mores, and taboos; provide examples of each; and discuss their sociological significance. (48-50)
11. Compare, contrast, and offer examples of dominant cultures, subcultures, and countercultures. (51-52)
12. List the core values in American society as identified by Robin Williams and supplemented by James Henslin. (53)
13. Explain what is meant by value clusters and value contradictions, and offer examples of some value clusters and value contradictions in American society. (56-57)
14. Understand how value contradictions can affect social change. (58)
15. Discuss the differences between "ideal" and "real" culture. (58)
16. Define and identify some cultural universals and discuss how carrying out universal human activities may differ from one group to another. (59)
17. List some current "new technologies" and talk about how they are changing social behaviors and relationships in the United States and around the world. (60)
18. Define and discuss cultural lag and cultural change (61)
19. Discuss the role that technology has played in cultural diffusion and cultural leveling. (61-62)

KEY TERMS
After studying the chapter, review the definition for each of the following terms.

counterculture: a group whose values, beliefs, and related behaviors place its members in opposition to the values of the broader culture (52)

cultural diffusion: the spread of cultural characteristics from one group to another (61)

cultural lag: William Ogburn's term for human behavior lagging behind technological innovations (61)

cultural leveling: the process by which cultures become similar to one another; refers especially to the process by which U.S. culture is being exported and diffused into other nations (62)

cultural relativism: not judging a culture, but trying to understand it on its own terms (41)

cultural universal: a value, norm, or other cultural trait that is found in every group (59)

culture: the language, beliefs, values, norms, behaviors, and even material objects that are passed from one generation to the next (38)

culture shock: the disorientation that people experience when they come in contact with a fundamentally different culture and can no longer depend on their taken-for-granted assumptions about life (39)

ethnocentrism: the use of one's own culture as a yardstick for judging the ways of other individuals or societies, generally leading to a negative evaluation of their values, norms, and behaviors (39)

folkways: norms that are not strictly enforced (50)

gestures: the ways in which people use their bodies to communicate with one another (44)

ideal culture: the ideal values and norms of a people, the goals held out for them (58)

language: a system of symbols that can be combined in an infinite number of ways and can represent not only objects but also abstract thought (45)

material culture: the material objects that distinguish a group of people, such as their art, buildings, weapons, utensils, machines, hairstyles, clothing, and jewelry (38)

mores: norms that are strictly enforced because they are thought essential to core values or the well-being of the group (50)

negative sanction: an expression of disapproval for breaking a norm, ranging from a mild, informal reaction such as a frown to a formal prison sentence or an execution (48)

new technology: the emerging technologies of an era that have a significant impact on social life (60)

nonmaterial culture: (also called symbolic culture) a group's ways of thinking (including its beliefs, values, and other assumptions about the world) and doing (its common patterns of behavior, including language and other forms of interaction) (38)

norms: the expectations, or rules of behavior, that reflect and enforce values (48)

pluralistic society: a society made up of many different groups (52)

positive sanction: a reward or positive reaction for following norms, ranging from a smile to a prize (48)

real culture: the norms and values that people actually follow (59)

sanctions: expressions of approval or disapproval given to people for upholding or violating norms (48)

Sapir-Whorf hypothesis: Edward Sapir and Benjamin Whorf's hypothesis that language creates ways of thinking and perceiving (48)

sociobiology: a framework of thought that views human behavior as the result of natural selection and considers biological characteristics to be the fundamental cause of human behavior (59)

subculture: the values and related behaviors of a group that distinguish its members from the larger culture; a world within a world (51)

symbol: something to which people attach meaning and then use to communicate with others (44)

symbolic culture: another term for nonmaterial culture (44)

taboo: a norm so strong that it brings revulsion if it is violated (50)

technology: in its narrow sense, tools; its broader sense includes the skills or procedures necessary to make and use those tools (60)

value clusters: a series of interrelated values that together form a larger whole (56)

value contradictions: values that conflict with one another; to follow the one means to come into conflict with the other (56)

values: the standards by which people define what is desirable or undesirable, good or bad, beautiful or ugly (48)

KEY PEOPLE
Review the major theoretical contributions or findings of these people.

Peter Conrad: He notes that not all homosexuals have the Xq28, "gay gene", and some people who have this gene are not homosexual. This gene does not determine behavior and social causes should be examined. (59-60)

Charles Darwin: Darwin studied the principles on which natural selection occurred. (59)

Robert Edgerton: Edgerton attacks the concept of cultural relativism, suggesting that because some cultures endanger their people's health, happiness, or survival, there should be a scale to evaluate cultures on their "quality of life." (42)

Douglas Massey: This sociologist has studied the impact that immigration is having on Miami, predicting that the city will become the first "truly bilingual" city. (47)

George Murdock: Murdock was an anthropologist who sought to determine which cultural values, norms, or traits, if any, were found universally across the globe. (59)

William Ogburn: Ogburn coined the term "cultural lag." He felt that sometimes the nonmaterial culture never catches up to the material changes. (61)

Edward Sapir and Benjamin Whorf: These two anthropologists argued that language not only reflects thoughts and perceptions, but that it actually shapes the way people think and perceive the world. (48)

JoEllen Shively: This sociologist's research demonstrated that Native Americans' identification with cowboys in Westerns was based on the symbolism of the West as a free, natural way of life. She discovered that they think of themselves as the real cowboys. (56)

William Sumner: Sumner developed the concept of ethnocentrism. (39)

Robin Williams: He identified twelve core U.S. values that are shared by most of the groups that make up U.S. society. (52-53)

Edward Wilson: Wilson is an insect specialist who claims that human behavior is also the result of natural selection. (59-60)

Eviatar Zerubavel: This sociologist offers an example of how language shapes our perceptions of the world (the *Sapir-Whorf hypothesis*). He notes that in his native Hebrew, there is no distinction made between the two forms of fruit spread — jams and jellies. It was only when he learned English that he was able to "see" the differences that were so obvious to English speakers. (48)

PRACTICE TEST

1. Clothing, jewelry, and hairstyles are examples of: (38)
    a. material culture.
    b. nonmaterial culture.
    c. folkways.
    d. technology.

2. An emphasis on the "culture within us" can often lead to: (39)
    a. ethnocentrism.
    b. cultural relativism.
    c. objectively understanding other cultures.
    d. only the negative consequences of ethnocentrism.

3. Which of these statements regarding culture is *not* true? (40-41)
    a. people generally are aware of the effects of their own culture.
    b. culture touches almost every aspect of who and what a person is.
    c. at birth, people do not possess culture.
    d. culture is the lens through which we perceive and evaluate what is going on around us.

4. Which area of the country did many of the Hmong immigrants move to? (40)
    a. Southern Florida
    b. Upstate New York
    c. Central Texas
    d. California's Central Valley

5. When we try to understand a culture on its own terms without judging elements of culture as superior or inferior to our own way of life, we are practicing: (41)
    a. stereotyping.
    b. cultural relativism.
    c. mores.
    d. bias.

6. What term is given to the ways that we can use our bodies to communicate without words? (44)
    a. sanctions
    b. signals
    c. gestures
    d. mores

7. All of the following statements are true regarding language **except**: (45-47)
    a. Language allows human experience to be cumulative.
    b. Language allows one culture to be superior to another.
    c. Language allows shared perspectives.
    d. Language allows complex, shared, goal-directed behavior.

8.   The Sapir-Wharf hypothesis is based on the belief that: (48)
     a.   some animals can be taught to speak.
     b.   only humans can have language.
     c.   common sense is our basis of understanding culture.
     d.   language is the basis of culture.

9.   The term *People of Color:* (49)
     a.   is a replacement for the rejected term *Colored People.*
     b.   is a term supported by Latinos but not by African Americans.
     c.   shows the dominant group imposing a name on racial and ethnic groups.
     d.   has neither political nor cultural meaning connected to it.

10. For every group, what is the term for the expectations that develop out of a group's values? (48)
     a.   ideal culture
     b.   real culture
     c.   norms
     d.   moral standards

11. An expression of approval given for following a norm is called a: (48)
     a.   folkway.
     b.   value.
     c.   positive sanction.
     d.   cultural universal.

12. Moral holidays are: (49)
     a.   times when people can break the norms and not be sanctioned.
     b.   often center around people getting drunk and being rowdy.
     c.   celebrations like Mardi Gras.
     d.   all of the above.

13.   Serving turkey for Thanksgiving dinner is an example of a: (50)
     a.   vice.
     b.   taboo.
     c.   core value.
     d.   folkway.

14. If a man walked down the street naked, what would he be violating? (50)
     a.   a more
     b.   a core value
     c.   a folkway
     d.   a moral holiday

15.   The author of your text cites having sex with one's parents as an example of: (50)
       a.   folkways.
       b.   mores.
       c.   taboos.
       d.   a behavior that is universally sanctioned.

16.   Subcultures: (51-52)
       a.   are a world within a world.
       b.   have values and related behaviors that set their members apart from the dominant culture.
       c.   include occupational groups.
       d.   are all of the above.

17.   The Ku Klux Klan is a: (52)
       a.   subculture.
       b.   counterculture.
       c.   sub-unit of the dominant culture.
       d.   dominant culture.

18.   U.S. society is made up of many different groups. Which of the following terms would a sociologist use to describe this type of society? (52)
       a.   a melting pot
       b.   a pluralistic society
       c.   a conflicted society
       d.   a counterculture

19.   Which of the following statements concerning core values is *incorrect*? (52-53)
       a.   they are shared by the many groups that make up U.S. society
       b.   they include achievement and success, individualism, and progress
       c.   they change over time
       d.   they rarely create much conflict as they change

20.   A value cluster of which four interrelated core values is emerging in the United States? (57)
       a.   achievement and success, activity and work, material comfort
       b.   individualism, freedom, democracy, equality
       c.   leisure, self-fulfillment, physical fitness, youngness
       d.   youngness, self-fulfillment, romantic love, material comfort

21.   Which of the following is the best example of value contradiction? (57)
       a.   the Great Depression that began in 1929
       b.   America's participation in World War II
       c.   the issue of slavery that helped lead to the Civil War
       d.   the War of 1812 against the British

22. Cultural universals: (59)
     a.   are present in all cultures, but specific customs differ from one group to another.
     b.   are found in all societies in both general and specific terms.
     c.   are found in specific terms for marriage, funerals, and incest.
     d.   stem from a biological imperative to forbid incest.

23. The printing press or the computer may be considered: (60)
     a.   inventive technologies
     b.   diffused technologies
     c.   examples of cultural leveling
     d.   new technologies

24. The custom of maintaining a nine-month school year in the U.S. even though this custom no longer matches the current technology would be considered: (61)
     a.   cultural diffusion
     b.   cultural leveling
     c.   cultural hindrance
     d.   cultural lag

25. Mexican piñatas often depict Mickey Mouse or Fred Flintstone. This is an example of: (52)
     a.   symbolic culture.
     b.   cultural lag.
     c.   cultural leveling.
     d.   cultural relativism.

Answer Key

1.   A
2.   A
3.   A
4.   D
5.   B
6.   C
7.   B
8.   D
9.   A
10.   C
11.   C
12.   D
13.   D
14.   A
15.   C
16.   D
17.   B
18.   B
19.   D
20.   C
21.   C
22.   A
23.   D
24.   D
25.   C

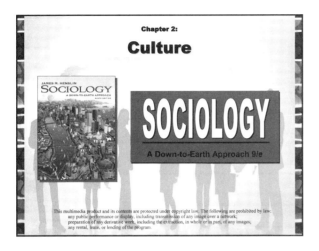

What is Culture?

❋ **Language, Beliefs, Values, Norms, Behavior Passed from One Generation to the Next**

❋ **Material vs. Nonmaterial Cultures**

Copyright © Allyn & Bacon 2008　　Chapter 2: Culture

Culture and Taken-for-Granted Orientations

❋ **What is Normal, Natural, or Usual?**

❋ **The Culture Within Us**

❋ **Culture as Lens**

❋ **Culture Shock**

❋ **Ethnocentrism**

Copyright © Allyn & Bacon 2008　　Chapter 2: Culture

Cultural Diversity in the United States - Example

Arrival of the Hmong
* The Trip Over
* The New Home
* The New Rules
* Isolation and the Regathering

Copyright © Allyn & Bacon 2008   Chapter 2: Culture   4

Practicing Cultural Relativism

* Understanding Cultures on Their Own Terms
* "Sick Cultures" - Robert Edgerton
* Confronting Contrasting Views of Reality

Copyright © Allyn & Bacon 2008   Chapter 2: Culture

Components of Symbolic Culture

Gestures
* Conveying Messages without Words
* Gestures' Meaning Differ Among Cultures
* Can Lead to Misunderstandings

Copyright © Allyn & Bacon 2008   Chapter 2: Culture

Figure 2.1 Gestures to Indicate Height, Southern Mexico

Chapter 2: Culture

Components of Symbolic Culture

Language

* Allows Human Experience to be Cumulative
* Provides Social or Shared Past
* Provides Social or Shared Future
* Allows Shared Perspective
* Allows Complex, Shared, Goal-Directed Behavior

Chapter 2: Culture

Language and Perception: Sapir-Whorf

* Language Has Embedded Within It

  Ways of Looking at the World

* Sapir-Whorf Reverses Common Sense

Chapter 2: Culture

Values, Norms, and Sanctions

* Values - What is Desirable in Life
* Norms - Expectations or Rules for Behavior
* Sanctions - Reaction to Following or Breaking Norms
  * Positive Sanctions
  * Negative Sanctions
* Moral Holidays and Places

Copyright © Allyn & Bacon 2008   Chapter 2: Culture

Folkways and Mores

* Folkways - Norms not Strictly Enforced
* Mores - Core Values: We Insist on Conformity
* Taboos

Copyright © Allyn & Bacon 2008   Chapter 2: Culture

Subcultures and Countercultures

* Subculture - A World Within the Dominant Culture
* Countercultures - Groups With Norms and Values at Odds With the Dominant Culture

Copyright © Allyn & Bacon 2008   Chapter 2: Culture

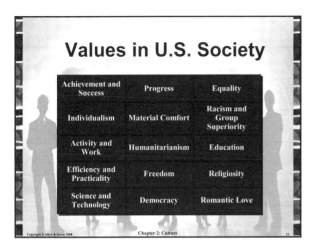

Values in U.S. Society

Achievement and Success	Progress	Equality
Individualism	Material Comfort	Racism and Group Superiority
Activity and Work	Humanitarianism	Education
Efficiency and Practicality	Freedom	Religiosity
Science and Technology	Democracy	Romantic Love

Values in U.S. Society

* Achievement and Success
* Individualism
* Activity and Work
* Efficiency and Practicality
* Science and Technology

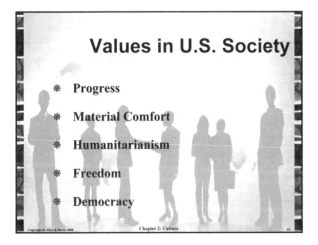

Values in U.S. Society

* Progress
* Material Comfort
* Humanitarianism
* Freedom
* Democracy

Values in U.S. Society

* Equality
* Racism and Group Superiority
* Education
* Religiosity
* Romantic Love

Copyright © Allyn & Bacon 2008   Chapter 2: Culture   16

Values in U.S. Society

* Value Clusters
* Value Contradictions

Copyright © Allyn & Bacon 2008   Chapter 2: Culture   14

Emerging Values

* Leisure
* Self-fulfillment
* Physical Fitness
* Youthfulness
* Concern for the Environment

Copyright © Allyn & Bacon 2008   Chapter 2: Culture   18

Values and Culture

❋ Culture Wars: When Values Clash

❋ Value as Blinders

❋ "Ideal" vs. "Real" Culture

Copyright © Allyn & Bacon 2008   Chapter 2: Culture   19

Cultural Universals

❋ Some Activities are Universal -

Courtship, Marriage, Funerals, Games

❋ Specific Customs Associated with

Activities Differ Between Groups

Copyright © Allyn & Bacon 2008   Chapter 2: Culture   20

Sociobiology

❋ Controversial View of Human Behavior

❋ Biology Cause of Human Behavior

❋ Charles Darwin and Natural Selection

❋ Sociologists and Social Biologists on

Opposite Sides

Copyright © Allyn & Bacon 2008   Chapter 2: Culture   21

Technology in the Global Village

✳ **The New Technology - New Tools**

✳ **Cultural Lag and Cultural Change**

✳ **Technology and Cultural Leveling**

Copyright © Allyn & Bacon 2008   Chapter 2: Culture   22

Chapter 2:

Culture

SOCIOLOGY

A Down-to-Earth Approach 9/e

CHAPTER 3
SOCIALIZATION

CHAPTER SUMMARY

- Scientists have attempted to determine how much of peoples' characteristics come from heredity and how much from the social environment. One way is to examine identical twins who have been reared apart. Observations of feral, isolated, and institutionalized children also help to answer this question, as well as the Harlow's research on deprived monkeys.

- Humans are born with the *capacity* to develop a self, but this self must be socially constructed through social interaction. Charles H. Cooley, George H. Mead, Jean Piaget, Sigmund Freud and Lawrence Kohlberg provide insights into the social development of human beings. The work of Cooley and Mead demonstrates that the self is created through our interactions with others. Piaget identified four stages in the development of our ability to reason. Freud defined the personality in terms of the id, ego, and superego and Kohlberg focused on stages of moral development.

- Socialization influences not only *how* we express our emotions, but *what* emotions we feel. These vary based on gender, culture, social class, and relationships.

- Gender socialization is a primary means of controlling human behavior and social institutions reinforce a society's ideals of sex-linked behaviors. Gender messages in the family, from peers, and in the mass media are very powerful influences in reinforcing gender roles.

- The main agents of socialization—family, the neighborhood, religion, day care, school, peer groups, the mass media, sports, and the workplace—all contribute to our socialization, enabling us to become full-fledged members of society.

- Resocialization is the process of learning new norms, values, attitudes and behaviors. Intense resocialization takes place in total institutions. Most resocialization is voluntary, but some is involuntary.

- Socialization, which begins at birth, continues throughout the life course; at each stage the individual must adjust to a new set of social expectations. Life course patterns, such as history, gender, race-ethnicity, and social class, vary by social location, as well as by individual experiences such as health and age at marriage.

- Although socialization creates the basic self and is modified by our social location, humans are not robots but rational beings who consider options and make choices.

LEARNING OBJECTIVES
After reading Chapter 3, you should be able to:

1. Discuss the ongoing debate over what most determines human behavior: "nature" (heredity) or "nurture" (social environment), and cite the evidence that supports one position or the other. (66-70)
2. Discuss how studies of feral, isolated, and institutionalized children show that social contact and interaction is essential for healthy human development. (67-70)
3. Identify key findings from Margaret and Harry Harlow's research on deprived monkeys and discuss the extent to which this research can be extrapolated to human beings. (69-70)
4. Explain Charles Horton Cooley's theory on the looking glass self. (70)
5. Discuss the stages that George Herbert Mead has identified in role taking. (71)
6. Explain Jean Piaget's research on the development of reasoning and identify what happens in each stage. (72-73)
7. Explain Freud's view on the development of personality and sociologists view of Freud's theory. (73-75)
8. Differentiate between Kohlberg and Gilligan's theory on the development of morality. (75-76)
9. Discuss how people are socialized into the expression of emotions and how these differ based on culture, social class, and relationships. (76-77)
10. Discuss how we are controlled by the society within us. (77)
11. Know what is meant by gender socialization and how the family, media, and other agents of socialization *teach* children, from the time of their birth, to act masculine or feminine based on their gender. (78-81)
12. Define the term agents of socialization. List the major agents of socialization in American society, and discuss how each of these teach—and influence—people's attitudes, behaviors, and other orientations toward life. (81-87)
13. Define the term resocialization and provide examples of situations that may require it. (87-88)
14. Discuss how a total institution is a more extreme form of resocialization. (88)
15. Identify the stages of the life course and explain how changes within society have impacted these stages. (89-92)
16. Explain the sociological significance of the life course. (93)
17. Discuss why human beings are not prisoners of socialization and provide examples of how people can and do exercise a considerable degree of freedom over which agents of socialization to follow and which cultural messages to accept. (93)

KEY TERMS

After studying the chapter, review the definition for each of the following terms.

agents of socialization: people or groups that affect our self-concept, attitudes, behaviors or other orientations towards life (81)

anticipatory socialization: because one anticipates a future role, one learns part of it now (87)

degradation ceremony: a term coined by Harold Garfinkel to describe an attempt to remake the self by stripping away an individual's self-identity and stamping a new identity in its place (88)

ego: Freud's term for a balancing force between the id and the demands of society (73)

feral children: children assumed to have been raised by animals, in the wilderness, isolated from other humans (67)

gender role: the behaviors and attitudes considered appropriate because one is male or female (80)

gender socialization: the ways in which society sets children onto different courses in life *because* they are male or female (78)

generalized other: the norms, values, attitudes, and expectations of people "in general"; the child's ability to take the role of the generalized other is a significant step in the development of a self (70)

id: Freud's term for our inborn basic drives (73)

latent functions: unintended beneficial consequences of people's actions (84)

life course: the stages of our life as we go from birth to death (88)

looking-glass self: a term coined by Charles Horton Cooley to refer to the process by which our self develops through internalizing others' reactions to us (70)

manifest functions: the intended consequences of people's actions designed to help some part of the social system (84)

mass media: forms of communication, such as radio, newspapers, and television that are directed to mass audiences (80)

peer group: a group of individuals of roughly the same age, linked by common interests (80)

resocialization: process of learning new norms, values, attitudes, and behaviors (87)

self: the unique human capacity to see ourselves "from the outside"; the views we internalize of how others see us (70)

significant other: an individual who significantly influences someone else's life (71)

social environment: the entire human environment, including direct contact with others (66)

social inequality: a social condition in which privileges and obligations are given to some but denied to others (81)

socialization: the process by which people learn the characteristics of their group—the attitudes, values, and actions thought appropriate for them (70)

superego: Freud's term for the conscience, the internalized norms and values of our social groups (73)

taking the role of the other: putting oneself in someone else's shoes; understanding how someone else feels and thinks and thus anticipating how that person will act (71)

total institution: a place in which people are cut off from the rest of society and are almost totally controlled by the officials who run it (88)

transitional adulthood: a term that refers to a period following high school when young adults have not yet taken on the responsibilities ordinarily associated with adulthood; also called adultolescence (91)

KEY PEOPLE

Review the major theoretical contributions or findings of these people.

Patricia and Peter Adler: These sociologists have documented how peer groups socialize children into gender-appropriate behavior. (86)

Charles Horton Cooley: Cooley is a symbolic interactionist who studied the development of the self, coining the term "the looking-glass self." (70)

Donna Eder: She studied conversations between middle school girls and examined how girls reinforce what they think is appropriate for females. (80)

Paul Ekman: This anthropologist studied emotions in several countries and concluded that people everywhere experience six basic emotions—anger, disgust, fear, happiness, sadness, and surprise. (76)

Sigmund Freud: Freud developed a theory of personality development that took into consideration inborn drives (id), the internalized norms and values of one's society (superego), and the individual's ability to balance the two (ego). (73-74)

Carol Gilligan: Gilligan was uncomfortable with Kohlberg's conclusions regarding the development of morality. She studied gender differences in morality, concluding that men and women use different criteria in evaluating morality. (75-76)

Erving Goffman: Goffman studied the process of resocialization in total institutions. (88)

Susan Goldberg and Michael Lewis: Two psychologists studied how parents' unconscious expectations about gender behavior are communicated to their young children. (78-79)

Harry and Margaret Harlow: These psychologists studied the behavior of monkeys raised in isolation to demonstrate the importance of early learning. (69-70)

Lawrence Kohlberg: This psychologist studied the development of morality, concluding that individuals go through a sequence of developmental stages. (75)

Melvin Kohn: Kohn has done extensive research on the social class differences in child-rearing between working- and middle-class parents. (83)

George Herbert Mead: Mead emphasized the importance of play in the development of the self, noting that children learn to take on the role of the other and eventually learn to perceive themselves as others do. (71-72)

Melissa Milkie: This sociologist studied how adolescent boys used media images such as movies and TV programs to develop their identities as males. (80)

Michael Messner: He notes that girls are more likely to construct their identities on meaningful relationships whereas boys' identity develops out of competitive success. (87)

Jean Piaget: Piaget studied the development of reasoning skills in children and identified four stages. (72-73)

H. M. Skeels and H. B. Dye: These psychologists studied how close social interaction affected the social and intellectual development of institutionalized children. (67-69)

PRACTICE TEST

1. Studies of isolated institutionalized children point out the importance of: (67-68)
    a. intimate early social interaction.
    b. education.
    c. proper nutrition.
    d. discipline.

2. The Harlows' studies of isolated rhesus monkeys demonstrate that: (69)
    a. the monkeys were able to adjust to monkey life after a time.
    b. they instinctively knew how to enter into "monkey interaction" with other monkeys.
    c. they knew how to engage in sexual intercourse.
    d. the monkeys were not able to adjust fully to monkey life and did not know instinctively how to enter into interaction with other monkeys.

3. According to Charles Horton Cooley's term the *looking-glass self*: (70)
    a. our sense of self develops from interaction with others.
    b. our concept of self depends on our good looks.
    c. when we look good we feel good.
    d. humans are instinctively vain.

4. According to Mead's theory, during which stage do children pretend to take the roles of specific people? (71-72)
    a. imitation
    b. play
    c. game
    d. generalized other

5. Jean Piaget focused on studying how children develop: (72)
    a. the ability to understand language.
    b. the ability to read.
    c. the ability to perform mathematical equations.
    d. the ability to reason.

6. What term does Sigmund Freud use to represent the "culture within us," the norms and values we have internalized for our social groups? (74)
    a. id
    b. superego
    c. eros
    d. ego

7. Which of the four stages of moral development are most people unlikely to ever reach, according to Kohlberg? (75)
    a. amoral
    b. preconventional
    c. conventional
    d. postconventional

8. Carol Gilligan's first reports of her research on gender differences in evaluating morality: (76)
    a. has been supported by other research.
    b. has actually been rejected by Gilligan herself.
    c. has not been researched by others to test Gilligan's conclusion.
    d. concludes that males form evaluations of morality almost exclusively based on personal relationships.

9. What did Ekman conclude about emotions? (76)
    a. every society expresses emotions in its own way
    b. they are built into our biology
    c. emotions are a result of socialization
    d. none of the above

10. Psychologists Susan Goldberg and Michael Lewis reached what conclusions after observing mothers with their six-month-old infants in a laboratory setting? (78-79)
    a. Mothers keep their male children closer to them.
    b. Mothers keep their male and female children about the same distance from them.
    c. Mothers touch and spoke more to their sons.
    d. Mothers unconsciously reward daughters for being passive and dependent.

11. Which of the following is a Japanese cartoon form targeted at children? (78)
    a. anime
    b. ifalgo
    c. sudoku
    d. keneshowa

12. What do middle-class parents try to develop in their children, according to Melvin Kohn? (83)
    a. outward conformity
    b. neatness and cleanliness
    c. curiosity, self-expression, and self-control
    d. obedience to rules

13. Which of the following statements is true? (84)
    a. 2 of 5 Americans attends a religious service in a typical week.
    b. 80% of Americans belong to a local congregation.
    c. 20% of Americans pray every day.
    d. 3 of 8 of Americans donate to their church each week.

14. According to the story in the textbook, what do many Latino immigrants face? (85)
    a.   being caught between two worlds
    b.   deportation for illegal immigration
    c.   working in substandard conditions
    d.   none of the above

15. What conclusions can be drawn about peer groups and academic achievement from Adler and Adler's research? (86-87)
    a.   Both boys and girls avoid doing well academically.
    b.   Boys want to do well academically in order to boost their standing in the peer group, but girls avoid being labeled as smart, because it will hurt their image
    c.   Both boys and girls believe that good grades will translate into greater popularity among their respective peer groups.
    d.   For boys, to do well academically is to lose popularity, while for girls, getting good grades increases social standing.

16. In the workplace, we may try out different jobs. This is known as: (87)
    a.   resocialization.
    b.   a competitive spirit.
    c.   a total institution.
    d.   a degradation ceremony.

17. When someone gets divorced they may to undergo: (87)
    a.   degradation.
    b.   resocialization.
    c.   leveling.
    d.   anticipatory socialization.

18. An attempt to strip a person of his or her identity so as to remake a new identity: (88)
    a.   is exemplified by one's being allowed to keep their personal identity kit.
    b.   applies to all institutions of society.
    c.   is an example of a positive sanction.
    d.   is part of a degradation ceremony.

19. Total institutions tend to: (85)
    a.   reinforce the expression of pre-existing statuses.
    b.   reinforce the expression of an individual's personal identity.
    c.   reinforce individuality by controlling daily activities.
    d.   reinforce resocialization by being physically isolated from the public.

20. Stages we experience from birth to death are called: (88)
    a.   the life course.
    b.   social locations.
    c.   statuses.
    d.   socialization.

21. The example of the Marine boot camp shows they are characterized by: (89)
    a. tactics to humiliate recruits in a subtle, low-keyed manner.
    b. tactics of degradation that can lead some recruits to suicidal tendencies.
    c. tactics of resocialization that are intense yet still try to maintain a persons societal and religious individual identities.
    d. tactics that offer ordinary everyday diversions, such as television, only on those days when recruits' behavior conform to staff expectations.

22. Which statement best describes childhood? (89-90)
    a. The role of children has remained the same over time.
    b. Industrialization transformed the way that we perceive children.
    c. Childhood is essentially biologically determined
    d. Children have always been seen as innocent and free from responsibility.

23. Which stage of the lifecourse is a period of extended youth? (91)
    a. childhood
    b. adolescence
    c. transitional adulthood
    d. pre-adolescence

24. Which stage do most people find to be the most comfortable period of their lives? (92)
    a. later middle years
    b. early middle years
    c. early older years
    d. later older years

25. Sociologists believe that the establishment of a sense of "self" is: (93)
    a. firmly done in early childhood and undergoes very little modification over time.
    b. dynamic and changes over time.
    c. a passive process whereby individuals are not actively involved in the construction of self.
    d. a process that has little effect on our behavior.

Answer Key

1.   A
2.   D
3.   A
4.   B
5.   D
6.   B
7.   D
8.   B
9.   B
10.   D
11.   A
12.   C
13.   A
14.   A
15.   D
16.   C
17.   B
18.   D
19.   D
20.   A
21.   B
22.   B
23.   C
24.   A
25.   B

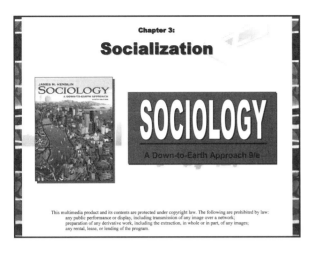

Chapter 3:
Socialization

SOCIOLOGY
A Down-to-Earth Approach 9/e

This multimedia product and its contents are protected under copyright law. The following are prohibited by law: any public performance or display, including transmission of any image over a network; preparation of any derivative work, including the extraction, in whole or in part, of any images; any rental, lease, or lending of the program.

What is Human Nature?

Nature vs. Nurture - Oscar and Jack

* **Feral Children**

* **Isolated Children**

* **Institutionalized Children**

* **Deprived Animals**

Copyright © Allyn & Bacon 2008   Chapter 3:Socialization   2

In Sum...

Society Makes Us Human

Copyright © Allyn & Bacon 2008   Chapter 3:Socialization   3

Socialization into the Self and Mind

Cooley and the Looking Glass Self

✷ **We Imagine How We Appear to Others**

✷ **We Interpret Others' Reactions**

✷ **We Develop a Self-Concept**

Copyright © Allyn & Bacon 2008   Chapter 3:Socialization

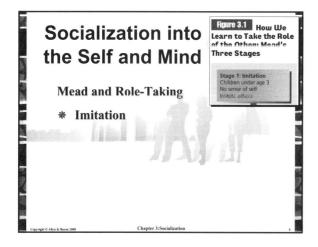

Socialization into the Self and Mind

Mead and Role-Taking

✷ **Imitation**

Figure 3.1 How We Learn to Take the Role of the Other: Mead's Three Stages

Stage 1: Imitation
Children under age 3
No sense of self
Imitate others

Copyright © Allyn & Bacon 2008   Chapter 3:Socialization

Socialization into the Self and Mind

Mead and Role-Taking

✷ **Imitation**

✷ **Play**

Figure 3.1 How We Learn to Take the Role of the Other: Mead's Three Stages

Stage 1: Imitation
Children under age 3
No sense of self
Imitate others

Stage 2: Play
Ages 3 to 6
Play "pretend" others
(princess, Spiderman, etc.)

Copyright © Allyn & Bacon 2008   Chapter 3:Socialization

Socialization into the Self and Mind

Mead and Role-Taking

　✻　**Imitation**

　✻　**Play**

　✻　**Games**

Figure 3.1 How We Learn to Take the Role of the Other: Mead's Three Stages

Stage 1: Imitation
Children under age 3
No sense of self
Imitate others

Stage 2: Play
Ages 3 to 6
Play "pretend" others
　　(princess, Spiderman, etc.)

Stage 3: Team Games
After about age 6 or 7
Team games
　　("organized play")
Learn to take multiple roles

Copyright © Allyn & Bacon 2008　　　Chapter 3:Socialization

Socialization into the Self and Mind

Piaget and the Development of Reasoning

　✻　**Sensorimotor Stage**

　✻　**Preoperational Stage**

　✻　**Concrete Operational Stage**

　✻　**Formal Operational Stage**

　✻　**Global Aspects of Self and Reasoning**

Copyright © Allyn & Bacon 2008　　　Chapter 3:Socialization

Learning Personality, Morality, and Emotions

　✻　**Freud and the Development of Personality**

　✻　**Kohlberg and the Development of Morality**

　✻　**Gilligan and Gender Differences in Morality**

Copyright © Allyn & Bacon 2008　　　Chapter 3:Socialization

Socialization into Emotions

* Global Emotions
* Expressing Emotions
* What We Feel
* Research Needed
* The Self and Emotions as Social Control - Society Within Us

Copyright © Allyn & Bacon 2008   Chapter 3:Socialization   10

Society Within Us

* The Self and Emotions as Social Control
* Are We Free?
* Expectations of Family and Friends
* Social Mirror

Copyright © Allyn & Bacon 2008   Chapter 3:Socialization   11

Socialization into Gender

* Gender Messages in the Family
* Gender Messages from Peers
* Gender Messages in the Mass Media
    * Advertising
    * Television
    * Video Games
    * Anime

Copyright © Allyn & Bacon 2008   Chapter 3:Socialization   12

Agents of Socialization

* **The Family**
  * The First Group with Impact
  * The Family and Social Class
* **The Neighborhood**

Copyright © Allyn & Bacon 2008   Chapter 3:Socialization   13

Agents of Socialization

* **Religion**
* **Day Care**
* **The School**
  * Manifest Function
  * Latent Functions
* **Peer Groups**

Copyright © Allyn & Bacon 2008   Chapter 3:Socialization   14

Agents of Socialization

* **Sports and Competitive Success**
* **The Workplace**
* **Resocialization**
  * Mild - New Boss
  * Intense - Alcoholics Anonymous
  * Total Institutions - Boot Camp

Copyright © Allyn & Bacon 2008   Chapter 3:Socialization   15

Socialization Through Life

❋ **Childhood - Birth to ~12 yrs**

❋ **Adolescence - 13 to 17 yrs**

❋ **Transitional Adulthood - 18 to 29 yrs**

Copyright © Allyn & Bacon 2008   Chapter 3:Socialization   16

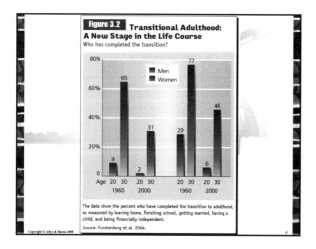

Figure 3.2 Transitional Adulthood: A New Stage in the Life Course

Who has completed the transition?

The data show the percent who have completed the transition to adulthood, as measured by leaving home, finishing school, getting married, having a child, and being financially independent.
Source: Furstenberg et al. 2004.

Copyright © Allyn & Bacon 2008   17

Socialization Through Life

The Middle Years - 30 to 65 yrs

❋ Early Middle Years - 30 to 49 yrs

❋ Later Middle Years - 50 to 65 yrs

Copyright © Allyn & Bacon 2008   Chapter 3:Socialization   18

Socialization Through Life

The Older Years ~65 yrs on

❀ Early Older Years

❀ Later Older Years

Copyright © Allyn & Bacon 2008   Chapter 3:Socialization   19

Sociological Significance of the Life Course

❀ Does Not Merely Represent Biology

❀ Social Factors Influence Life Course

❀ Social Location Very Significant

Copyright © Allyn & Bacon 2008   Chapter 3:Socialization   20

Are We Prisoners of Socialization?

❀ Sociologists Do Not Think So

❀ Individuals Are Actively Involved

in the Construction of the Self

Copyright © Allyn & Bacon 2008   Chapter 3:Socialization   21

Chapter 3:

Socialization

SOCIOLOGY

A Down-to-Earth Approach 9/e

_____

_____

_____

_____

_____

_____

_____

CHAPTER 4
SOCIAL STRUCTURE AND SOCIAL INTERACTION

CHAPTER SUMMARY

- There are two levels of sociological analysis: macrosociology investigates the large-scale features of social structure, while microsociology focuses on social interaction. Functional and conflict theorists tend to use a macrosociological approach, while symbolic interactionists are more likely to use a microsociological approach.

- The term social structure refers to a society's framework, that which guides our behavior. The individual's location in the social structure affects his or her perceptions, attitudes, and behaviors. Culture, social class, social status (both ascribed and achieved), roles, groups, and social institutions are the major components of social structure.

- Social status refers to the position that one occupies. All of us occupy a number of positions at the same time. Status can be ascribed or achieved: Ascribed status is involuntary and often present at birth while achieved statuses are those positions that are earned or accomplished.

- Roles are the behaviors and privileges that are attached to a status. The groups to which we belong play a powerful role in our life depending on our experience and interaction with that group.

- Social institutions are the organized and standard means that a society develops to meet its basic needs. Functionalists view social institutions as established ways of meeting universal group needs; however, conflict theorists see social institutions as the primary means by which the elite maintains its privileged position.

- Over time, social structure undergoes changes. Sometimes this change is very dramatic, as illustrated by Durkheim's concepts of mechanical and organic solidarity and Tönnies' constructs of *Gemeinschaft* and *Gesellschaft*.

- In contrast to functionalist and conflict theorists who, as macrosociologists, focus on the "big picture," symbolic interactionists tend to be microsociologists and look at social interaction in everyday life. They examine how people look at things and how that, in turn, affects their behavior.

- Microsociologists may study stereotypes or they may study personal space. Personal space varies from one culture to another. Americans have four different "distance zones": intimate, personal, social, and public.

- The dramaturgical analysis provided by Erving Goffman analyzes everyday life in terms of it's stage. At the core of this approach is the analysis of the impressions we attempt to make on others by using *sign-vehicles* (setting, appearance, and manner), *teamwork*, and *face-saving behavior*.

- Ethnomethodologists try to uncover the background assumptions which provide us with basic ideas about the way life is. The social construction of reality refers to how we each create a view, or understanding, of our world.

- Both macrosociology and microsociology are needed to understand human behavior because we must grasp both social structure and social interaction.

LEARNING OBJECTIVES
After reading Chapter 4, you should be able to:

1. Differentiate between the macrosociological and microsociological approach to studying social life. (98)
2. Define social structure and discuss how it guides people's behaviors. (98)
3. Understand the concepts of culture, social class, social status, roles, and groups, and the role they play in social structure. (99-103)
4. Differentiate between ascribed, achieved, and master status. (99-100)
5. Identify the social institutions common to industrial and postindustrial societies and summarize their basic features. (104-105)
6. Understand the role of the media as an emerging institution. (104)
7. Compare and contrast functionalists and conflict theorists over the purposes for, and effects of, social institutions. (106-107)
8. Differentiate between Emile Durkheim's concepts of mechanical and organic solidarity and Ferdinand Tönnies' constructs of *Gemeinschaft* and *Gesellschaft*, and understand why they continue to be relevant. (107-108)
9. Explain what microsociologists might study and how they differ from macrosociologists. (110)
10. Discuss stereotypes, personal space, touching, eye contact, smiling, and applied body language and how they may differ from one culture to another. (110-113))
11. Differentiate between the front and back stage, role conflict, role exit and role strain, and provide examples of each. (113-114)
12. Know the key components of dramaturgy and discuss how people try to control other people's impressions of them through sign-vehicles, teamwork, and face-saving behavior. (112-113)
13. Explain how we can become the roles that we play and apply impression management. (117-118)
14. Understand how people use background assumptions to make sense out of everyday life. (118-119)
15. Explain what is meant by the "social construction of reality" and how it relates to the "Thomas theorem." (119-120)
16. Know why both macrosociology and microsociology are essential to understanding social life. (121-124)

KEY TERMS
After studying the chapter, review the definition for each of the following terms.

achieved statuses: positions that are earned, accomplished, or involve at least some effort or activity on the individual's part (101)

ascribed statuses: positions an individual either inherits at birth or receives involuntarily later in life (101)

back stage: where people rest from their performances, discuss their presentations, and plan future performances (113)

background assumptions: deeply embedded common understandings of how the world operates and of how people ought to act (118)

body language: the ways in which people use their bodies to give messages to others, much of which is done subconsciously (113)

division of labor: the splitting of a group's or society's tasks into specialties (107)

dramaturgy: an approach, pioneered by Erving Goffman, in which social life is analyzed in terms of drama or the stage; also called *dramaturgical analysis* (113)

ethnomethodology: the study of how people use background assumptions to make sense of life (118)

face-saving behavior: techniques used to salvage a performance that is going sour (115)

front stage: where performances are given (113)

functional requisites: the major tasks that a society must fulfill if it is to survive (106)

Gemeinschaft: a type of society in which life is intimate; a community in which everyone knows everyone else and people share a sense of togetherness (108)

Gesellschaft: a type of society dominated by impersonal relationships, individual accomplishments, and self-interest (108)

group: people who have something in common and believe that it is significant; also called a *social group* (103)

impression management: people's efforts to control the impressions that others receive of them (113)

macrosociology: analysis of social life that focuses on broad features of society, such as social class and the relationships of groups to one another; usually used by functionalist and conflict theorists (98)

master status: a status that cuts across the other statuses that an individual occupies (100)

mechanical solidarity: Durkheim's term for the unity (a shared consciousness) that people feel as a result of performing the same or similar tasks (107)

microsociology: analysis of social life focusing on social interaction; typically used by symbolic interactionists (98)

organic solidarity: Durkheim's term for the interdependence that results from the division of labor; people needing others to fulfill their jobs (107)

role: the behaviors, obligations, and privileges attached to a status (103)

role conflict: conflict that someone feels *between* roles because the expectations attached to one role are incompatible with the expectations of another role (114)

role performance: the ways in which someone performs a role, showing a particular "style" or "personality" (114)

role strain: conflicts that someone feels *within* a role (114)

sign vehicles: the term used by Goffman to refer to how people use social setting, appearance, and manner to communicate information about the self (115)

social class: according to Weber, a large group of people who rank close to one another in wealth, power and prestige; according to Marx, one of two groups: capitalists who own the means or production or workers who sell their labor (101)

social construction of reality: the process by which people use their background assumptions and life experiences to define what is real (120)

social institution: the organized, usual, or standard ways by which society meets its basic needs (104)

social integration: the degree to which members of a group or a society feel united by shared values and other social bonds; also known as social cohesion (107)

social interaction: people's interaction with one another (98)

social structure: the framework that surrounds us, consisting of the relationships of people and groups to one another, which give direction to and set limits on behavior (99)

status: the position that someone occupies in society or a social group (101)

status inconsistency: ranking high on some dimensions of social class and low on others, also called *status discrepancy* (102)

status set: all of the statuses or positions that an individual occupies (101)

status symbols: items used to identify a status (101)

stereotype: assumptions of what people are like, whether true or false (110)

teamwork: the collaboration of two or more persons to manage impressions jointly (115)

Thomas theorem: William I. and Dorothy S. Thomas' classic formulation of the definition of the situation: "If people define situations as real, they are real in their consequences." (119)

KEY PEOPLE
Review the major theoretical contributions or findings of these people.

Elijah Anderson: In a series of books, Anderson has studied the lives of inner city residents (*Streetwise* and *Code of the Streets*) and suggests that their world is organized around the same norms and beliefs that characterize our wider society. (98)

William Chambliss: Chambliss used macrosociology and microsociology to study high school gangs and found that social structure and interaction explained the patterns of behavior in these groups. (121-124)

Emile Durkheim: Durkheim identified mechanical and organic solidarity as the keys to social cohesion. As societies get larger, how they divide up work becomes more specialized and this division of labor makes people depend on one another. (107)

Helen Ebaugh: Ebaugh interviewed people who were no longer performing a role that had once been central in their lives. She found that many of them struggled to define their identity as a result of the loss of these roles. (117-118)

Harold Garfinkel: Garfinkel is the founder of ethnomethodology; he conducted experiments in order to uncover people's background assumptions. (118-119)

Erving Goffman: Goffman developed dramaturgy, the perspective within symbolic interactionism that views social life as a drama on the stage. (113-116)

Edward Hall: This anthropologist found that personal space varied from one culture to another and that North Americans use four different "distance zones." (112)

James Henslin and Mae Biggs: The author of your text, along with gynecological nurse Biggs, researched how doctors and patients constructed the social reality of vaginal examinations in order to define these exams as nonsexual. (120-121)

Elliot Liebow: This sociologist studied street-corner men and found that their lives are not disorganized, but influenced by the same norms and beliefs of the larger society. (98)

Mark Snyder: Snyder carried out research in order to test whether stereotypes are self-fulfilling. (111)

W. I. Thomas and Dorothy S. Thomas: These sociologists said that "If people define situations as real, they are real in their consequences." (119-120)

Ferdinand Tönnies: Tönnies analyzed different types of societies that existed before and after industrialization. He used the terms *Gemeinschaft* and *Gesellschaft* to describe the two types of societies. (108)

PRACTICE TEST

1.   When studying street corner men, which is likely to focus on the men's rules or "codes" for getting along? (98)
    a.   macrosociology theory
    b.   microsociology theory
    c.   mesosociology theory
    d.   social structure

2.   The significance of social structure to the experience of a student in a   classroom in a college or university is such that: (99)
    a.   a street person would never be affected by that social structure.
    b.   the same social structure influences both the instructor and the student.
    c.   the influence of social structure is more important for its effect on the instructor than on the student.
    d.   social structure would not be guiding behavior in a college or university   setting since they are specialized settings.

3.   To a sociologist the term "status" means: (101)
    a.   a person's occupational prestige level.
    b.   a person's position in a society or social group.
    c.   a social group's prestige level.
    d.   a social group's position in society.

4.   Your race or ethnicity is known as your: (101)
    a.   ascribed status.
    b.   achieved status.
    c.   status symbol.
    d.   role.

5.   A master status: (102)
    a.   is independent of one's ascribed status.
    b.   cuts across other statuses one might hold.
    c.   can stem only from one's achieved status.
    d.   is subordinate to one's individual ascribed and achieved statuses.

6.   A contradiction or mismatch between an individual's statuses: (102)
    a.   is known as status inconsistency.
    b.   leads to a smooth unfolding of the relationship between status and social interaction.
    c.   is in conformity with the modern expectations of everyday society for   most statuses.
    d.   is independent of norms.

7.   People who regularly interact with one another and believe they have something in common are known as a: (103)
    a.   group.
    b.   social institution.
    c.   buddy system.
    d.   master race.

8.   The behaviors, obligations, and privileges attached to a status are called: (103)
    a.   status symbols.
    b.   master status indicators.
    c.   roles.
    d.   limitations.

9.   In industrial societies, social institutions tend to be: (104)
    a.   smaller.
    b.   less formal.
    c.   more formal
    d.   non-existentant.

10.   The organized ways a society meets its basic needs are called: (104)
    a.   social institutions.
    b.   roles.
    c.   groups.
    d.   status assignments.

11.   The best example of an emerging social institution is: (105)
    a.   the mass media.
    b.   the family.
    c.   religion.
    d.   medicine.

12.   According to _____, social institutions are used by the elite for its own advantage. (106)
    a.   functionalists
    b.   conflict theorists
    c.   symbolic interactionists
    d.   dramaturgists

13.   The Amish in the United States represent an example of: (109)
    a.   organic solidarity.
    b.   Gesellschaft.
    c.   Gemeinschaft.
    d.   a deviant subculture that is not legally protected in our society.

14.   Which of the following statements about stereotypes is incorrect? (110-111)
a.   When you first meet someone, the assumptions you have about certain social characteristics have a tendency to shape your first impressions of that person.
b.   Stereotypes are unlikely to be self-fulfilling.
c.   Stereotypes can have an impact on what we are able to accomplish because they influence how others' behave toward us.
d.   People are able to resist stereotypes and change outcomes.

15.   Hall's four different distance zones conclude that the correct assessment of how North Americans view physical distance from themselves to others is: (112)
a.   an intimate distance that extends about eighteen inches.
b.   a narrow public distance that is less than three feet.
c.   a personal distance that extends well beyond five feet.
d.   a social distance that extends twelve to eighteen feet.

16.   A smile by Walmart clerks in Germany was interpreted by the customers as: (113)
a.   flirting.
b.   that the clerk was being arrogant.
c.   that the clerk was laughing at them.
d.   annoying.

17.   What is the concept that refers to the situation when a student tries to excel in   class but is criticized for making classmates look bad? (114)
a.   role exit
b.   face-saving behavior
c.   ethnomethodology
d.   role strain

18.   According to Goffman, where do we go when we want to be ourselves? (114)
a.   front stage
b.   back stage
c.   inside the drama
d.   outside the drama

19.   Which of the following statements apply to social setting, appearance, and manner? (114-115)
a.   They are less important than role performance for impression management.
b.   They are sign-vehicles used by individuals for managing impressions.
c.   They are more important for females than males.
d.   They are techniques for saving face when a performance fails.

20. If you went to your doctor's office and he/she started cutting your hair, this would be an example of violating: (118)
    a. face-saving behavior.
    b. impression management.
    c. a master status.
    d. background assumption.

21. One of the recommendations given by career counselors to executive women is: (118)
    a. to wear brightly colored clothing.
    b. to place their hands on the table during executive sessions.
    c. to speak loudly to get their point across.
    d. to use a dominant stance.

22. Which of the following encouraged his students to act as though they did not understand the basic rules of social life? (119)
    a. Harold Garfinkel
    b. Erving Goffman
    c. Edward Hall
    d. W. I. Thomas

23. The Thomas Theorem states that: (119)
    a. if something can go wrong, it will.
    b. work expands to fill the time one has to complete it.
    c. if people define situations as real, they are real in their consequences.
    d. people rise to their level of incompetence.

24. The social construction of reality: (120)
    a. is based on the effects society and social groups have in defining particular views of life even if such views go against the actual objective truth.
    b. confirms that objective, scientifically proven phenomenon, such as germs causing illness, are accepted as fact by all societies.
    c. is something that is independent of subjective interpretation.
    d. is present as a definition of reality only for people who are in subcultures.

25. What did the research on the Saints and the Roughnecks demonstrate? (121)
    a. Social class is unimportant when it comes to encounters with teachers, police, and the general community.
    b. The reputations that the boys acquired as teenagers disappeared once they reached adulthood.
    c. The Saints were significantly less delinquent than the Roughnecks because they came from more solid middle-class families.
    d. To understand what happened to the boys in the study, William Chambliss analyzed both the social structure and the patterns of social interaction that characterized their lives.

Answer Key

1.   B
2.   B
3.   B
4.   A
5.   B
6.   A
7.   A
8.   C
9.   D
10. A
11. A
12. B
13. C
14. B
15. A
16. A
17. D
18. B
19. B
20. D
21. B
22. A
23. C
24. A
25. D

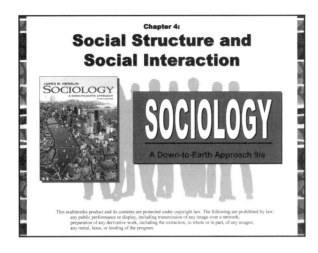

Levels of Sociological Analysis

✳ **Macrosociology**

✳ Large-Scale Features of Social Life

✳ **Microsociology**

✳ Focus on Social Interaction

Copyright © Allyn & Bacon 2008   Chapter 4: Social Structure and Social Interaction   2

The Macrosociological Perspective

✳ **Sociological Significance of Social Structure**

✳ Guides Our Behavior

✳ Behavior Decided by Location in Social Structure

✳ **Culture**

✳ **Social Class**

Copyright © Allyn & Bacon 2008   Chapter 4: Social Structure and Social Interaction   3

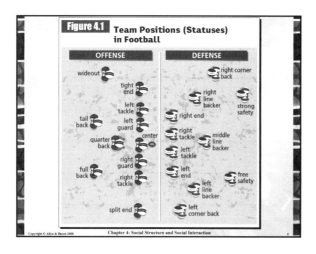

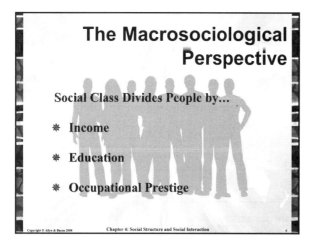

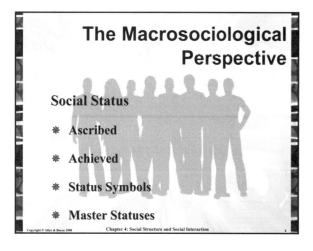

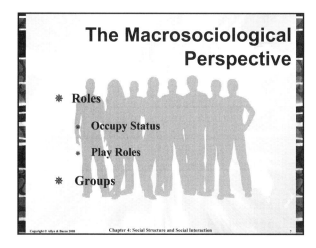

The Macrosociological Perspective

❋ **Roles**

   ❋ **Occupy Status**

   ❋ **Play Roles**

❋ **Groups**

Copyright © Allyn & Bacon 2008   Chapter 4: Social Structure and Social Interaction   7

Social Institutions

❋ **Sociological Significance of Social Institutions**

❋ **Ten Social Institutions in Industrialized Societies**

Copyright © Allyn & Bacon 2008   Chapter 4: Social Structure and Social Interaction   8

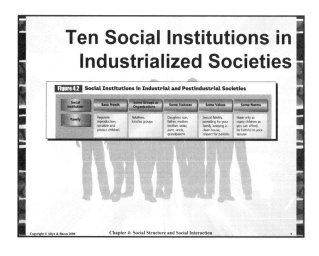

Ten Social Institutions in Industrialized Societies

Figure 4.2	Social Institutions in Industrial and Postindustrial Societies				
Social Institution	Basic Needs	Some Groups or Organizations	Some Statuses	Some Values	Some Norms
Family	Regulate reproduction, socialize and protect children	Relatives, kinship groups	Daughter, son, father, mother, brother, sister, aunt, uncle, grandparent	Sexual fidelity, providing for your family, keeping a clean house, respect for parents	Have only as many children as you can afford, be faithful to your spouse

Copyright © Allyn & Bacon 2008   Chapter 4: Social Structure and Social Interaction   9

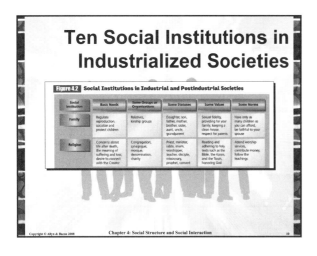

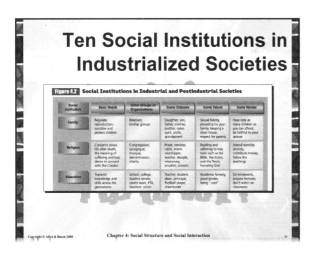

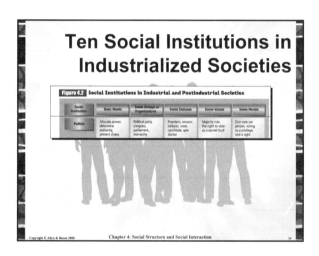

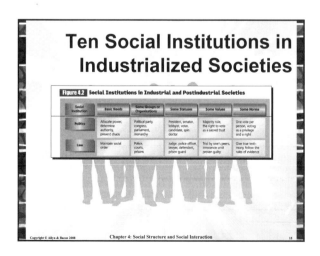

Social Institutions

* **Mass Media as an Emerging Social Institution**
* **Comparing Functionalist and Conflict Perspectives**

Copyright © Allyn & Bacon 2008   Chapter 4: Social Structure and Social Interaction   19

Functionalist Perspective

* **Replacing Members**
* **Socializing New Members**
* **Producing and Distributing Goods and Services**
* **Preserving Order**
* **Providing a Sense of Purpose**

Copyright © Allyn & Bacon 2008   Chapter 4: Social Structure and Social Interaction   20

Conflict Perspective

* **Powerful Groups Control Institutions**
* **Small Groups Garner Lion's Share of Wealth**
* **Social Institutions Affect Gender Relations**
* **Main Purpose is to Preserve Social Order**

Copyright © Allyn & Bacon 2008   Chapter 4: Social Structure and Social Interaction   21

Changes in Social Order

❋ **What Holds Society Together?**

  ❋ Mechanical and Organic Solidarity

  ❋ Gemeinschaft and Gesellschaft

❋ **How Relevant Today?**

Copyright © Allyn & Bacon 2008   Chapter 4: Social Structure and Social Interaction   22

Microsociological Perspective:
Social Interaction in Everyday Life

❋ **Examine Face-to-Face Interactions**

❋ **Symbolic Interaction**

  ❋ Symbols People Use

  ❋ How People Look at Things

  ❋ How it Affects Behavior and Orientations to Life

Copyright © Allyn & Bacon 2008   Chapter 4: Social Structure and Social Interaction   23

Microsociological Perspective:
Social Interaction in Everyday Life

Stereotypes

❋ **Assumptions About What People Are Like**

❋ **Classify Others By Visible Characteristics**

❋ **Ideas About Characteristics Guide Our Behavior**

Copyright © Allyn & Bacon 2008   Chapter 4: Social Structure and Social Interaction   24

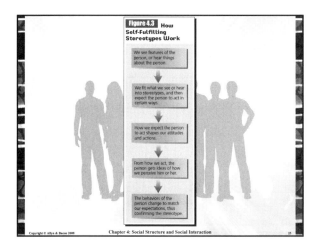

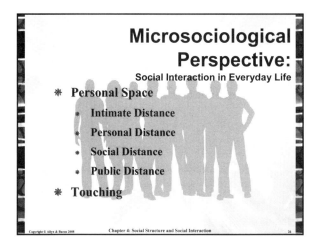

Dramaturgy:
The Presentation of Self in Everyday Life

Erving Goffman

* **Dramaturgy**
* **Impression Management**
* **Front and Back Stages**
* **Role Performance**
* **Role Strain Between and Within Roles**

Copyright © Allyn & Bacon 2008 — Chapter 4: Social Structure and Social Interaction — 28

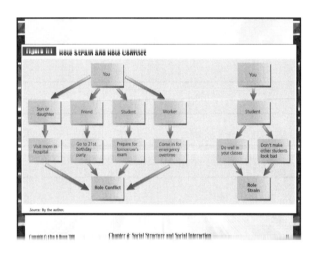

Dramaturgy:
The Presentation of Self in Everyday Life

* **Sign-Vehicles**
  * **Social Setting**
  * **Appearance**
  * **Manner**
* **Teamwork and Face Saving Behavior**
* **We Become the Roles we Play**
* **Applying Impression Management**

Copyright © Allyn & Bacon 2008 — Chapter 4: Social Structure and Social Interaction — 30

Ethnomethodology:
Uncovering Background Assumptions

* The Study of How People Do Things

* Harold Garfinkle's Experiments

Copyright © Allyn & Bacon 2008   Chapter 4: Social Structure and Social Interaction   31

Social Construction of Reality

* Definition of the Situation – Thomas Theorem

* Objective Reality vs. Subjective Interpretation

* Gynecological Examinations

Copyright © Allyn & Bacon 2008   Chapter 4: Social Structure and Social Interaction   32

Need for Macrosociology and Microsociology

* Understanding Incomplete Without Both

* Consider the Example of Groups Studied by William Chambliss

Copyright © Allyn & Bacon 2008   Chapter 4: Social Structure and Social Interaction   33

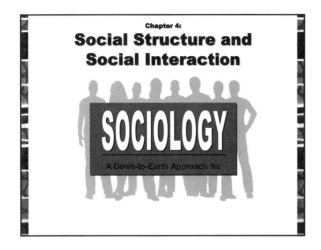

CHAPTER 5
HOW SOCIOLOGISTS DO RESEARCH

CHAPTER SUMMARY

- Sociologists conduct research about almost every area of human behavior. The choice of research topics depends on the sociologist's interests, the availability of subjects, the appropriateness of methods, and ethical considerations.

- Sociological research is needed because common sense ideas are often incorrect and based on limited information.

- Eight basic steps are included in scientific research: (1) selecting a topic, (2) defining the problem, (3) reviewing the literature, (4) formulating a hypothesis, (5) choosing a research method, (6) collecting the data, (7) analyzing the results, and (8) sharing the results.

- Sociologists use six research methods (or research designs) for gathering data: (1) surveys, (2) participant observations, (3) secondary analysis, (4) documents, (5) unobtrusive measures, and (6) experiments. The choice of a research method depends on the research questions, the researcher's access to potential subjects, the resources available, the researcher's background and training, and ethical considerations.

- Sociologists often find themselves researching controversial topics. Sometimes they poke into private lives, which might upset some people. Even a task like trying to count the homeless population can land sociologists in the middle of controversy.

- In the past, sociologists used to ignore the world of women, although that is no longer the case. However, the gender of the researcher can affect the findings in some kinds of research.

- Ethics are of concern to sociologists. Research ethics requires openness, honesty, truth, and protecting subjects.

- Research and theory are related to one another. Theory is used to generate research questions and interpret the data collected; when research findings don't match what is expected, theories are modified.

LEARNING OBJECTIVES
After reading Chapter 5, you should be able to:

1. Discuss what areas of human behavior and aspects of social life are valid topics for sociological research. (128)
2. Explain why there is a need for sociological research and common sense alone isn't enough. (128)
3. List and describe the eight basic steps for conducting scientific research. (128-130)

4. Know and discuss the six research methods that sociologists use, the tools that they employ, and the strengths and limitations of each. (131-141)
5. Cite the four primary factors that determine which research method or methods a sociologist uses to conduct his or her research. (141)
6. Discuss why sociological research can be controversial. (141)
7. Define, describe, and discuss the significance of the following terms associated with the research process: hypothesis, variable, independent variable, dependent variable, correlation, spurious correlation, operational definitions, validity, reliability, causation, replication, and generalizability. (131-139)
8. Define, describe, and discuss the significance of the following terms associated with the six research methods: survey, population, sample, random sample, stratified random sample, questionnaires, self-administered questionnaires, interview, interviewer bias, structured interviews, closed-ended questions, unstructured interviews, open-ended questions, rapport, participant observation, secondary analysis, documents, unobtrusive measures, experiment, experimental group, and control group. (131-139)
9. Understand the Hawthorne effect and its significance in conducting research. (140)
10. Distinguish between quantitative and qualitative research methods. (141)
11. Discuss the role that gender can and often does play in sociological research. (141)
12. Know the ethical guidelines that sociologists are expected to follow and the ethical issues raised in Mario Brajuha's and Laud Humphrey's research. (145-146)
13. Explain how and why research and theory need to work together in order to fully explore and understand human behavior. (146-148)

KEY TERMS
After studying the chapter, review the definition for each of the following terms.

closed-ended questions: questions followed by a list of possible answers to be selected by the respondent (136)

control group: the group of subjects not exposed to the independent variable in the study (138)

dependent variable: a factor that is changed by an independent variable (138)

documents: in its narrow sense, written sources that provide data; in its extended sense, archival material of any sort, including photographs, movies, CD's, DVD's, and so on (137)

experimental group: the group of subjects exposed to the independent variable in a study (138)

generalizability: the extent to which the findings from one group (or sample) can be generalized or applied to other groups (or populations) (137)

hypothesis: a statement of the expected relationship between variables according to predictions from a theory (129)

independent variable: a factor that causes a change in another variable, called the dependent variable (138)

interview: direct questioning of respondents (135)

interviewer bias: effects that interviewers have on respondents that lead to biased answers (135)

open-ended questions: questions that respondents answer in their own words (136)

operational definition: the way in which a researcher measures a variable (130)

participant observation (or fieldwork): research in which the researcher participates in a research setting while observing what is happening in that setting (136)

population: the target group to be studied (131)

qualitative research method: research in which the emphasis is placed on observing, describing, and interpreting people's behavior (141)

quantitative research method: research in which the emphasis is placed on measurement, the use of statistics, and numbers (141)

questionnaires: a list of questions to be asked of respondents (135)

random sample: a sample in which everyone in the target population has the same chance of being included in the study (132)

rapport: a feeling of trust between researchers and the subjects that they are studying (136)

reliability: the extent to which research produces consistent or dependable results (130)

replication: repeating a study in order to test its findings (130)

research method (or research design): one of six procedures sociologists used to collect data: surveys, participant observation, secondary analysis, documents, experiments, and unobtrusive measures (130)

respondents: people who respond to a survey, either in interviews or self-administered questionnaires (133)

sample: the individuals intended to represent the population to be studied (131)

secondary analysis: the analysis of data already collected by other researchers (137)

self-administered questionnaire: questionnaires that respondents fill out (135)

stratified random sample: a sample from select subgroups of the target population in which everyone in these subgroups has an equal chance of being included in the research (133)

structured interviews: interviews that use closed-ended questions (136)

survey: the collection of data by having people answer a series of questions (131)

unobtrusive measures: ways of observing people who do not know they are being studied (141)

unstructured interviews: interviews that use open-ended questions (136)

validity: the extent to which an operational definition measures what it was intended to measure (130)

variable: a factor thought to be significant for human behavior, which varies or changes from one case to another (129)

KEY PEOPLE
Review the major theoretical contributions or findings of these people.

Chloe Bird and Patricia Rieker: These sociologists caution against assuming that research findings that apply to one gender apply to the other because women's and men's lives differ significantly. (144)

Mario Brajuha: During an investigation into a restaurant fire, this sociologist refused to hand over field notes he had taken. He had promised to keep the information confidential. (145)

Laud Humphreys: This sociologist carried out doctoral research on homosexual activity but ran into problems when he misrepresented himself to his research subjects. Although he earned his doctorate degree, he was fired from his position because of his questionable ethics. (145-146)

Elton Mayo: Mayo is famous for his research at the Western Electric Company Hawthorne plant during the 1920s. He concluded that workers adjusted their productivity because they knew they were being observed. This phenomenon came to be known as the *Hawthorne effect.* (140)

C. Wright Mills: Mills argued that research without theory is of little value; simply a collection of unrelated "facts," and theory without research is abstract and empty. (146)

Peter Rossi: Rossi produced a controversial piece of research related to counting the homeless, which revealed that the average number of homeless on any given night was far less than homeless advocates had been stating. (141-143)

Diana Scully and Joseph Marolla: These two sociologists interviewed convicted rapists in prison and found that rapists are not sick or overwhelmed by uncontrollable urges, but rather, are men who have learned to view rape as appropriate in various circumstances. (147)

PRACTICE TEST

1.   A valid topic for sociological research is: (128)
   a.   any human behavior that is not considered to be one's personal, private behavior.
   b.   any human behavior that is not considered to be personally disreputable.
   c.   any human behavior.
   d.   any human behavior that can be studied, but only if it can be studied by the use of surveys and interviews.

2.   In which step of the research model do you predict relationships between or among variables? (128-129)
   a.   reviewing the literature
   b.   defining the problem
   c.   formulating a hypothesis
   d.   collecting the data

3.   What is the term used to predict a relationship between variables according to predictions from a theory? (129)
   a.   operational definition
   b.   hypothesis
   c.   assertion
   d.   topic statement

4.   A factor significant for human behavior that can vary from one case to another is: (129)
   a.   a variable.
   b.   a standard topic.
   c.   a hypothesis.
   d.   an operational definition.

5.   Which of the following is *not* a reason why researchers review the literature?   (129)
   a.   to help them narrow down the problem by pinpointing particular areas to examine.
   b.   to develop ideas about how to do their own research.
   c.   to insure that their research findings will confirm their hypotheses.
   d.   to determine whether the problem has been answered already.

6.   Which of the following best describes the extent to which research produces consistent results? (130)
   a.   justification
   b.   reliability
   c.   bias
   d.   validity

7. The target group for a study is called a: (131)
    a.   sample.
    b.   population.
    c.   stratified random sample.
    c.   model.

8. What is the name given to a sample whereby everyone in the population has an equal chance of being included in the study? (132)
    a.   stratified random sample
    b.   random sample
    c.   median
    d.   full sample

9. Based on in your text, all of the following are ways to measure "average" *except*: (133)
    a.   medial.
    b.   mean.
    c.   median.
    d.   mode.

10. Why might a researcher "load the dice" in designing a research project? (134)
    a.   The researcher doesn't know any better.
    b.   The researcher may have a vested interest in the outcome of the research.
    c.   The researcher is short on time and money but still wants to get the desired results.
    d.   All of the above.

11. Which technique allows a large number of people to be sampled at a lower cost? (135)
    a.   self-administered questionnaires
    b.   telephone interviews
    c.   personal interviews
    d.   experiments

12. Sometimes when a researcher is asking questions to a respondent face-to-face or over the telephone, the person may feel compelled to give "socially acceptable" answers. This outcome is due to: (136)
    a.   asking open-ended questions.
    b.   rapport between the respondent and researcher.
    c.   interviewer bias.
    d.   interviewee bias.

13. When researchers analyze data collected by others, they are using: (137)
    a.   secondary analysis.
    b.   primary research.
    c.   generalizability.
    d.   plagiarism.

14. Sources such as newspapers, diaries, bank records, police reports, household accounts, and immigration files are all considered: (137)
    a. unreliable data sources.
    b. documents that provide useful information for investigating social life.
    c. useful for doing quantitative research but not valid when doing qualitative analysis.
    d. of limited validity because it would be difficult to replicate the study.

15. In an experiment, the group not exposed to the independent variable in the study is: (138)
    a. the guinea pig group.
    b. the control group.
    c. the experimental group.
    d. the maintenance group.

16. When you analyze your data you find that men who abuse women are often drunk at the time the abuse takes place. How do sociologists refer to the simultaneous presence of both alcohol and abuse? (139)
    a. simulation
    b. correlation
    c. association
    d. intervening variable

17. Billboards are being developed that can read information from a chip in your car key. Then the billboard will display your name and a message. This is an example of: (141)
    a. unobtrusive measures.
    b. survey.
    c. bias in research.
    d. participation.

18. How do sociologists decide what research method to use? (141)
    a. By matching methods with available resources.
    b. By determining if they have access to subjects.
    c. By deciding what their background and training is in a particular method.
    d. All of the above.

19. Surveys are more likely to be used by researchers trained in: (141)
    a. social psychology.
    b. ethnomethodology.
    c. quantitative research methods.
    d. qualitative research methods.

20. Having taken a good part of its tradition from sociological research, marketing research: (142)
    a. combines both qualitative and quantitative methods.
    b. does not use a symbolic interactionist perspective to interpret focus groups.
    c. utilizes survey research as opposed to any form of small group research.
    d. never uses quantitative techniques to analyze data.

21. Peter Rossi's research counting the homeless involved using: (143)
    a. participant observation.
    b. secondary analysis.
    c. a stratified random sample.
    d. biased sampling.

22. Why is it important to consider gender in planning and conducting research?   (144)
    a. The gender of the interviewer might produce interviewer bias.
    b. It cannot be assumed that men and women experiences the social work in the same way, so both need to be studied in order to have a complete picture.
    c. Gender is a significant factor in social life.
    d. All of the above.

23. Research ethics require: (145)
    a. openness.
    b. that a researcher not falsify results or plagiarize someone else's work.
    c. that research subjects should not be harmed by the research.
    d. all of the above.

24. What researcher would not hand over his field notes in an investigation of a fire? (145)
    a. Laud Humphreys
    b. Robin Williams
    c. Mario Brajuha
    d. Lewis Coser

25. The relationship between research and theory in sociology is that: (146)
    a. research stimulates the development of theory but not the need for further research.
    b. research always precedes the development of theory.
    c. theory and research must be truly independently pursued to maintain objectivity in research.
    d. research and theory are both essential for sociology.

Answer Key

1. C
2. C
3. A
4. A
5. C
6. B
7. B
8. B
9. A
10. B
11. A
12. C
13. A
14. B
15. B
16. B
17. A
18. D
19. C
20. A
21. C
22. D
23. D
24. C
25. D

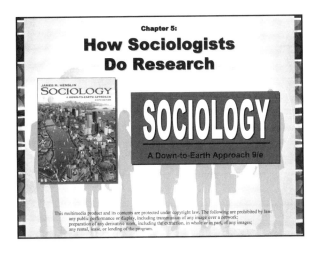

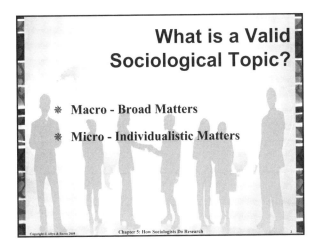

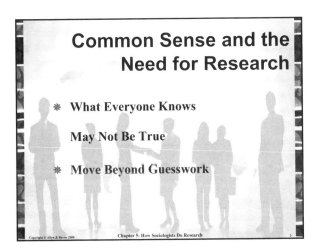

A Research Model

* Selecting a Topic

* Defining a Problem

* Reviewing the Literature

* Formulating a Hypothesis

Copyright © Allyn & Bacon 2008 — Chapter 5: How Sociologists Do Research

A Research Model

* Choosing a Research Method

* Collecting Data

* Analyzing Results

* Sharing Results

Copyright © Allyn & Bacon 2008

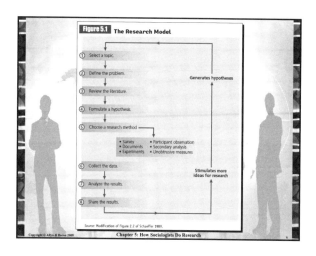

Figure 5.1 The Research Model

1. Select a topic.
2. Define the problem.
3. Review the literature.
4. Formulate a hypothesis.
5. Choose a research method
   - Survey
   - Documents
   - Experiments
   - Participant observation
   - Secondary analysis
   - Unobtrusive measures
6. Collect the data.
7. Analyze the results.
8. Share the results.

Generates hypotheses

Stimulates more ideas for research

Source: Modification of Figure 2.2 of Schaefer 1989.

Copyright © Allyn & Bacon 2008 — Chapter 5: How Sociologists Do Research

Research Methods

Surveys

* Selecting a Sample
  * Random Sample
  * Stratified Random Sample
* Asking Neutral Questions

Chapter 5: How Sociologists Do Research

Research Methods

Questionnaires

* Self-Administered
* Allow the Largest Sample
* Low Cost
* Loss of Researcher Control

Chapter 5: How Sociologists Do Research

Research Methods

* Interviews
  * More Researcher Control
  * Time Consuming
  * Interviewer Bias
* Structured Interviews
  * Open-Ended Questions
* Establishing Rapport

Chapter 5: How Sociologists Do Research

Research Methods

Participant Observation (Fieldwork)

✳ **Researcher Participates**

✳ **Problems with Generalizability**

✳ **Done for Exploratory Work**

✳ **Generates Hypotheses**

Copyright © Allyn & Bacon 2008   Chapter 5: How Sociologists Do Research   10

Research Methods

Secondary Analysis

✳ **Analyze Data Collected by Others**

✳ **Researcher Cannot Be Sure of Data Quality**

Copyright © Allyn & Bacon 2008   Chapter 5: How Sociologists Do Research   11

Research Methods

Documents

✳ **Examine Books, Newspapers, Diaries, etc.**

✳ **Limited Scope**

✳ **Cannot Study Topic Unless Access is Granted**

Copyright © Allyn & Bacon 2008   Chapter 5: How Sociologists Do Research   12

Research Methods

Experiments

* **Experimental Group**
* **Control Group**
* **Independent Variables**
* **Dependent Variables**

Copyright © Allyn & Bacon 2008   Chapter 5: How Sociologists Do Research   13

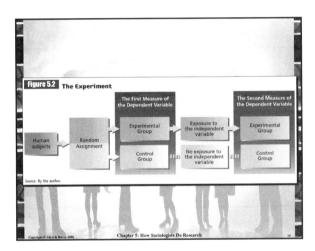

Figure 5.2 The Experiment

Human subjects → Random Assignment → Experimental Group / Control Group → The First Measure of the Dependent Variable → Exposure to the independent variable / No exposure to the independent variable → The Second Measure of the Dependent Variable → Experimental Group / Control Group

Source: By the author.

Copyright © Allyn & Bacon 2008   Chapter 5: How Sociologists Do Research   14

Research Methods

Unobtrusive Measures

* **Observe People Without Them Knowing**
* **Question of Ethics**
* **Hawthorne Effect**

Copyright © Allyn & Bacon 2008   Chapter 5: How Sociologists Do Research   15

Deciding Which Method to Use

* Available Resources

* Access to Subjects

* Purpose of Research

* Researcher's Background and Training

Copyright © Allyn & Bacon 2008   Chapter 5: How Sociologists Do Research   16

Deciding Which Method to Use

* Quantitative Research Methods
  * Emphasis on Precise Measurement
  * Uses Statistics and Numbers
* Qualitative Research Methods
  * Emphasis on Observing, Describing, and Interpreting Behavior

Copyright © Allyn & Bacon 2008   Chapter 5: How Sociologists Do Research

Controversy in Sociological Research

* Poke into Private Areas of Lives

* Threatens Those with a Stake

Copyright © Allyn & Bacon 2008   Chapter 5: How Sociologists Do Research   18

Gender in Sociological Research

❋ Affects Orientation and Attitudes

❋ Interviewer Bias

❋ Women and Men Lead Different Lives

Copyright © Allyn & Bacon 2008   Chapter 5: How Sociologists Do Research   19

Ethics in Sociological Research

❋ Openness, Honesty, and Truthfulness

  ❋ Forbids Falsifying Results

  ❋ Condemns Plagiarism

❋ Subjects' Informed Consent

❋ Subjects' Anonymity

Copyright © Allyn & Bacon 2008   Chapter 5: How Sociologists Do Research   20

Ethics in Sociological Research

❋ Protecting Subjects: The Brajuha Research

❋ Misleading Subjects: The Humphreys Research

Copyright © Allyn & Bacon 2008   Chapter 5: How Sociologists Do Research   21

101

How Research and Theory Work Together

❋ **Neither Research nor Theory can Stand Alone**

❋ **Theories Must Be Tested**

❋ **Findings Must be Explained with Theory**

Copyright © Allyn & Bacon 2008   Chapter 5: How Sociologists Do Research   22

Chapter 5:

How Sociologists Do Research

SOCIOLOGY

A Down-to-Earth Approach 9/e

CHAPTER 6
SOCIETIES TO SOCIAL NETWORKS

CHAPTER SUMMARY

- Groups are the essence of life in society. We become who we are by our membership in groups. Essential features of groups are that members have a sense of belonging and interact with one another. Society is the largest and most complex group that sociologists study.

- On the way to postindustrial society, humans passed through four types of societies, each due to a social revolution that was linked to new technology. The societies that have existed are (1) hunting and gathering; (2) pastoral and horticultural, the result of the domestication revolution; (3) agricultural, the result of the invention of the plow; and (4) industrial, the result of the Industrial Revolution.

- Today's postindustrial society, based on information, services, and technology, has emerged with the invention of the computer chip. Another new type of society, the bioeconomic society, may be emerging and will center on applying and altering both plant and animal genetic structures.

- The following types of groups exist within society: primary groups, secondary groups, in-groups and out-groups, reference groups, and social networks. Changing technology has given birth to a new type of group — the electronic community.

- Group dynamics examines the ways in which individuals affect groups and how groups affect individuals. Group size is a significant aspect of group dynamics: As a group grows larger, it becomes more stable but the intensity or intimacy of the group decreases.

- Leaders can be either instrumental (task-oriented) or expressive (socioemotional); both are essential for the functioning of the group. The three main leadership styles are authoritarian, democratic, and laissez-faire. Different situations require different styles of leadership.

- The Asch experiment demonstrated the influence of peer groups over their members, while the Milgram experiment showed how powerfully people are influenced by authority. Groupthink, which occurs when political leaders become cut off from information that does not support their opinion, poses a serious threat to society's well-being. The circulation of independent research conducted by social scientists is one of the keys to preventing group think.

LEARNING OBJECTIVES

After reading Chapter 6, you should be able to:

1. Know the essential features of what comprises a group. (152)
2. Identify the five types of societies that have developed in the course of human history, understand how they evolved, and cite their distinct forms of social division, social labor, and social inequality. (153-158)
3. Identify the four technological innovations that were most responsible for the social transformations of society and understand their respective roles in those transformations. (153-158)
4. Discuss how recent advances in human genetics, such as cloning and bioengineering, may be transforming society into a biotech society. (157-158)
5. Distinguish between the terms "aggregate," "category," and "group." (159)
6. Describe the social characteristics, relationships, and/or functions that are associated with primary groups, secondary groups, in-groups and out-groups, reference groups, social networks, and electronic communities. (159-165)
7. Know what is meant by "group dynamics" and discuss the effect of group size on the stability and intimacy within the group. (165-168)
8. Describe how group size can affect attitudes, behavior, and willingness to help. (167-168)
9. Identify and compare the two types of group leaders and the three types of leadership styles that are typically found within groups. (168-170)
10. Discuss the methodology, findings, and implications of the Asch experiment and the Milgram experiment as they relate, respectively, to peer pressure and obedience to authority. (170-172)
11. Define the term "groupthink," talk about why it is dangerous, and discuss what can —and should— be done to prevent it. (173-174)

KEY TERMS
After studying the chapter, review the definition for each of the following terms.

aggregate: individuals who temporarily share the same physical space but do not see themselves as belonging together (159)

agricultural revolution: the second social revolution, based on the invention of the plow, which led to agricultural societies (154)

agricultural society: a society based on large-scale agriculture; plows drawn by animals are the source of food production (151)

authoritarian leader: a leader who leads by giving orders (169)

biotech society: a society whose economy increasingly centers around the application of genetics—human genetics for medicine, and plant and animal genetics for the production of food and materials (157)

category: people who have similar characteristics (159)

clique: a cluster of people within a larger group who choose to interact with one another; an internal faction (163)

coalition: the alignment of some members of a group against others (166)

democratic leader: a leader who leads by trying to reach a consensus (169)

domestication revolution: the first social revolution, based on the domestication of plants and animals, which led to pastoral and horticultural societies (154)

dyad: the smallest possible group, consisting of two persons (165)

electronic community: individuals who regularly interact with one another on the Internet and who think of themselves as belonging together (165)

expressive leader: an individual who increases harmony and minimizes conflict in a group; also known as a *socioemotional leader* (169)

group: people who have something in common and believe that what they have in common is significant; also called a social group (152)

group dynamics: the ways in which individuals affect groups and groups affect individuals (165)

groupthink: a narrowing of thought by a group of people, leading to the perception that there is only one correct answer; to even suggest alternatives becomes a sign of disloyalty (173)

horticultural society: a society based on cultivating plants by the use of hand tools (154)

hunting and gathering society: a human group dependent on hunting and gathering for its survival (153)

Industrial Revolution: the third social revolution, occurring when machines powered by fuels replaced most animal and human power (154)

industrial society: a society based on the harnessing of machines powered by fuels (156)

in-groups: groups toward which one feels loyalty (161)

instrumental leader: an individual who tries to keep the group moving toward its goals; also known as a *task-oriented leader* (169)

laissez-faire leader: an individual who leads by being highly permissive (169)

leader: someone who influences other people (168)

leadership styles: ways in which people express their leadership (169)

networking: using one's social networks for some gain (165)

out-groups: groups toward which one feels antagonisms (161)

pastoral society: a society based on the pasturing of animals (154)

postindustrial society: a society based on information, services, and high technology, rather than on raw materials and manufacturing (156)

primary group: a group characterized by intimate, long-term, face-to-face association and cooperation (159)

reference group: Herbert Hyman's term for the groups we use as standards to evaluate ourselves (162)

secondary group: compared with a primary group, a larger, relatively temporary, more anonymous, formal, and impersonal group based on some interest or activity. Its members are likely to interact on the basis of specific statuses (159)

shaman: the healing specialist of a tribe who attempts to control the spirits thought to cause a disease or injury; commonly called a witch doctor (153)

small group: a group small enough for everyone to interact directly with all the other members (165)

social network: the social ties radiating outward from the self that link people together (162)

society: people who share a culture and a territory (152)

triad: a group of three persons (166)

KEY PEOPLE

Review the major theoretical contributions or findings of these people.

Solomon Asch: Asch is famous for his research on conformity to peer pressure. (170-171)

Herbert Blumer: He describes an industrial society as one in which goods are no longer produced by the brute force of humans or animals but by machines powered by fuels. (156)

Elise Boulding: This sociologist hypothesized that women's status in agricultural societies declined sharply once men were put in charge of plowing and cattle. (155)

Charles H. Cooley: It was Cooley who noted the central role of primary groups in the development of one's sense of self. (159)

John Darley and Bibb Latané: These researchers investigated how group size affects members' attitudes and behaviors. They found that as the group grew larger, an individuals' sense of personal responsibility decreased. (168)

Emile Durkheim: Durkheim viewed the small group as a buffer between the individual and society, helping to prevent anomie. (159)

Lloyd Howells and Selwyn Becker: These social psychologists found that factors such as location within a group underlie people's choices of leaders. (169)

Irving Janis: Janis coined the term "groupthink" to refer to the tunnel vision that a group of people sometimes develop. (173-174)

Ronald Lippitt and Ralph White: These social psychologists carried out a classic study on leadership styles and found that the style of leadership affected the behavior of group members. (169-170)

Robert Merton: Merton observed that the traits of in-groups become viewed as virtues, while those same traits in out-groups are seen as vices. (161)

Stanley Milgram: Milgram's research has contributed greatly to sociological knowledge of group life. He did research on social networks and individual conformity to group pressure. (163, 171-172)

Georg Simmel: This early sociologist was one of the first to note the significance of group size; he used the terms dyad and triad to describe small groups. (165-166)

PRACTICE TEST

1. What term is used to describe people who interact with one another and think of themselves as belonging together? (152)
    a. assembly
    b. aggregate
    c. category
    d. group

2. The largest and most complex group that sociologists study is a: (152)
    a. group.
    b. society.
    c. triad.
    d. state.

3. Which type of society typically has a shaman? (153)
    a   pastoral
    b. industrial
    c. hunting and gathering
    d. agricultural

4. How many hunting and gathering groups remain in the world? (154)
    a. fewer than 300
    b. 1000
    c. about 5000
    d. 7000

5. On what are pastoral societies based? (154)
    a. The cultivation of plants.
    b. The pasturing of animals.
    c. The invention of the plow.
    d. The use of large-scale agriculture.

6. As group life moves from fewer to more possessions, one sees: (155)
    a. less horticultural societies and more pastoral societies.
    b. a move to greater social economic inequality.
    c. a move towards greater egalitarianism.
    d. a move towards less complexity in its development of social organization.

7. Most of the early part of the Industrial Revolution was marked by: (156)
    a. a high degree of toleration for the worker's struggle for equality.
    b. no legal rights for safe working conditions, nor for unionizing.
    c. no illegal use of force against American workers.
    d. an imposing of the feudal-type system on American workers.

8.	In an industrial society, which of the following was an indicator of increasing equality? (156)
	a.	better housing
	b.	the abolition of slavery
	c.	a move toward more representative political systems
	d.	all of the above

9.	Which society has information as a basic component? (156-157)
	a.	industrial
	b.	postindustrial
	c.	biotech
	d.	none of the above

10.	Which society has goats whose milk contains spider silk and no-sneeze cats? (157)
	a.	bionic society
	b.	industrial society
	c.	postindustrial society
	d.	biotech society

11.	According to Cooley, which group is essential to an individual's psychological well-being? (159)
	a.	primary group
	b	secondary group
	c.	therapy group
	d.	interpersonal group

12.	People waiting at a red light are an example of: (156)
	a.	an in-group.
	b.	a category.
	c.	an aggregate.
	d.	a group.

13.	What are some of the consequences of in-group membership? (161)
	a.	discrimination
	b.	hatred
	c	killing
	d.	all of the above

14.	The groups we use as standards to evaluate ourselves are called: (162)
	a.	primary groups.
	b.	reference groups.
	c.	voluntary groups
	d.	looking-glass groups.

15. How are some college students finding new ways to meet friends electronically? (164)
    a. through cliques
    b. facebooking
    c. telecommuting
    d. face saving

16. Which of the following is *not* a characteristic of a triad? (166)
    a. The introduction of a third person into a dyad reduces the intensity of the interactions.
    b. A triad is inherently unstable because coalitions can form.
    c. One of the members of the group often acts as an arbitrator or mediator.
    d. The continuation of the group depends on the success of the arbitrator in settling disputes.

17. When some group members align themselves against one another, this is known as a: (166)
    a. triadic allegiance.
    b. secondary group.
    c. coalition.
    d. primary group.

18. As long as a small group does not grow too large, the general pattern is that as it gets larger: (167)
    a. it becomes less stable but more intimate.
    b. it becomes both less stable and less intimate.
    c. it becomes more stable but less intimate.
    d. it becomes both more stable and more intimate.

19. A diffusion of responsibility occurs: (168)
    a. when someone does not identify with a reference group.
    b. when someone feels excluded from a coalition.
    c. when a group is larger than a dyad and each member feels that someone else will act.
    d. when the leadership is authoritarian.

20. According to sociologists, leaders tend to have certain characteristics that may include: (168)
    a. that they are more outgoing.
    b. that they tend to be taller and are judged better-looking than others.
    c. where they sit in a group.
    d. all of the above.

21.   An expressive leader: (169)
       a.   tries to keep the group moving toward its goals.
       b.   is also known as a task-oriented leader.
       c.   increases harmony and minimizes conflict in a group.
       d.   is the director of the drama club.

22.   Leaders who are task-oriented and try to keep their group on-track are known as: (169)
       a.   instrumental leaders.
       b.   laissez-faire leaders.
       c.   democratic leaders.
       d.   expressive leaders.

23.   Of the 50 people that Solomon Asch tested, what percentage stuck to their guns and always gave the right answer? (171)
       a.   25 percent
       b.   33 percent
       c.   40 percent
       d.   53 percent

24.   What was the significance of Stanley Milgram's "electric shock" experiment? (171-172)
       a.   Learners were able to retain more of what they learned.
       b.   Intelligent adults followed orders given by someone "in authority" even when they thought that following these orders applied painful, even possibly deadly shocks to individuals being studied.
       c.   Intelligent adults will not follow orders that harm others unless they fear they themselves will be physically punished.
       d.   It is acceptable to violate codes of ethics to gather important data.

25.   When the U.S. Justice Department ruled that the U.S. was not bound by the Geneva Convention that prohibits torturing, it was an example of: (174)
       a.   group solidarity.
       b.   diffusion of responsibility.
       c.   groupthink.
       d.   group dynamics.

Answer Key

1. D
2. B
3. C
4. A
5. B
6. B
7. B
8. D
9. B
10. D
11. A
12. C
13. D
14. B
15. B
16. D
17. C
18. C
19. C
20. D
21. C
22. A
23. A
24. B
25. C

Chapter 6:
Societies to Social Networks

SOCIOLOGY

SOCIOLOGY

A Down-to-Earth Approach 9/e

What is a Group?

"People who interact with one another and think of themselves as belonging together."

Copyright © Allyn & Bacon 2008   Chapter 6: Societies to Social Networks   2

Societies and Their Transformation

Domestication Revolution

* **Hunting and Gathering**

* **Pastoral and Horticultural**

* **Agricultural**

Copyright © Allyn & Bacon 2008   Chapter 6: Societies to Social Networks   3

Societies and Their Transformation

✳ **Industrial Revolution**

✳ **Postindustrial (Information)**

✳ **Biotech – New Type?**

Copyright © Allyn & Bacon 2008   Chapter 6: Societies to Social Networks

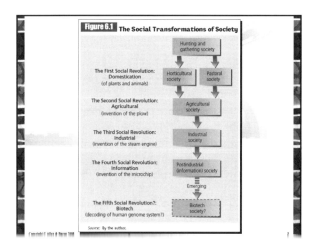

Figure 6.1 The Social Transformations of Society

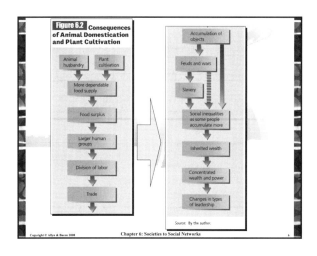

Figure 6.2 Consequences of Animal Domestication and Plant Cultivation

Groups Within Society

Not to be Confused with Groups...

* **Aggregate**

* **Category**

Groups Within Society

* **Primary Groups**
    * Face-to-Face
    * The Family
    * Friends
* **Producing a Mirror Within**

Groups Within Society

Secondary Groups

* **Larger, More Anonymous**

* **Members Interact Based on Statuses**

* **Fail to Satisfy Need for Intimate Association**

Groups Within Society

In-Groups and Out-Groups

❋ Loyalty to In-Groups

❋ Antagonism Towards Out-Groups

Groups Within Society

❋ In-Groups and Out-Groups Produce...

  ✴ Loyalty

  ✴ Sense of Superiority

  ✴ Rivalries

❋ Implications for Socially Diverse Society

Groups Within Society

Reference Groups

❋ Evaluating Ourselves

❋ Expose Us to Contradictory

Standards

Groups Within Society

✳ **Social Networks**

✳ **The Small World Phenomenon**

✳ **Is the Small World Phenomenon a Myth?**

Copyright © Allyn & Bacon 2008   Chapter 6: Societies to Social Networks   13

Groups Within Society

✳ **Implications for Socially Diverse Society**

✳ **Implications for Science**

Copyright © Allyn & Bacon 2008   Chapter 6: Societies to Social Networks   14

Groups Within Society

✳ **Electronic Communities**

    ✳ **People Connect Online**

    ✳ **Newsgroups**

    ✳ **Online Chat Rooms**

✳ **Some Meet Definition of Group**

Copyright © Allyn & Bacon 2008   Chapter 6: Societies to Social Networks   15

Group Dynamics

* **Group Size Affects Stability and Intimacy**
  * **Dyad**
  * **Triad**
  * **Coalitions**
* **As Size Increases, So Does Stability**
* **As Size Increases, Intensity and Intimacy Decrease**

Copyright © Allyn & Bacon 2008   Chapter 6: Societies to Social Networks   16

Group Dynamics

* **Effects of Group Size on Attitudes and Behavior**
* **The Larger the Group…**
  * **Greater Diffusion of Responsibility**
  * **Increase in Formality**
  * **Division into Smaller Groups**

Copyright © Allyn & Bacon 2008   Chapter 6: Societies to Social Networks   17

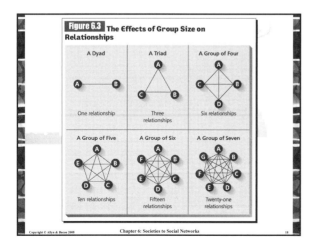

Copyright © Allyn & Bacon 2008   Chapter 6: Societies to Social Networks   18

Leadership

* Who Becomes a Leader?
* Types of Leaders
  * Instrumental
  * Expressive

Leadership

* Leadership Styles
  * Authoritarian
  * Democratic
  * Laissez-Faire
* Leadership Styles in Changing Situations

Group Dynamics

* Power of Peer Pressure—Asch Experiment
  * Study on Conformity

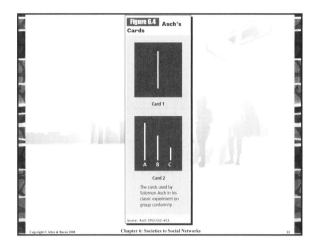

Group Dynamics

❋ **Power of Peer Pressure—Asch Experiment**

  ✴ **Study on Conformity**

❋ **Power of Authority—Milgram Experiment**

  ✴ **Administering Shocks**

Chapter 6: Societies to Social Networks

Groupthink - Global Consequences

❋ **Irving Janis Coined the Term**

❋ **Examples of Groupthink**

❋ **Preventing Groupthink**

Copyright © Allyn & Bacon 2008   Chapter 6: Societies to Social Networks   24

Chapter 6:
Societies to Social Networks

SOCIOLOGY
A Down-to-Earth Approach 9/e

_____

_____

_____

_____

_____

_____

_____

CHAPTER 7
BUREAUCRACY AND FORMAL ORGANIZATIONS

CHAPTER SUMMARY

- The rationalization of society refers to a major transformation in the way people think—from a desire to protect time-honored ways of thinking to a concern with efficiency and practical results. Max Weber traced the rationalization of society to Protestantism, while Marx attributed it to capitalism.

- As a result of the emphasis on rationality, formal organizations have become a central feature of our society. Their most common form is a bureaucracy characterized by Weber as having a hierarchy of authority, a division of labor, written rules, written communications, and impersonality. Weber's characteristics of bureaucracy are an "ideal type" that may not accurately describe any real organization.

- The dysfunctions of bureaucracies include alienation, red tape, a lack of communication between units, goal displacement, and incompetence. In Weber's view, the impersonality of bureaucracies tends to produce alienation among workers. In Marx's view, workers experience alienation when they lose control of the work process and are cut off from the finished product of their labor.

- In the United States voluntary associations (groups made up of volunteers who organize on the basis of some mutual interest) have proliferated. Voluntary associations play an important role in society, furthering interests, offering people an identity and a sense of purpose, and helping to govern and maintain social order. The iron law of oligarchy—the tendency of formal organizations to be dominated by a small, self-perpetuating elite—is a problem in voluntary associations.

- The concept of corporate culture refers to the organization's traditions, values, and unwritten norms. Much of this culture is invisible. It can affect its members, either negatively or positively, depending on the opportunities for members to achieve.

- Greater emphasis is now being placed on humanizing work settings to develop rather than impede human potential. The development of quality circles, work teams, corporate day care, and employee stock ownership plans represent attempts by organizations to humanize the workplace.

- The Japanese corporate model provides a contrast to that in America, although the reality of life in a Japanese corporation is at variance with the model that is generally presented.

LEARNING OBJECTIVES

After reading Chapter 7, you should be able to:

1. Define the rationalization of society and discuss its ramifications. (178)
2. Differentiate between the views of Karl Marx and Max Weber on what led to the rationalization of society and which view is correct. (179-180)
3. Define the term bureaucracy and how it emerged. (181)
4. List and discuss the characteristics of bureaucracies. (1818-183)
5. Explain the difference between "ideal" and "real" bureaucracy. (183-184)
6. Cite and discuss examples of the dysfunctions of bureaucracies. (184-187)
7. Discuss goal displacement and the perpetuation of bureaucracies. (187-188)
8. Explain the sociological significance of bureaucracies. (188)
9. Contrast bureaucracies with voluntary organizations. (188)
10. Discuss the functions of voluntary organizations (188)
11. Explain the "iron law of oligarchy" within voluntary associations. (190-191)
12. Understand the hidden corporate culture and its ramifications on women and minority employees. (191-192)
13. Describe and evaluate the different steps many corporations have taken to humanize their work settings and maximize the potential of their employees. (193-195)
14. Discuss the conflict perspective's critique of corporate attempts to humanize the work setting. (195)
15. Explain the fads in corporate culture, including ideas such as quality circles and "corporate cook-offs". (195)
16. Explain the role technology currently plays in the control of workers and how that role may soon be expanding. (195196)
17. Compare and contrast the Japanese and American corporate models. (196-198)
18. Discuss myth versus reality in the Japanese model. (198)

KEY TERMS
After studying the chapter, review the definition for each of the following terms.

alienation: Marx's term for workers' lack of connection to the product of their labor (being assigned repetitive tasks on a small part of a product leads to a sense of powerlessness and normlessness); others use the term in the general sense of not feeling a part of something (186)

bureaucracy: a formal organization with a hierarchy of authority, a clear division of labor, and impersonality of positions; emphasis on written rules, communications, and records (181)

capitalism: an economic system characterized by private ownership of the means of production, the pursuit of profit, and market competition (180)

formal organization: a secondary group designed to achieve explicit objectives (181)

goal displacement: the adoption of new goals by an organization; also known as *goal replacement* (187)

humanizing a work setting: organizing a workplace in such a way that it develops rather than impedes human potential (193)

iron law of oligarchy (the): Robert Michels's phrase for the tendency of formal organizations to be dominated by a small, self-perpetuating elite (190)

Peter Principle: a tongue-in-cheek observation that the members of an organization are promoted for their accomplishments until they reach their level of incompetence; there they cease to be promoted, remaining at the level at which they can no longer do good work (187)

rationality: using rules, efficiency, and practical results as the right way to approach human affairs (178)

rationalization of society: a widespread acceptance of rationality and the social organizations that are built largely around this idea (179)

traditional orientation: the idea that the past is the best guide for the present; characterizes tribal, peasant, and feudal societies (178)

voluntary association: a group made up of people who voluntarily organize on the basis of some mutual interest; also known as *voluntary memberships* and *voluntary organizations* (188)

KEY PEOPLE
Review the major theoretical contributions or findings of these people.

Peter Evans and James Rauch: These sociologists examined government bureaucracies in 35 developing nations and found that those with centralized bureaucracies in which workers are hired on the basis of merit were more prosperous than those that lacked such organization. (187)

Elaine Fox and George Arquitt: These sociologists studied local posts of the Veterans of Foreign Wars (VFW); they found three types of members and evidence of the iron law of oligarchy. (190-191)

Rosabeth Moss Kanter: Kanter studied the hidden corporate culture and found that for the most part it continually reproduces itself by promoting those workers who fit the elite's stereotypical views. (191)

Gary Marx: Marx has written about the "maximum-security" workplace, given the increased use of computers to control workers. (196)

Karl Marx: Marx believed that the emergence of rationality was due to capitalism. He believed that capitalism changed the way people thought about life rather than people's orientation to life producing capitalism. (179-180)

Robert Michels: Michels first used the term "the iron law of oligarchy" to describe the tendency for the leaders of an organization to become entrenched. (190)

William Ouchi: Ouchi studied the characteristics of the Japanese corporation. (196-198)

George Ritzer: Ritzer coined the term the "McDonaldization of society" to describe the increasing standardization of modern social life. (184)

David Sills: Sills studied goal displacement in the March of Dimes, as well as identifying four additional functions that some voluntary groups perform. (187-189)

Alexis de Tocqueville: This Frenchman traveled across the United States in the 1830s in order to observe the customs of the new nation. One of his observations was that Americans have a tendency to join voluntary associations. (188)

Max Weber: Weber studied the rationalization of society by investigating the link between Protestantism and capitalism and identifying the characteristics of bureaucracy. (180-187)

PRACTICE TEST

1. Underlying our information age is an emphasis on: (178)
   a. rationality.
   b. the stability of traditional beliefs.
   c. strong government regulations.
   d. primary personal relationships.

2. Karl Marx believed that capitalism resulted in: (179)
   a. decreasing efficiency.
   b. breaking the bonds of tradition.
   c. discouraging investment of capital.
   d. a lessening in the production of goods.

3. In reconciling Weber's and Marx's views on rationality, sociologists feel that: (180)
   a. Weber was most correct.
   b. Marx was most correct.
   c. Weber and Marx were both incorrect.
   d. no analyst has yet reconciled the opposing views to their satisfaction.

4. All of the following statements are true about formal organizations **except:** (181)
   a. with industrialization, secondary groups became common.
   b. throughout time there have been many formal organizations.
   c. with rationality came the development of formal organizations.
   d. none of the above.

5. All of the following are characteristics of bureaucracy, *except*: (181-183)
   a. a division of labor.
   b. a hierarchy with assignments flowing upward and accountability flowing downward.
   c. written rules, communications, and records.
   d. impersonality.

6. Which characteristic of a bureaucracy believes that the office, not the individual who holds the office, is important? (183)
   a. clear levels of organization
   b. written rules
   c. impersonality
   d. written communications

7. The first theorist to identify the essential characteristics of an "ideal" bureaucracy was: (183)
   a. August Comte.
   b. Karl Marx.
   c. Max Weber.
   d. Emile Durkheim.

8. What did George Ritzer mean when he said our lives had been "McDonaldized?" (184)
   a. Americans eat unhealthy amounts of fast food.
   b. Fast food is responsible for obesity in America.
   c. Americans traded individuality and spontaneity for rationality, efficiency, and dependability.
   d. College students have developed an expectation that their professors should devote more and more time to critical discussions on social issues.

9. Dysfunctions of bureaucracies include: (184-187)
   a. alienation.
   b. bureaucratic incompetence.
   c. red tape.
   d. all of the above.

10. Max Weber warned that a loss of workers' control over their work would lead to: (186)
    a. bureaucratic alienation.
    b. stress.
    c. McDonaldization.
    d. incompetence.

11. *The Peter Principle* states that workers are promoted to their: (187)
    a. level of greatest success.
    b. level of incompetence.
    c. level of education.
    d. area of greatest interest.

12. The March of Dimes' shift from curing polio to lessening birth defects is an example of: (187)
    a. bureaucratic redefinition.
    b. goal conflict.
    c. goal displacement.
    d. goal transformation.

13. The sociological significance of bureaucracy is that it: (183)
    a. has always existed as a way of organizing human activity.
    b. reflects the best way of organizing work.
    c. is more dysfunctional than functional.
    d. represents a fundamental change in the way people relate to one another.

14. Who noted that Americans join a lot of voluntary organizations? (188)
    a. Max Weber
    b. Emile Durkheim
    c. Robin Williams
    d. Alexis de Tocqueville

15.   According to David Sills, which one of the following functions applies only to some voluntary associations, organizations, or groups? (189)
   a.   Voluntary organizations advance a particular interest.
   b.   Voluntary groups offer people an identity.
   c.   Voluntary associations help maintain social order.
   d.   Voluntary groups mediate between the government and the individual.

16.   What did sociologists Elaine Fox and George Arquitt describe as an example of an iron law of oligarchy? (190)
   a.   the March of Dimes
   b.   only the strong survive
   c.   rigid rules are necessary for bureaucracies
   d.   the VFW

17.   Kanter maintains that the "hidden values" of corporate culture result in: (191)
   a.   an objective use of merit as the basis for promotions and raises.
   b.   corporate leaders who end up on the "fast track" to promotions.
   c.   "fast track" promoted people ending up with less access to information.
   d.   seeking "outsiders" because of their strong abilities.

18.   Kanter's emphasis on the corporate "showcasing" of women and minorities refers to: (191)
   a.   their being put on the "fast track" assignments.
   b.   their gaining stronger acceptance from corporate bosses.
   c.   their being put in visible positions with little power.
   d.   their being given an ever increasing access to top management.

19.   What percent of U.S. senators who choose to run are reelected? (192)
   a.   60%
   b.   82%
   c.   90%
   d.   93%

20.   Pepsi executives are a good example of: (192)
   a.   modeling diversity training in the workplace.
   b.   promoting primarily within the organization.
   c.   maintaining "hidden values" within the corporation.
   d.   none of the above.

21.   Humanizing a work setting means organizing work in such a way that: (193)
   a.   it develops, rather than impedes, human potential.
   b.   it leads to promotion based on criteria other than ability and contributions.
   c.   it leads to promotion based on personal characteristics.
   d.   it leads to an inequality of distribution of power within a corporation.

22. Research on the costs and benefits of employer-financed day care demonstrated that: (194)
    a. such a benefit is costly to the employer because of strict government regulations that must be met.
    b. such a benefit cuts into stockholders' dividends by eating up profits.
    c. few employees took advantage of the benefit.
    d. such a benefit can save the employer money by reducing turnover and absenteeism.

23. Which of the following is an example of a fad in corporate culture? (195)
    a. corporate cook-offs
    b. cooperatives
    c. collectives
    d. corporate day care

24. According to sociologist Gary Marx, what type of workplace are we moving towards? (196)
    a. a corporate lock-down
    b. a laissez-faire workplace
    c. a maximum-security workplace
    d. a cyber-space workplace

25. Which of the following statements best describes the Japanese workers' access to lifetime job security? (196)
    a. Almost all Japanese workers enjoy lifetime job security.
    b. About one half of Japanese workers, who are employed in small firms, have lifetime job security.
    c. Lifetime job security is elusive, and only about one-third of workers have it.
    d. Lifetime job security is restricted to top management only.

Answer Key

1. A
2. B
3. D
4. B
5. B
6. C
7. C
8. C
9. D
10. A
11. B
12. C
13. D
14. D
15. D
16. D
17. B
18. C
19. C
20. A
21. A
22. D
23. A
24. C
25. C

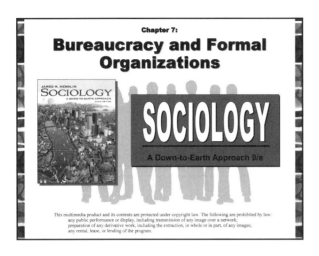

Chapter 7:
Bureaucracy and Formal Organizations

SOCIOLOGY
A Down-to-Earth Approach 9/e

This multimedia product and its contents are protected under copyright law. The following are prohibited by law: any public performance or display, including transmission of any image over a network; preparation of any derivative work, including the extraction, in whole or in part, of any images; any rental, lease, or lending of the program.

The Rationalization of Society

"The idea that efficiency and practical results should dominate human affairs."

Copyright © Allyn & Bacon 2008   Chapter 7: Bureaucracy and Formal Organizations   2

Why Did Society Change?

Prior - Traditional Orientation

* Past Best Guide for Present

* Protect Status Quo

* Bases on Personal Relationships

Copyright © Allyn & Bacon 2008   Chapter 7: Bureaucracy and Formal Organizations   3

Why Did Society Change?

Post - Industrialization- Capitalism

❋ **Rationality - Most Efficient**

   Going Forward

❋ **Attention to Bottom Line**

Copyright © Allyn & Bacon 2008   Chapter 7: Bureaucracy and Formal Organizations   4

Table 7.1 A Model of Production in Traditional and Nontraditional Societies

Traditional Societies (Horticultural, Agricultural)	Nontraditional Societies (Industrial, Postindustrial)
PRODUCTION	
1. Production is done by family members and same-sex groups (men's and women's groups).	1. Production is done by workers hired for the job.
2. Production takes place in the home, or in fields and other areas adjacent to the home.	2. Production takes place in a centralized location. (Some decentralization is occurring in the information society.)
3. Tasks are assigned according to personal relationships (men, women, and children do specific tasks based on custom).	3. Tasks are assigned according to agreements and training.
4. The "how" of production is not evaluated; the attitude is, "We want to keep doing it the way we've always done it."	4. The "how" of production is evaluated; the attitude is, "How can we make this more efficient?"

Copyright © Allyn & Bacon 2008   Chapter 7: Bureaucracy and Formal Organizations

---

Table 7.1 A Model of Production in Traditional and Nontraditional Societies

Traditional Societies (Horticultural, Agricultural)	Nontraditional Societies (Industrial, Postindustrial)
PRODUCTION	
1. Production is done by family members and same-sex groups (men's and women's groups).	1. Production is done by workers hired for the job.
2. Production takes place in the home, or in fields and other areas adjacent to the home.	2. Production takes place in a centralized location. (Some decentralization is occurring in the information society.)
3. Tasks are assigned according to personal relationships (men, women, and children do specific tasks based on custom).	3. Tasks are assigned according to agreements and training.
4. The "how" of production is not evaluated; the attitude is, "We want to keep doing it the way we've always done it."	4. The "how" of production is evaluated; the attitude is, "How can we make this more efficient?"
RELATIONSHIPS	
5. Relationships are based on history ("the way it's always been").	5. Relationships are based on contracts, which change as the situation changes.
6. Relationships are diffuse (vague, covering many areas of life).	6. Relationships are specific; contracts (even if not written) specify conditions.
7. Relationships are long-term, often lifelong.	7. Relationships are short-term, for the length of the contract.

Copyright © Allyn & Bacon 2008   Chapter 7: Bureaucracy and Formal Organizations

Table 7.1 A Model of Production in Traditional and Nontraditional Societies

Traditional Societies (Horticultural, Agricultural)	Nontraditional Societies (Industrial, Postindustrial)
PRODUCTION	
1. Production is done by family members and same-sex groups (men's and women's groups).	1. Production is done by workers hired for the job.
2. Production takes place in the home, or in fields and other areas adjacent to the home.	2. Production takes place in a centralized location. (Some decentralization is occurring in the information society.)
3. Tasks are assigned according to personal relationships (men, women, and children do specific tasks based on custom).	3. Tasks are assigned according to agreements and training.
4. The "how" of production is not evaluated; the attitude is, "We want to keep doing it the way we've always done it."	4. The "how" of production is evaluated; the attitude is, "How can we make this more efficient?"
RELATIONSHIPS	
5. Relationships are based on history ("the way it's always been").	5. Relationships are based on contracts, which change as the situation changes.
6. Relationships are diffuse (vague, covering many areas of life).	6. Relationships are specific; contracts (even if not written) specify conditions.
7. Relationships are long-term, often lifelong.	7. Relationships are short-term, for the length of the contract.
EVALUATIONS	
8. It is assumed that arrangements will continue indefinitely.	8. Arrangements are evaluated periodically, to decide whether to continue or to change them.
9. People are evaluated according to how they fulfill their traditional roles.	9. People are evaluated according to the "bottom line" (the organization's goals).

Note: This model is an ideal type. Rationality is never totally absent from any society, and no society (or organization) is based entirely on rationality. Even the most rational organizations (those that most carefully and even ruthlessly compute the "bottom line") have traditional components. To properly understand this table, consider these nine characteristics as being "more" or "less" present.

Copyright © Allyn & Bacon 2008 Chapter 7: Bureaucracy and Formal Organizations 7

Why Did Society Change?

❋ **Marx: Capitalism Broke Tradition**

❋ **Weber: Religion Broke Tradition**

❋ **The Two Views Today**

Copyright © Allyn & Bacon 2008 Chapter 7: Bureaucracy and Formal Organizations 8

What Are Formal Organizations?

"Secondary groups designed to achieve explicit objectives."

Copyright © Allyn & Bacon 2008 Chapter 7: Bureaucracy and Formal Organizations 9

Formal Organizations and Bureaucracy

Characteristics of Bureaucracies

❋ **Clear Levels**

❋ **Division of Labor**

❋ **Written Rules**

❋ **Written Communication and Records**

❋ **Impersonality & Replaceability**

Copyright © Allyn & Bacon 2008   Chapter 7: Bureaucracy and Formal Organizations   10

Figure 7.1 The Typical Bureaucratic Structure of a Medium-Sized University

This is a scaled-down version of a university's bureaucratic structure. The actual lines of a university are likely to be much more complicated than those depicted here. A large university may have a chancellor and several presidents under the chancellor, with each president responsible for a particular campus. Although in this figure extensions of authority are shown only for the vice president for administration and the College of Social Sciences, each of the other vice presidents and colleges has similar positions. If the figure were to be extended, departmental secretaries would be shown, and eventually, somewhere, even students.

Formal Organizations and Bureaucracy

❋ **"Ideal" vs. "Real" Bureaucracy**

❋ **Extent of Bureaucracy - A Matter of Degree**

❋ **Ideal vs. Actual Organizational Chart**

Copyright © Allyn & Bacon 2008   Chapter 7: Bureaucracy and Formal Organizations   12

Dysfunctions of Bureaucracies

* Red Tape - A Rule is a Rule

* Lack of Communication Between Units

* Bureaucratic Alienation

Copyright © Allyn & Bacon 2008   Chapter 7: Bureaucracy and Formal Organizations   13

Dysfunctions of Bureaucracies

* Resisting Alienation

* The Alienated Bureaucrat

* Bureaucratic Incompetence

Copyright © Allyn & Bacon 2008   Chapter 7: Bureaucracy and Formal Organizations   14

Bureaucracies

* Goal Displacement

* Perpetuation of Bureaucracies

* Social Significance of Bureaucracies

Copyright © Allyn & Bacon 2008   Chapter 7: Bureaucracy and Formal Organizations   15

Voluntary Associations

* **Functions of Voluntary Associations**
  * Advance Particular Interests
  * Offer People Identity
  * Govern Nations and Maintain Social Order
* **These Apply to All or Most Voluntary Associations**

Copyright © Allyn & Bacon 2008   Chapter 7: Bureaucracy and Formal Organizations   16

Voluntary Associations

* **Functions of Voluntary Associations**
  * Mediate Between Government and Individuals
  * Help Individuals Climb Occupational Ladder
  * Bring People into Political Mainstream
  * Pave Way for Social Change
* **These Apply to Only Some Voluntary Associations**

Copyright © Allyn & Bacon 2008   Chapter 7: Bureaucracy and Formal Organizations   17

Voluntary Associations

* **Shared Interests**
  * Motivations for Joining Differ
  * Experience High Turnover
* **The Problem of Oligarchy**
  * Leaders Grow Distant from Members
  * Iron Law of Oligarchy

Copyright © Allyn & Bacon 2008   Chapter 7: Bureaucracy and Formal Organizations   18

Working for the Corporation

* Self-Fulfilling Stereotypes and Promotions
* Stereotypes and the Iron Law of Oligarchy

Copyright © Allyn & Bacon 2008   Chapter 7: Bureaucracy and Formal Organizations   19

Humanizing the Corporate Culture

* Develop Rather than Impede Potential
* Access to Opportunities
* Distribute Power More Evenly
* Can Bureaucracies Adapt?
* What is the Cost of Change?

Copyright © Allyn & Bacon 2008   Chapter 7: Bureaucracy and Formal Organizations   20

Humanizing the Corporate Culture

* Work Teams
* Corporate Day Care
* Employee Stock Ownership
* The Conflict Perspective
* Fads in the Workplace

Copyright © Allyn & Bacon 2008   Chapter 7: Bureaucracy and Formal Organizations   21

Technology and the Control of Workers

✳ **The Rise of the Microchip**

✳ **Surveillance in the Workplace**

✳ **Monitoring Computer Use**

Copyright © Allyn & Bacon 2008   Chapter 7: Bureaucracy and Formal Organizations   22

U.S. and Japanese Corporations

How They Differ

✳ **Hiring and Promoting Teams**

✳ **Lifetime Security**

✳ **Almost Total Involvement**

✳ **Broad Training**

✳ **Decision-Making by Consensus**

Copyright © Allyn & Bacon 2008   Chapter 7: Bureaucracy and Formal Organizations   23

U.S. and Japanese Corporations

Myth vs. Reality

✳ **Most Don't Find Lifelong Job Security**

✳ **Management by Consensus False**

Copyright © Allyn & Bacon 2008   Chapter 7: Bureaucracy and Formal Organizations   24

Chapter 7:
Bureaucracy and Formal Organizations

SOCIOLOGY

A Down-to-Earth Approach 9/e

CHAPTER 8
DEVIANCE AND SOCIAL CONTROL

CHAPTER SUMMARY

- Deviance, which refers to violations of social norms, is relative; what people consider deviant varies from one culture to another and from group to group within a society. It is not the act itself but the reaction to the act that makes it deviant.

- To explain deviance, biologists and psychologists look for reasons within individuals, such as genetic predispositions or personality disorders, while sociologists look for explanations outside of the individual such as socialization and social class.

- Symbolic interactionists use differential association theory, control theory, and labeling theory to analyze how group membership influences people's behaviors and views of the world. There are several techniques of neutralization that people who commit deviant acts use in order to continue to think of themselves as conformists.

- Functionalists state that deviance is functional, using strain theory and illegitimate opportunity structures to argue that widespread socialization into norms of material success accounts for much of the crime committed by the poor.

- Conflict theorists argue that the group in power imposes its definitions on other groups—that is, the ruling class directs the criminal justice system against the working class, which commits highly visible property crimes, while it diverts its own criminal activities away from the criminal justice system.

- In reacting to criminal deviance, the U.S. has adopted a "get-tough" policy, imprisoning millions of people.

- The causes for the decline in violent crime have been controversial among sociologists. While crime has declined, the rearrest rate, or recidivism rate, remains high. The death penalty is the most extreme measure that the state can take.

- The conclusions of both symbolic interactionists and conflict theorists cast doubts on the accuracy of official crime statistics.

- Society may deal with deviance by medicalizing and calling it mental illness. Thomas Szasz disagrees, claiming that deviance is just problem behavior, not mental illness.

- With deviance inevitable, the larger issues are how to protect people from deviant behaviors that are harmful to their welfare, to tolerate those that are not, and to develop systems of fair treatment for deviants.

LEARNING OBJECTIVES

After reading Chapter 8, you should be able to:

1. Define "deviance" and explain why deviance is relative, according to the sociological perspective. (204)
2. Explain why norms are necessary and describe how a system of social control is used to enforce norms. (205-206)
3. Describe some of the sanctions human groups use to enforce norms, including shaming and degradation ceremonies. (206)
4. Differentiate between the biological, psychological, and sociological explanations of why people violate norms. (208-209)
5. Describe and apply deviance to the symbolic interactionist perspective, which includes differential association theory, control theory, and labeling theory. (209-213)
6. List and discuss the five techniques of neutralization found in labeling theory. (211-212)
7. List the functions deviance fulfills for society, according to Emile Durkheim. (213-214)
8. Explain strain theory and discuss the four deviant paths in response to it. (214-216)
9. Describe the different ways street crime and white-collar crime are perceived by the public and treated by the criminal justice system. (216-218)
10. Discuss from the conflict perspective how the criminal justice system legitimates and perpetuates social inequality. (219-221)
11. Discuss the reasons for, and implications of, "get tough" policies on crime in the United States. (223-224)
12. Discuss the decline in crime and the recidivism rate. (224-225)
13. Talk about the gender, social class, and racial and ethnic biases in the application of the death penalty. (225-228)
14. Explain why crime statistics may be misleading and should be interpreted with caution. (229)
15. Know what is meant by the medicalization of deviance and why some sociologists view mental illness as more of a social, rather than biological, condition. (230-231)
16. Explain why the United States needs to develop a fairer and more humane approach to dealing with deviance. (232)

KEY TERMS
After studying the chapter, review the definition for each of the following terms.

capital punishment: the death penalty (225)

capitalist class: the wealthy who own the means of production and buy the labor of the working class (220)

control theory: the idea that two control systems, inner and outer controls, work against our tendencies to deviate (210)

corporate crime: crimes committed by executives in order to benefit the corporation (216)

crime: the violation of norms that are written into law (204)

criminal justice system: the system of police, courts, and prisons set up to deal with people who are accused of having committed a crime (219)

cultural goals: the legitimate objectives held out to the members of a society (215)

degradation ceremony: a term coined by Harold Garfinkel to describe rituals designed to remake the self by stripping away an individual's particular self-identity and stamping a new one in its place (206)

deviance: the violation of rules or norms (204)

differential association: Edwin Sutherland's term to indicate that associating with some groups results in learning an "excess of definitions" of deviance, and, by extension, in a greater likelihood that one will become deviant (209)

genetic predisposition: inborn tendencies; in this context, to commit deviant acts (208)

hate crime: crimes to which more severe penalties are attached because they are motivated by hatred (dislike, animosity) of someone's race-ethnicity, religion, sexual orientation, disability, or national origin (229)

illegitimate opportunity structures: opportunities for crimes woven into the texture of life (216)

institutionalized means: approved ways of reaching cultural goals (215)

labeling theory: the view that the labels people are given affect their own and others' perceptions of them, thus channeling their behavior either into deviance or into conformity (211)

marginal working class: the most desperate members of the working class, who have few skills, little job security, and are often unemployed (220)

medicalization of deviance: to make deviance a medical matter, a symptom of some underlying illness that needs to be treated by physicians (230)

negative sanction: an expression of disapproval for breaking a norm, ranging from a mild, informal reaction such as a frown to a formal reaction such as a prison sentence or an execution (206)

personality disorders: the view that a personality disturbance of some sort causes an individual to violate social norms (208)

police discretion: the practice of the police, in the normal course of their duties, to arrest someone for an offense or to overlook the matter (229)

positive sanction: a reward or positive reaction for following norms, ranging from a smile to a prize (206)

recidivism rate: the proportion of released convicts who are rearrested (224)

serial murder: the killing of several victims in three or more separate events (227)

social control: a group's formal and informal means of enforcing norms (205)

social order: a group's usual and customary social arrangements, on which its members depend and on which they base their lives (205)

stigma: "blemishes" that discredit a person's claim to a "normal" identity (204)

strain theory: Robert Merton's term for the strain engendered when a society socializes large numbers of people to desire a cultural goal (such as success) but withholds from many the approved means of reaching that goal; one adaptation to the strain is crime, the choice of an innovative means (one outside the approved system) to attain the cultural goal (215)

street crime: crimes such as mugging, rape, and burglary (208)

techniques of neutralization: ways of thinking or rationalizing that help people deflect (or neutralize) society's norms (211)

white-collar crime: Edwin Sutherland's term for crimes committed by people of respectable and high social status in the course of their occupations; for example, bribery of public officials, securities violations, embezzlement, false advertising, and price fixing (216)

working class: those who sell their labor to the capitalist class (220)

KEY PEOPLE
Review the major theoretical contributions or findings of these people.

Howard Becker: Becker observed that an act is not deviant in and of itself, but only when there is a reaction to it. (204)

William Chambliss: Chambliss demonstrated the power of the label in his study of two youth gangs—the Saints and the Roughnecks. (212-213)

Richard Cloward and Lloyd Ohlin: These sociologists identified the illegitimate opportunity structures that are woven into the texture of life in urban slums and provide an alternative set of opportunities for slum residents when legitimate ones are blocked. (214-215)

Emile Durkheim: Durkheim noted three ways in which deviance is functional for society. (213-214)

Robert Edgerton: This anthropologist's studies document how different human groups react to similar behaviors, demonstrating that what is deviant in one context is not in another. (205)

Harold Garfinkel: Garfinkel used the term degradation ceremonies to describe formal attempts to mark an individual with the status of an outsider. (206)

Erving Goffman: Goffman used the term stigma to refer to characteristics that discredit people. (204)

Travis Hirschi: Hirschi studied the strength of the bonds an individual has to society in order to understand the effectiveness of inner controls. (210-211)

Ruth Horowitz: This sociologist conducted participant observation in a Chicano neighborhood in Chicago. She found that attitudes about honor, which were common among residents, helped to propel young men into deviance. (210)

Martin Sánchez-Jankowski: Jankowski studied gangs and identified traits that characterize gang members and the functions that gangs play in urban neighborhoods. (217)

Robert Merton: Merton developed strain theory to explain patterns of deviance within a society. (215-216)

Donald Partington: This lawyer examined executions for rape and attempted rape in Virginia between 1908 and 1963 and found that only Black men were executed for these crimes during those years. (227)

Walter Reckless: Reckless developed control theory, suggesting that our behavior is controlled by two different systems, one external (like the police, family and friends) and the other internal (like our conscience, religious principles, and ideas of right and wrong). (210-211)

Edwin Sutherland: Sutherland not only developed differential association theory, but was the first to study and give a name to crimes that occur among the middle class in the course of their work—white collar crime. (209-210, 216-217)

Gresham Sykes and David Matza: These sociologists studied the different strategies delinquent boys use to deflect society's norms—techniques of neutralization. (211-212)

Thomas Szasz: Szasz argued that mental illness represents the medicalization of deviance. (230-231)

Mark Watson: Watson studied motorcycle gangs and found that these people actively embraced the deviant label. (212)

PRACTICE TEST

1. The violation of rules written into law is known as: (204)
   a. deviance.
   b. an aberrance.
   c. crime.
   d. a stigma.

2. Becker stresses the sociological perspective that deviance is: (204)
   a. established by the act itself, not the reaction of others.
   b. a violation of the formal, written laws of a society.
   c. defined by the same guidelines in every modern culture.
   d. defined by the reaction of others to the act.

3. Goffman's conception of "stigma" refers to the fact that deviance: (204)
   a. is a label that can be used even if a person has not done anything deviant.
   b. refers to violations of one's action rather than violations of one's ability.
   c. is independent of a person's master status.
   d. is independent of ascribed factors such as being born with a facial birth mark.

4. Frowns, gossip, and crossing people off guest lists all examples of: (206)
   a. retribution.
   b. degradation ceremonies.
   c negative sanctions.
   d. institutionalized means to achieve goals.

5. Being able to look online at people who have committed deviant acts is: (202)
   a. a stigmatization ritual.
   b. a degradation ceremony.
   c. shaming.
   d. a rite of passage ritual.

6. Sociobiologists explain deviance by looking for its causes: (208)
   a. outside of the individual.
   b. as dependent on psychological theories.
   c. as dependent on genetic pre-dispositions.
   d. as dependent on social inequality.

7. According to differential association theory, someone become a deviant because: (209)
   a. of genetic predispositions.
   b. of personality disorders.
   c. of a lack of opportunities to engage in conventional activities.
   d. he learns to deviate from or conform to society's norms.

8. The idea that two control systems, inner and outer controls, work against our tendencies toward deviance is called: (210)
   a. conflict theory.
   b. differential association theory.
   c. control theory.
   d. strain theory.

9. According to Travis Hirschi, the effectiveness of our inner controls is known as: (211)
   a. self-respect.
   b. our willingness to cooperate.
   c. self-control.
   d. labeling .

10. All of the following are techniques of neutralization EXCEPT a: (211 212)
    a. denial of a victim.
    b. denial the act occurred.
    c. denial of responsibility.
    d. denial of a right to appeal to higher authorities.

11. Functionalists like Emile Durkheim believe deviance: (213-214)
    a. hinders social unity.
    b. promotes social change.
    c. confuses what a society's moral boundaries entail.
    d. negates societal norms.

12. Which deviant path do teachers who are experiencing burnout, but remain in the classroom, take? (215)
    a. rebellion
    b. innovation
    c. reticalism
    d. ritualism.

13. In strain theory, seeing goals as legitimate, but means as illegitimate is called: (215)
    a. retreatism.
    b. rebellion.
    c. ritualism.
    d. innovation.

14. Illegitimate crime opportunity structures are such that: (216)
    a. the poor are punished for white collar crime, but the privileged are not.
    b. white-collar crime is committed against all social classes.
    c. white-collar crime is functional for society only when committed by the poor.
    d. the privileged can commit only white-collar crime.

15.   Which of the following would sociologists term a white-collar crime? (216)
      a.   robbery
      b.   burglary
      c.   embezzlement
      d.   prostitution

16.   "Crime in the suites" vs. "crime in the street" shows that: (217)
      a.   violent crime is actually higher among the upper class.
      b.   white-collar crime is a rare phenomenon.
      c.   street crime costs far more, in dollars, than white-collar crime.
      d.   white collar crime costs far more, in dollars, than street crime.

17.   Conflict theorists believe that in the U.S. criminal justice system: (220)
      a.   there is a significant focus on crimes by owners of corporations.
      b.   the law does not operate impartially.
      c.   the capitalist class is totally ignored in terms of being prosecuted for crime.
      d.   courts imprison more white-collar crime offenders than street crime offenders.

18.   What country's prison has no walls, fences, or bars? (221)
      a.   Nigeria
      b.   Australia
      c.   Greenland
      d.   Malaysia

19.   A comparison between inmates in U.S. prisons and those incarcerated in other nations shows that the U.S.: (222)
      a.   has both more prisoners and a larger percentage of its population in prison.
      b.   has a lower number of inmates than many other nations.
      c.   has a lower percentage of its population in prison.
      d.   has about the same percentage of its population in prison as Iran and China.

20.   Which of the following statements is true? (222-223)
      a.   About one out of 6 African American men ages 20 to 34 are in jail or prison.
      b.   About one of every 500 people in the U.S. is in jail or prison.
      c.   About three-fourths of the prison population are African American.
      d.   About 95% of prisoners are men.

21.   Who is disproportionately at risk of being put to death under the death penalty?   (227)
      a.   whites
      b.   African Americans
      c.   Latinos
      d.   Asian Americans

22. According to statistics on hate crimes, which group is most likely to be   victimized? (229)
    a. African Americans
    b. whites
    c. Latinos
    d. Asian Americans

23. A routine part of police work is: (229)
    a. finding those who have committed hate crimes.
    b. trying to ignore the affect of social class.
    c. stereotyping individuals.
    d. deciding whether to follow up on a matter or arrest someone.

24. Szasz feels that the best critique of the medicalization of deviance would be found in an empasis on: (230)
    a. trying to see how people learn deviant behavior.
    b. understanding the "sub-conscious mind."
    c. seeing deviant behavior as a mental illness.
    d. medical research rather than sociological research.

25. With deviance inevitable, the author of your textbook suggests that one measure of a society is: (232)
    a. how low the overall rates of deviance are.
    b. what types of deviance exist.
    c. what gets defined as deviance and what doesn't.
    d. how deviants are treated.

Answer Key

1. C
2. D
3. A
4. C
5. C
6. C
7. D
8. C
9. C
10. D
11. B
12. D
13. D
14. B
15. C
16. D
17. B
18. C
19. A
20. A
21. B
22. A
23. D
24. A
25. D

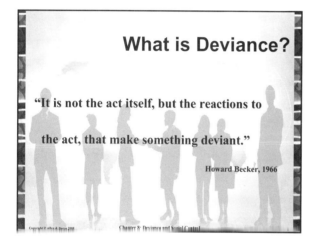

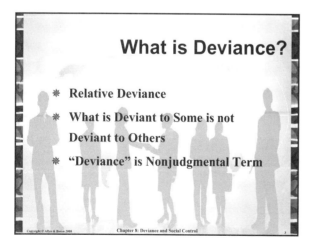

Deviance Terminology

- ❋ Crime
  - ✳ Violation of Norms as Laws
- ❋ Deviance
  - ✳ Violation of Rules or Norms
- ❋ Stigma
  - ✳ Blemishes on "Normal" Identity

Copyright © Allyn & Bacon 2008   Chapter 8: Deviance and Social Control   4

Norms Make Social Life Possible

- ❋ Makes Behavior Predictable
- ❋ No Norms - Social Chaos
- ❋ Social Control
  - ✳ Group's Formal and Informal Means of Enforcing Norms

Copyright © Allyn & Bacon 2008   Chapter 8: Deviance and Social Control   5

Sanctions

- ❋ Negative Sanctions
- ❋ Positive Sanctions

Copyright © Allyn & Bacon 2008   Chapter 8: Deviance and Social Control   6

Shaming and Degradation Ceremonies

※ **Shaming is a Sanction**

※ **Can Be Centerpiece of Public Ritual**

※ **Degradation Ceremony**

Copyright © Allyn & Bacon 2008   Chapter 8: Deviance and Social Control

Explanations of Deviance

Sociobiology

※ **Look for Answers Inside Individuals**

※ **Genetic Predispositions**

Copyright © Allyn & Bacon 2008   Chapter 8: Deviance and Social Control

Explanations of Deviance

Psychology

※ **Focuses on Abnormalities Within Individuals**

※ **Personality Disorders**

※ **Deviant Personalities**

Copyright © Allyn & Bacon 2008   Chapter 8: Deviance and Social Control

Explanations of Deviance

Sociology

* **Look for Answers Outside Individuals**
  * **Socialization**
  * **Membership in Subcultures**
* **Social Class**

Chapter 8: Deviance and Social Control

Symbolic Interactionist Perspective

Differential Association Theory

* **Families**
* **Friends, Neighbors**
* **Subcultures**
* **Prison or Freedom?**

Chapter 8: Deviance and Social Control

Symbolic Interactionist Perspective

Control Theory

Inner Controls

* **Morality**
* **Conscience**
* **Religious Principles**

Chapter 8: Deviance and Social Control

Symbolic Interactionist Perspective
Control Theory

Outer Controls

✳ Attachments

✳ Commitments

✳ Involvements

✳ Beliefs that Actions are Morally Wrong

Copyright © Allyn & Bacon 2008   Chapter 8: Deviance and Social Control   13

Symbolic Interactionist Perspective
Labeling Theory

✳ Focuses on the Significance of Labels

✳ Labels Become Part of Self-Concept

✳ Propel Towards or Away from Deviance

Copyright © Allyn & Bacon 2008   Chapter 8: Deviance and Social Control

Symbolic Interactionist Perspective
Rejecting Labels

✳ Denial of Responsibility

✳ Denial of Injury

✳ Denial of a Victim

Copyright © Allyn & Bacon 2008   Chapter 8: Deviance and Social Control   15

Symbolic Interactionist Perspective
Rejecting Labels

❋ **Condemnation of Condemners**

❋ **Appeal to Higher Loyalties**

Copyright © Allyn & Bacon 2008   Chapter 8: Deviance and Social Control   16

Symbolic Interactionist Perspective
Labeling Theory

❋ **Embracing Labels - Outlaw Bikers**

❋ **The Power of Labels - Saints and Roughnecks**

Copyright © Allyn & Bacon 2008   Chapter 8: Deviance and Social Control   17

Functionalist Perspective
Can Deviance Be Functional?

❋ **Clarifies Moral Boundaries and Affirms Norms**

❋ **Promotes Social Unity**

❋ **Promotes Social Change**

Copyright © Allyn & Bacon 2008   Chapter 8: Deviance and Social Control   18

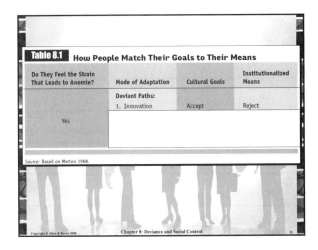

Table 8.1 — How People Match Their Goals to Their Means

Do They Feel the Strain That Leads to Anomie?	Mode of Adaptation	Cultural Goals	Institutionalized Means
	Deviant Paths:		
Yes	1. Innovation	Accept	Reject

Source: Based on Merton 1968.

Chapter 8: Deviance and Social Control

Table 8.1 — How People Match Their Goals to Their Means

Do They Feel the Strain That Leads to Anomie?	Mode of Adaptation	Cultural Goals	Institutionalized Means
	Deviant Paths:		
	1. Innovation	Accept	Reject
Yes	2. Ritualism	Reject	Accept

Source: Based on Merton 1968.

Chapter 8: Deviance and Social Control

Table 8.1 — How People Match Their Goals to Their Means

Do They Feel the Strain That Leads to Anomie?	Mode of Adaptation	Cultural Goals	Institutionalized Means
	Deviant Paths:		
	1. Innovation	Accept	Reject
Yes	2. Ritualism	Reject	Accept
	3. Retreatism	Reject	Reject

Source: Based on Merton 1968.

Chapter 8: Deviance and Social Control

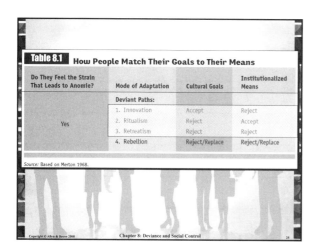

Table 8.1 How People Match Their Goals to Their Means

Do They Feel the Strain That Leads to Anomie?	Mode of Adaptation	Cultural Goals	Institutionalized Means
	Deviant Paths:		
Yes	1. Innovation	Accept	Reject
	2. Ritualism	Reject	Accept
	3. Retreatism	Reject	Reject
	4. Rebellion	Reject/Replace	Reject/Replace

Source: Based on Merton 1968.

Functionalist Perspective
Illegitimate Opportunity Structures

* Unequal Access to Institutional Means to Success
* Street Crime
* White-Collar Crime
* Gender and Crime

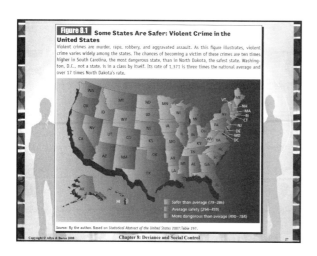

Figure 8.1 Some States Are Safer: Violent Crime in the United States

Violent crimes are murder, rape, robbery, and aggravated assault. As this figure illustrates, violent crime varies widely among the states. The chances of becoming a victim of these crimes are ten times higher in South Carolina, the most dangerous state, than in North Dakota, the safest state. Washington, D.C., not a state, is in a class by itself. Its rate of 1,371 is three times the national average and over 17 times North Dakota's rate.

Safer than average (79–286)
Average safety (294–459)
More dangerous than average (490–784)

Source: By the author. Based on Statistical Abstract of the United States 2007:Table 297.

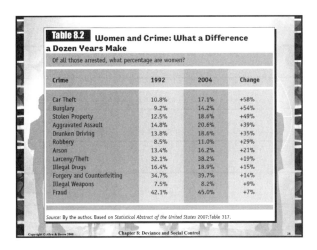

Table 8.2 **Women and Crime: What a Difference a Dozen Years Make**

Of all those arrested, what percentage are women?

Crime	1992	2004	Change
Car Theft	10.8%	17.1%	+58%
Burglary	9.2%	14.2%	+54%
Stolen Property	12.5%	18.6%	+49%
Aggravated Assault	14.8%	20.6%	+39%
Drunken Driving	13.8%	18.6%	+35%
Robbery	8.5%	11.0%	+29%
Arson	13.4%	16.2%	+21%
Larceny/Theft	32.1%	38.2%	+19%
Illegal Drugs	16.4%	18.9%	+15%
Forgery and Counterfeiting	34.7%	39.7%	+14%
Illegal Weapons	7.5%	8.2%	+9%
Fraud	42.1%	45.0%	+7%

Source: By the author. Based on *Statistical Abstract of the United States* 2007:Table 317.

Copyright © Allyn & Bacon 2008 — Chapter 8: Deviance and Social Control

---

The Conflict Perspective

* **Class, Crime, and the Criminal Justice System**
* **Power and Inequality**
    * **Capitalist Class**
    * **Working Class**
    * **Marginal Working Class**
* **The Law as an Instrument of Oppression**

Copyright © Allyn & Bacon 2008 — Chapter 8: Deviance and Social Control

---

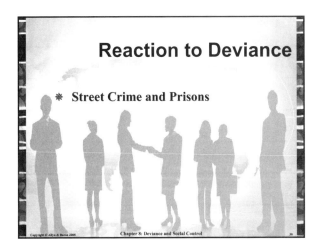

Reaction to Deviance

* **Street Crime and Prisons**

Copyright © Allyn & Bacon 2008 — Chapter 8: Deviance and Social Control

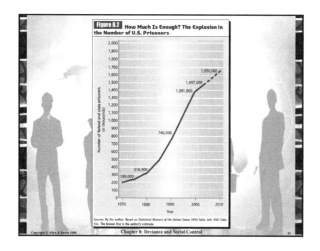

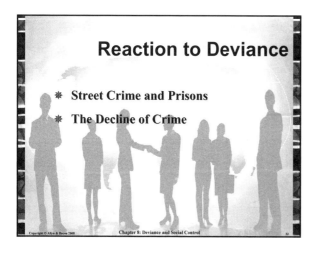

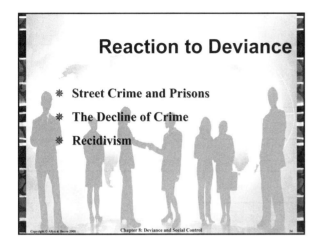

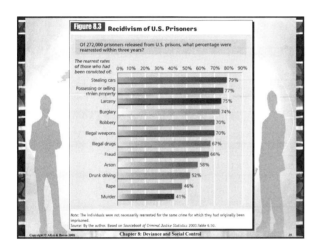

Figure 8.3 Recidivism of U.S. Prisoners

Of 272,000 prisoners released from U.S. prisons, what percentage were rearrested within three years?

The rearrest rates of those who had been convicted of:

Stealing cars	79%
Possessing or selling stolen property	77%
Larceny	75%
Burglary	74%
Robbery	70%
Illegal weapons	70%
Illegal drugs	67%
Fraud	66%
Arson	58%
Drunk driving	52%
Rape	46%
Murder	41%

Note: The individuals were not necessarily rearrested for the same crime for which they had originally been imprisoned.
Source: By the author. Based on Sourcebook of Criminal Justice Statistics 2003: table 6.50.

Reaction to Deviance

* Street Crime and Prisons
* The Decline of Crime
* Recidivism
* The Death Penalty Bias

Chapter 8: Deviance and Social Control

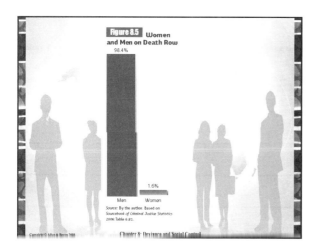

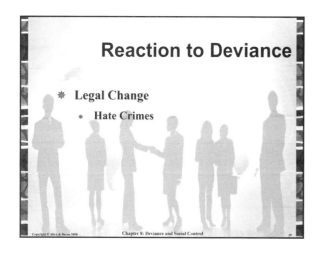

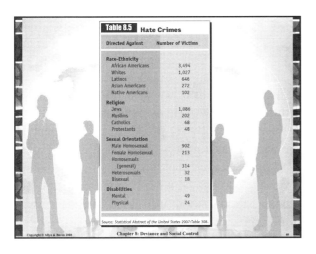

Table 8.5	Hate Crimes
Directed Against	**Number of Victims**
Race-Ethnicity	
African Americans	3,494
Whites	1,027
Latinos	646
Asian Americans	272
Native Americans	102
Religion	
Jews	1,086
Muslims	202
Catholics	68
Protestants	48
Sexual Orientation	
Male Homosexual	902
Female Homosexual	213
Homosexuals (general)	314
Heterosexuals	32
Bisexual	18
Disabilities	
Mental	49
Physical	24

Source: Statistical Abstract of the United States 2007:Table 308.

Copyright © Allyn & Bacon 2008   Chapter 8: Deviance and Social Control   40

Reaction to Deviance

❁ **Legal Change**

  ✳ **Hate Crimes**

❁ **Trouble with Statistics**

❁ **Medicalization of Deviance**

  ✳ **Neither Mental nor Illness?**

  ✳ **Homeless Mentally Ill**

❁ **Need for More Humane Approach**

Copyright © Allyn & Bacon 2008   Chapter 8: Deviance and Social Control   41

Chapter 8:
Deviance and Social Control

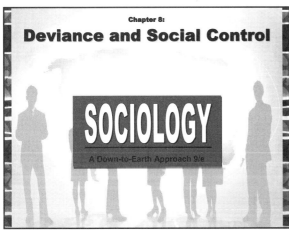

SOCIOLOGY

A Down-to-Earth Approach 9/e

CHAPTER 9
GLOBAL STRATIFICATION

CHAPTER SUMMARY

- Social stratification is a system in which people are divided into layers according to their relative power, property, and prestige. The nations of the world, as well as the people within a nation, are stratified into groups based on relative power, prestige, and property. In every society men, as a group, are placed above women as a group.

- Four major systems of social stratification include (1) slavery—owning other people; (2) caste—lifelong status determined by birth; (3) estate—feudal society divided into nobility, clergy, and commoners; and (4) class—based on monetary or material possessions.

- Early sociologists disagreed about the meaning of social class. Karl Marx argued that a person's relationship to the means of production was the only factor determining social class. Max Weber argued that three elements—property, prestige, and power—dictate an individual's standing in society.

- Various arguments have been developed to explain the universal presence of stratification. Kingsley Davis and Wilbert Moore argued that society must offer rewards in order to assure that important social positions are filled by the most competent people. Gaetano Mosca believed that the stratification of society by power is inevitable. Conflict theorists see that stratification is the consequence of group struggles for scarce resources.

- Gerhard Lenski combined the functional and conflict perspectives differently to explain the historical evolution of stratification systems.

- To maintain stratification within a nation, the ruling class controls ideas and information, technology, and the police and military.

- In Britain, the most striking features of the class system are differences in speech, accent, and education. In the former Soviet Union, communism resulted in one set of social classes being replaced by another.

- The model of global stratification presented in this text divides nations into three groups: the "Most Industrialized," the "Industrializing," and the "Least Industrialized" Nations. The oil-rich nations fit into their own category known as the oil rich, nonindustrialized nations.

- The major theories explaining the origins of global stratification are colonialism, world system theory, and the culture of poverty. Most sociologists agree with colonialism and the world system theory.

- International stratification is maintained through neocolonialism, the ongoing dominance of the Least Industrialized Nations by the Most Industrialized Nations, and multinational corporations which operate across national boundaries.

- The new technology gives advantage to the world's Most Industrialized Nations. However, countries like India and China are adopting high technology at a rapid pace.

- Global stratification affects each individual's life chances.

LEARNING OBJECTIVES
After reading Chapter 9, you should be able to:

1. Define social stratification and explain its sociological significance. (237)
2. Describe and provide examples of the four major systems of social stratification. (237-242)
3. Discuss the relationship between gender and social stratification. (243)
4. Describe the major points of disagreement between Karl Marx and Max Weber regarding the meaning of social class in industrialized societies. (243-245)
5. According to the functionalist view articulated by Kingsley Davis and Wilbert Moore, list the functions that social stratification provides for society. (245)
6. List and discuss Melvin Tumin's counter-arguments to the functionalist view of social stratification. (246)
7. Talk about the conflict perspective of social stratification as it relates to class conflict and scarce resources. (247)
8. Discuss and evaluate Gerhard Lenski's attempt to synthesize the functionalist and conflict perspectives on social stratification. (247-248)
9. Discuss how ideology rather than force is more effective for the elite classes in maintaining social stratification. (248)
10. Compare the social stratification systems in Great Britain and the former Soviet Union to the social stratification system in the United States. (249-251)
11. Identify the major characteristics associated with the Most Industrialized Nations, Industrializing Nations, and Least Industrialized Nations. (251-255)
12. Discuss why modifications may be necessary in classifying nations into level of industrialization. (255-258)
13. Describe and evaluate the major theories pertaining to the origins and maintenance of global stratification. (258-261)
14. Explain how technology leads to global domination. (263)

KEY TERMS
After studying the chapter, review the definition for each of the following terms.

apartheid: the separation of races as was practiced in South Africa (241)

bonded labor or indentured service: a contractual system in which someone sells his or her body (services) for a specified period of time in an arrangement very close to slavery, except that it is entered into voluntarily (238)

bourgeoisie: Karl Marx's term for the people who own the means of production (243)

caste system: a form of social stratification in which one's status is determined by birth and is lifelong (240)

class consciousness: Marx's term for awareness of a common identity based on one's position in the means of production (244)

class system: a form of social stratification based primarily on the possession of money or material possessions (242)

colonialism: the process by which one nation takes over another nation, usually for the purpose of exploiting its labor and natural resources (258)

culture of poverty: the assumption that the values and behaviors of the poor are different from other people, that these factors are largely responsible for their poverty, and that parents perpetuate poverty across generations by passing these characteristics to their children (261)

divine right of kings: the idea that the king's authority comes directly from God (248)

endogamy: the practice of marrying within one's own group (240)

estate stratification system: the stratification system of medieval Europe, consisting of three groups or estates; the nobility, the clergy, and commoners (242)

false class consciousness: Marx's term to refer to workers identifying with the interests of capitalists (244)

globalization of the capitalism: capitalism (investing to make profits within a rational system) becoming the globe's dominant economic system (259)

ideology: beliefs about the way things ought to be that justify social arrangements (238)

means of production: the tools, factories, land, and investment capital used to produce wealth (243)

meritocracy: a form of social stratification in which all positions are awarded on the basis of merit (246)

multinational corporations: companies that operate across many national boundaries; also called *transnational corporations* (262)

neocolonialism: the economic and political dominance of the Least Industrialized Nations by the Most Industrialized Nations (261)

proletariat: Karl Marx's term for the exploited class, the mass of workers do not own the means of production (243)

slavery: a form of social stratification in which some people own other people (237)

social mobility: movement up or down the social class ladder (242)

social stratification: the division of large numbers of people into layers according to their relative power, property, and prestige; applies to both nations and to people within a nation, society, or other group (237)

world system theory: economic and political connections that tie the world's countries together (259)

KEY PEOPLE
Review the major theoretical contributions or findings of these people.

Kingsley Davis and Wilbert Moore: According to these functionalists, stratification of a society is inevitable because it motivates the most qualified members of society to strive for the most important social positions. (245)

W. E. B. Du Bois: This sociologist wrote about slavery in the United States, noting that over time the South became committed to keeping African Americans in slavery and killing those who rebelled against this institution. (238)

John Kenneth Galbraith: This economist argued that the Least Industrialized Nations remain poor because their own culture, or way of life, perpetuates poverty from one generation to the next. (261)

Michael Harrington: Harrington argued that colonialism had been replaced by neocolonialism. (261)

Martha Huggins: This sociologist investigated poverty in Brazil. (254-255)

Gerhard Lenski: Lenski offered a synthesis of functionalist and conflict views of stratification which focused on surpluses that groups accumulate. (247-248)

Gerda Lerner: This historian noted that women were usually the first enslaved by war and conquest. (237)

Oscar Lewis: This anthropologist was among the first to write about the culture of poverty. (261)

Karl Marx: Marx concluded that social class depended exclusively on the means of production; an individual's social class was determined by whether or not he owned the means of production. (243-244,247)

Gaetano Mosca: Mosca argued that every society is inevitably stratified by power. (247)

Melvin Tumin: Tumin was the first to offer a criticism of the functionalist view on stratification. (246)

Immanuel Wallerstein: This historian proposed a world system theory to explain global stratification. (259)

Max Weber: Weber argued that social class was based on three components: property, prestige, and power (244-245)

PRACTICE TEST

1. What term applies to the division of large numbers or groups of people into layers according to their relative power, property, and prestige? (237)
    a. diversification
    b. networking
    c. stratification
    d. structure

2. Which of the following statements is true? (237)
    a. Most societies have a system of social stratification.
    b. Some societies use gender a way to stratify members.
    c. Social stratification has little to do with how we see life.
    d. Every society stratifies its members.

3. Which of the following statements is true regarding slavery? (238)
    a. was not usually based on racism
    b. was justified in the Koran, but not in the Judaic/Christian traditions in the Bible
    c. was more common among hunters and gatherers than it was in those engaged in agricultural activities
    d. was always inherited from one generation to another

4. The historic pattern of American slavery shows that: (238)
    a. indentured servants usually became slaves.
    b. slavery was inherited from one generation to another.
    c. patterns of legal discrimination became illegal after the Civil War.
    d. slavery led to the development of racist attitudes.

5. Which country provides the best example of a caste system? (240)
    a. India
    b. China
    c. Russia
    d. Sweden

6. When slavery ended in the United States: (241-242)
    a. patterns of legal discrimination ended.
    b. a racial caste system appeared.
    c. slavery remained an inheritable trait
    d. whites considered themselves to have a higher status than African Americans only if they had a higher income and education than African Americans.

7. In the estate system, the third system consisted of the: (236)
    a. clergy.
    c. nobility.
    c. those who held public office.
    c. commoners.

8. Karl Marx called the group that controlled the means of production the: (243)
    a. bourgeoisie.
    b. proletariat.
    c. estate class.
    d. upper class.

9. According to Karl Marx, the term for workers' mistaken identification of themselves with the capitalists is: (244)
    a. class error.
    b. false advancement.
    c. false consciousness.
    d. upward mobility.

10. Which of these statements is consistent with the functionalist view of   stratification? (245)
    a. Stratification is dysfunctional for society.
    b. Stratification is the outcome of conflict between different social classes.
    c. Stratification will disappear in societies that are characterized by a meritocracy.
    d. Stratification is an inevitable feature of social organization.

11. What is the best predictor of who will go to college? (246)
    a. family income
    b. merit
    c. ability
    d. the highest ranked students in high school

12. Conflict theory, as applied to social stratification, would maintain that: (247)
    a. labor represents a united concept both in theory and in practice regarding unions.
    b. African Americans are no longer pitted against whites regarding wages.
    c. capitalists are triumphing on a global level.
    d. conflict between men and women is no longer over power but is now strictly over a matter of wealth.

13. In order to maintain their relative position in society, the ruling elites in contemporary society must: (248)
   a.   manipulate the media to selectively release information.
   b.   conform outwardly to the controlling ideas.
   c.   pay no attention to checks and balances that exist in society.
   d.   rely less and less on technology to scrutinize security.

14. The classification *Most Industrialized Nations* includes: (251)
   a.   Canada, Brazil, and the United States.
   b.   the United States, Switzerland, and South Africa.
   c.   France, Germany, and Australia.
   d.   Japan, Kuwait, and the United States.

15. In Brazil, *death squads:* (254)
   a.   are a myth perpetuated to scare small children into behaving.
   b.   beat children but do not actually kill them.
   c.   are hired by parents to protect their children from street crime.
   d.   murder children, as do the police.

16. One significant characteristic of the Least Industrialized Nations is the fact that: (255)
   a.   they occupy three-fourths of the land's surface.
   b.   they represent over two-thirds of the world's population.
   c.   most residents now have access to trained physicians.
   d.   these countries have a low percentage of the overall growth rate of the world population.

17. Why is it difficult to know how to classify some nations into a global system of stratification? (255)
   a.   It is difficult because the lines that separate the three levels—Most Industrialized, Industrializing, and Least Industrialized—are soft.
   b.   Some nations have moved beyond industrialization, becoming "postindustrial" nations.
   c.   Some nations have not yet industrialized but are still extremely wealthy.
   d.   All of the above reflect problems with classifying nations into a global system.

18. In what way did U.S. colonialism differ from that of European nations? (258)
   a.   The United States restricted its invasions to Asian nations like the Philippines or Hawaii.
   b.   The United States usually chose to plant corporate flags rather than national flags.
   c.   Colonialism undertaken by the United States was on a much larger scale than that of other industrialized nations.
   d.   The United States was always sensitive to the cultural and religious differences of its colonies.

19. Immanuel Wallerstein's theory on world system notes that: (259)
    a. periphery nations develop more than core nations.
    b. Germany was the first to become a core nation.
    c. most African countries are fringe nations.
    d. Britain, Holland, and France are core nations.

20. According to world system theory, all of the following are groups of interconnected nations, *except*: (259)
    a. core nations.
    b. nations on the semiperiphery.
    c. nations on the periphery.
    d. nations in the internal area that have extensive connections with the core nations.

21. The culture of poverty theory was used to analyze global stratification by: (261)
    a. Immanuel Wallerstein.
    b. Max Weber.
    c. John Kenneth Galbraith.
    d. Karl Marx.

22. Which theories of stratification are sociologists most likely to agree with? (261)
    a. neocolonialism and culture of poverty
    b. world system theory and the culture of poverty
    c. colonialism and the culture of poverty
    d. colonialism and world system theory

23. According to the neocolonialist argument, why do so many of the Least Industrialized Nations remain poor? (261-262)
    a. The Most Industrialized Nations set the prices they will pay for these nations' raw materials and natural resources.
    b. The Most Industrialized Nations sell these nations weapons and manufactured goods on credit.
    c. The capital needed to develop the industrial capacity of these nations is used to pay off their debts to the Most Industrialized Nations.
    d. All of the above.

24. Which of the following countries have been able to enter the race for global domination because of technology and outsourced labor? (263)
    a. Korea and India
    b. China and India
    c. Russia and Yugoslavia
    d. Hungary and Hong Kong

25.   Some celebrities been able to accomplish: (263)
    a.   getting the G-8 to forgive the debt of some of the poorest of the world's nations.
    b.   nearly ending world hunger.
    c.   getting the U.S. to remain a world power.
    d.   getting the United Nations to put child slavery as a top priority.

Answer Key

1.   C
2.   D
3.   A
4.   D
5.   A
6.   B
7.   D
8.   A
9.   C
10.   D
11.   A
12.   C
13.   B
14.   C
15.   D
16.   B
17.   D
18.   B
19.   D
20.   D
21.   C
22.   D
23.   D
24.   B
25.   A

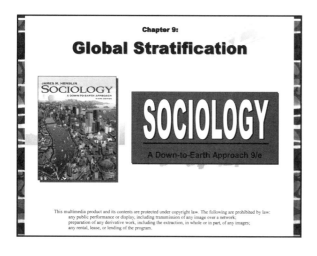

Chapter 9:
Global Stratification

SOCIOLOGY
A Down-to-Earth Approach 9/e

This multimedia product and its contents are protected under copyright law. The following are prohibited by law:
any public performance or display, including transmission of any image over a network;
preparation of any derivative work, including the extraction, in whole or in part, of any images;
any rental, lease, or lending of the program.

What is Social Stratification?

"A system of relative privilege based on

power, property, and prestige."

Chapter 9: Global Stratification

Systems of Social Stratification - Slavery

❋ **Causes**
❋ **Conditions**
  ＊ Temporary
  ＊ Not Necessarily Inheritable
  ＊ Not Necessarily Powerless and Poor
❋ **Slavery in the New World**
❋ **Slavery Today**

Copyright © Allyn & Bacon 2008   Chapter 9: Global Stratification

Systems of Social Stratification - Other

* **Estate**
  * Three Estates
  * Women in the Estate System
* **Class and Social Mobility**
* **Global Stratification and Status of Females**

Copyright © Allyn & Bacon 2008   Chapter 9: Global Stratification

Determinants of Social Class

Karl Marx:

* The Means of Production

* Bourgeoisie

* Proletariat

* Class Consciousness

Copyright © Allyn & Bacon 2008   Chapter 9: Global Stratification

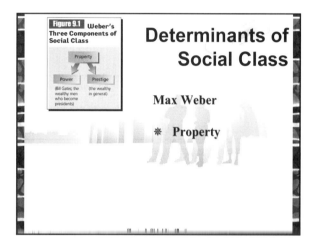

Determinants of Social Class

Max Weber

* Property

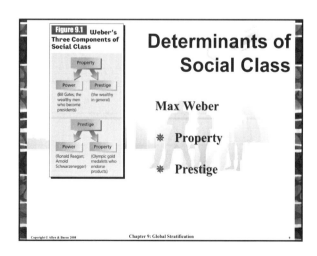

Determinants of Social Class

Max Weber

* Property

* Prestige

Copyright © Allyn & Bacon 2008   Chapter 9: Global Stratification

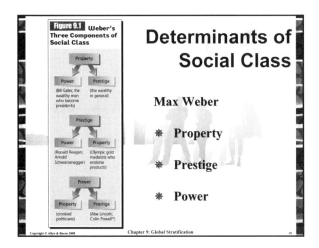

Determinants of Social Class

Max Weber

❋ Property

❋ Prestige

❋ Power

Why is Social Stratification Universal? Functionalist View

Davis and Moore's Explanation

❋ Society Must Make Sure all Positions are Filled

❋ Some Positions are More Important than Others

Why is Social Stratification Universal? Functionalist View

Davis and Moore's Explanation

❋ More Important Positions Filled by More Qualified People

❋ To Motivate Qualified People, They Must Be Rewarded

Why is Social Stratification Universal? Functionalist View

Tumin's Critique of Davis and Moore

* How do We Know Positions Most Important?

* Stratification Should = Meritocracy

* It Ought to Benefit Everyone

Copyright © Allyn & Bacon 2008   Chapter 9: Global Stratification   13

Why is Social Stratification Universal? Conflict Perspective

Mosca's Argument

* No Society Can Exist Unless Organized

* Leadership Means Inequalities of Power

* Human Nature is Self-Centered

Chapter 9: Global Stratification   11

Why is Social Stratification Universal? Conflict Perspective

Marx's Argument

* Functionalist Explanation is Ideology of the Elite

* Class Consciousness Will Overcome Blinding Ideology

Copyright © Allyn & Bacon 2008   Chapter 9: Global Stratification   15

Why is Social Stratification Universal? Conflict Perspective

❋ Current Applications of Conflict Theory

❋ Lenski's Synthesis

Copyright © Allyn & Bacon 2008   Chapter 9: Global Stratification   16

How Do Elites Maintain Stratification?

Ideology vs. Force

❋ Ideas Controlling the Masses

❋ Ideas Controlling the Elites

❋ Controlling Information and

Using Technology

Copyright © Allyn & Bacon 2008   Chapter 9: Global Stratification   17

Comparative Social Stratification

❋ Social Stratification in

Great Britain

❋ Social Stratification in

Former Soviet Union

Copyright © Allyn & Bacon 2008   Chapter 9: Global Stratification   18

Global Stratification: Three Worlds (Old Model)

* First World - Industrialized Capitalist Nations
* Second World - Communist Nations
* Third World - Nations that Don't Fit in First Two

Copyright © Allyn & Bacon 2008   Chapter 9: Global Stratification   19

Global Stratification: Three Worlds

* Most Industrialized Nations

* Industrializing Nations

* Least Industrialized Nations

Table 9.2 Distribution of the World's Land and Population

	Land	Population
Most Industrialized Nations	31%	16%
Industrializing Nations	20%	16%
Least Industrialized Nations	49%	68%

Sources: Computed from Kurian 1990, 1991, 1992.

Copyright © Allyn & Bacon 2008   Chapter 9: Global Stratification   21

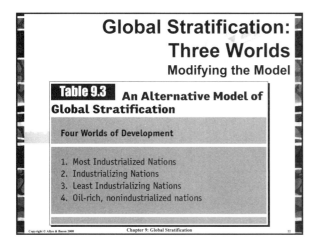

**Global Stratification:
Three Worlds**
Modifying the Model

Table 9.3 An Alternative Model of Global Stratification

Four Worlds of Development

1. Most Industrialized Nations
2. Industrializing Nations
3. Least Industrializing Nations
4. Oil-rich, nonindustrialized nations

Copyright © Allyn & Bacon 2008   Chapter 9: Global Stratification   22

**How Did World's Nations
Become Stratified?**

✳ **Colonialism**

✳ **World System Theory**

✳ **Culture of Poverty**

✳ **Evaluating the Theories**

Copyright © Allyn & Bacon 2008   Chapter 9: Global Stratification   23

**Maintaining Global
Stratification**

✳ **Neocolonialism**

✳ **Multinational Corporations**

✳ **Technology and Global Domination**

  ✳ **Race Outcome Predetermined**

  ✳ **Unintended Public Relations**

Copyright © Allyn & Bacon 2008   Chapter 9: Global Stratification   24

Chapter 9:
Global Stratification

SOCIOLOGY
A Down-to-Earth Approach 9/e

_____

_____

_____

_____

_____

_____

_____

CHAPTER 10
SOCIAL CLASS IN THE UNITED STATES

CHAPTER SUMMARY

- Most sociologists have adopted Weber's definition of social class as a large group of people who rank closely to one another in terms of wealth, power, and prestige. Wealth consists of property and income; power is defined as the ability to carry out one's will despite the resistance of others; and prestige is a measure of the regard or respect accorded an individual or social position.

- Status refers to social ranking. Most people are status consistent, meaning that they rank high or low on all three dimensions of social class. People who rank high on some dimensions and low on others are status inconsistent.

- Sociologists use two models to portray the social class structure. Erik Wright developed a four class model based on the ideas of Karl Marx. Dennis Gilbert and Joseph Kahl developed a six class model based on the ideas of Max Weber.

- Social class leaves no aspect of life untouched. Class membership affects physical and mental health, family life, educational attainment, religious affiliation, political participation and contact with crime and the criminal justice system.

- Each class is also affected by the globalization of capital and the changing economy.

- In studying the mobility of individuals within society, sociologists look at intergenerational mobility, exchange mobility, and structural mobility.

- Poverty is unequally distributed in the United States. Minorities, children, female-headed households, and the rural poor are more likely to be poor. Sociologists generally focus on structural factors, such as employment opportunities, in explaining poverty. Sociologists argue that life orientations are a consequence, not the cause, of people's position in the class structure.

- The Horatio Alger myth encourages people to strive to get ahead, and blames failures on individual shortcomings.

LEARNING OBJECTIVES
After reading Chapter 10, you should be able to:

1. Define social class and the components that comprise social class. (268)
2. Differentiate between wealth and property and how each is distributed in the United States. (268-271)
3. Discuss what defines power and who has power in the U.S. (271-272)
4. Discuss the relationship between occupations and prestige. (272-274)
5. Define status inconsistency and discuss its implications. (274)

6. Compare Erik Wright's model of social class with Marx's model of social class. (274-276)
7. Describe each of the six classes in Gilbert and Kahl's model of social class. (276-280)
8. Using Gilbert and Kahl's model, describe social class in the automobile industry. (280)
9. Know the consequences of social class on physical health, mental health, family life, education, religion, politics, and crime. (280-284)
10. Understand the relationship between social class and the changing economy. (284)
11. Describe and distinguish between the three types of social mobility. (284-285)
12. Explore women and social mobility. (285)
13. Discuss the role of statistics when examining social mobility. (285-286)
14. Discuss the pain that either upward or downward social mobility can bring. (286)
15. Know how the United States government defines poverty and the implications of that definition. (286-287)
16. Discuss the myths associated with the poor and how those myths can be dispelled. (288)
17. Identify the major characteristics of the poor in the United States. (289-290)
18. Describe how race and poverty are related in children. (291)
19. Describe how long poverty might last. (292)
20. Compare structural explanations of poverty in the United States to individual explanations of poverty. (292)
21. Talk about recent changes in welfare policy in the United States and the controversies associated with those changes. (293-294)
22. Discuss the advantages or disadvantages of deferred gratification. (294)
23. Identify the social functions of the Horatio Alger myth and discuss the myth's sociological implications. (294-295)

KEY TERMS
After studying the chapter, review the definition for each of the following terms.

anomie: Durkheim's term for a condition of society in which people become detached from the norms that usually guide their behavior (274)

contradictory class location: Erik Wright's term for a position in the class structure that generates contradictory interests (276)

culture of poverty: the assumption that the values and behaviors of the poor make them fundamentally different from other people; that these factors are largely responsible for their poverty, and that parents perpetuate poverty across generations by passing these characteristics on to their children (292)

deferred gratification: forgoing something in the present in the hope of achieving greater gains in the future (294)

downward social mobility: movement down the social class ladder (284)

exchange mobility: about the same numbers of people moving up and down the social class ladder such that, on balance, the social class system shows little change (285)

feminization of poverty: a trend in U.S. poverty whereby most poor families are headed by women (290)

Horatio Alger myth: the belief that due to limitless possibilities anyone can get ahead if he or she tries hard enough (295)

income: money received, usually from a job, business, or assets (268)

intergenerational mobility: the change that family members make in social class from one generation to the next (284)

poverty line: the official measure of poverty; calculated to include those whose incomes are less than three times a low-cost food budget (286)

power: the ability to carry out your will, even over the resistance of others (271)

power elite: C. Wright Mills' term for the top people in U.S. corporations, military, and politics who make the nation's major decisions (271)

prestige: respect or regard (272)

property: material possessions (286)

social class: according to Weber, a large group of people who rank close to one another in wealth, power, and prestige; according to Marx, one of two groups: capitalists who own the means of production and workers who sell their labor (268)

status: the position that someone occupies in society or a social group (274)

status consistency: ranking high or low on all three dimensions of social class (274)

status inconsistency: ranking high on some dimensions of social class and low on others; also known as *status discrepancy* (274)

structural mobility: movement up or down the social class ladder because of changes in the structure of society, not to individual efforts (285)

underclass: a small group of people for whom poverty persists year after year and across generations (279)

upward social mobility: movement up the social class ladder (284)

wealth: the total value of everything someone owns, minus the debts (268)

KEY PEOPLE
Review the major theoretical contributions or findings of these people.

William Domhoff: Drawing upon the work of C. Wright Mills, Domhoff states that the power elite is so powerful that no major decisions in the U.S. government is made without its approval. (271-272)

Dennis Gilbert and Joseph Kahl: These sociologists developed a more contemporary stratification model based on Max Weber's work. (276)

Ray Gold: Gold did research on the status inconsistency of apartment-house janitors who earned more than the tenants whose garbage they took out. (274)

Daniel Hellinger and Dennis Judd: These sociologists identified the average citizen's belief that he/she exercises political power through the voting process as the "democratic façade" that conceals the real source of power in the United States. (271)

Elizabeth Higgenbotham and Lynn Weber: These sociologists studied the mobility patterns for women. (285)

Melvin Kohn: Kohn studied social class differences in child-rearing patterns. (282-283)

Steph Lawler: This sociologist interviewed British women who achieved upward mobility but felt caught between their working class background and their middle class life. (286)

Elliot Liebow: In 1967, this sociologist studied black street-corner men. He noted that their circumstances made it difficult for them to save for the future, since whatever funds they had were needed to survive in the present. (294)

Gerhard Lenski: Lenski noted that everyone wants to maximize their status, but that others often judge an individual on the basis of his lowest status despite the individual's efforts to be judged on the basis of his highest status. (274)

Karl Marx: Marx believed that there were only two social classes—the capitalists and the workers. Membership is based on a person's relationship to the means of production. (274-275)

C. Wright Mills: Mills used the term "power elite" to describe the top decision-makers in the nation. (271)

Daniel Moynihan: In the 1960s, this sociologist attributed the high rate of childhood poverty in the African American community to the breakdown of the family. (291)

Richard Sennett and Jonathan Cobb: Sennett and Cobb studied the impact that a child's upward mobility had on his relationship with his parents. (286)

Max Weber: Weber developed the definition of social class that is used by most sociologists. He noted that social class is made up of a large group of people who rank close to one another in terms of wealth, power, and prestige. (268)

Erik Wright: Wright proposed an updated version of Marx's theory of stratification. (276)

PRACTICE TEST

1. According to your text, on what do most sociologists agree concerning social class? (268)
    a.   It has a clear-cut, accepted definition in sociology.
    b.   It is best defined by the two classes as set out by Marx.
    c.   It is best defined by Weber's dimensions of social class.
    d.   It has no clear-cut, accepted definition and thus is used differently by all sociologists.

2. Which group in America is one of the wealthiest? (270)
    a.   professors
    b.   airline pilots
    c.   Presidents of small companies
    d.   CEO's of the nations' largest corporations

3. Which of the following statements best describes changes in the distribution of U.S. income? (270)
    a.   The income distribution has remained virtually unchanged across time.
    b.   The percentage of income going to the richest 20 percent of U.S. families has declined while the percentage going to the poorest 20 percent has increased.
    c.   The percentage of income going to the middle income groups has increased at the expense of groups at both the top and bottom of the income scale.
    d.   The percentage of income going to the richest 20 percent of U.S. families has increased while the percentage going to the poorest 20 percent has decreased.

4. What term do Hellinger and Judd use to describe the myth that the average citizen exercises power when he or she votes for representatives to Congress or the U.S. president? (271)
    a.   democratic charade
    b.   popular façade
    c.   democratic façade
    d.   political power myth

5. C. Wright Mills' notion of the power elite in America refers to: (271)
    a.   a concentration of power that contradicts America's ideology of equality.
    b.   its' giving input for domestic policy, but not foreign policy.
    c.   Domhoff's idea that no one group could become so powerful.
    d.   the idea that its members do not share like-minded values or vested interests.

6. Which of the statements regarding the jobs that have the most prestige is *not* true? (273)
    a.   They pay more.
    b.   They require more education.
    c.   They require special talent or skills.
    d.   They offer greater autonomy.

7. If apartment-house janitors unionize and make more money than some of the people whose garbage they carried out, this outcome would be an example of: (274)
    a. status inconsistency.
    b. status consistency.
    c. contradictory class location.
    d. derogatory class location.

8. Which of the following is not one of the social classes identified by Erik Wright? (276)
    a. capitalists
    b. petty bourgeoisie
    c. workers
    d. underclass

9. Joseph Kahl and Dennis Gilbert's concept of the Capitalist Class: (276-277)
    a. includes only those people who are referred to as "old money."
    b. says the prestige of its members is independent of its length of time in the Capitalist Class.
    c. applies to the means of production and the controlling of businesses that have little ownership of the mass media.
    d. is seen as a perpetuation of the privileged class in America's society.

10. According to Gilbert and Kahl, the members of which social class are laborers, service workers, and low paid retail workers? (279)
    a. the capitalist class
    b. the working poor
    c. the lower middle class
    d. the working class

11. Which of the following statements best describes the place of the homeless in our system today? (279-280)
    a. they are on the lowest rung with little or no chance of climbing anywhere.
    b. they are the "fallout" of our developing postindustrial economy.
    c. in another era, they would have had plenty of work as unskilled laborers.
    d. all of the above.

12. What factor or factors explain the social class difference in death rates? (281)
    a. two-tiered system of medical care
    b. lifestyle differences
    c. unequal access to medical care
    d. all of the above

13. Which of the following statements about social class differences in mental health is *correct*? (281-282)
    a. The rich have less control over their wealth since it is invested in the stock market, so they worry more about becoming poor.
    b. The poor have less job security and lower wages than the nonpoor, which contribute to higher levels of stress.
    c. The rich experience more divorce and alcoholism, which can undermine their mental health.
    d. The middle class is squeezed by higher and higher taxes, which produces feelings of discontent and poor mental health.

14. According to Melvin Kohn, middle-class parents are concerned that their children: (274)
    a. are conformists.
    b. will follow rules.
    c. are creative
    d. all of the above.

15. Which of the following religions is most likely to attract members from the upper and middle classes? (283)
    a. Quaker (Society of Friends)
    b. Methodist
    c. Episcopal
    d. Baptist

16. In terms of politics, members of the working class are likely to be: (283)
    a. conservative on economic issues and liberal on social issues.
    b. liberal on economic issues and conservative on social issues.
    c. conservative on both economic and social issues.
    d. liberal on both economic and social issues.

17. Which social class is most likely to be robbed, burglarized or murdered? (283- 284)
    a. capitalist
    b. lower
    c. upper-middle
    d. elitist

18. Children who end up in a lower social class than their parents have experienced: (284)
    a. downward social mobility.
    b. intragenerational mobility.
    c. horizontal mobility.
    d. intergenerational mobility.

19. All of the following are examples of the myths about the American poor *except*: (288)
    a. that the poor are trapped in a cycle of poverty that few escape.
    b. most of the poor are white.
    c. most of the poor are single mothers with children.
    d. most of the poor live in the inner cities of our country.

20. The pattern of poverty for those in rural areas is such that: (289)
    a. they are more likely to be single parents than to be married.
    b. they are more skilled and better educated than most of those in poverty.
    c. they have a rate of poverty higher than that of the national average.
    d. the greatest predictor of poverty in America is where one is geographically as opposed to one's education level or gender.

21. One of the best indicators whether a family is poor or not is: (290)
    a. the number of members living in the family.
    b. the education levels of the parents.
    c. the race of the family.
    d. family structure.

22. As compared to other age groups, the elderly are _____ to be in poverty. (290)
    a. less likely
    b. more likely
    c. equally likely
    d. most likely

23. What percent of women with less than a high school education will give birth as a single woman? (283)
    a. 15%
    b. 37%
    c. over 50%
    d. about 80%

24. A conflict theorist would believe that: (293-294)
    a. the welfare system exists to reward the poor.
    b. the welfare system exists to maintain an army of workers in reserve.
    c. the welfare system helps the poor overcome the oppression of the rich.
    d. most poor do not deserve to collect welfare.

25. The Horatio Alger myth: (295)
    a. is beneficial for society, according to the functionalists.
    b. reduces pressures on the social system.
    c. motivates people to try harder to succeed because anything is possible.
    d. all of the above.

Answer Key

1.   D
2.   D
3.   A
4.   C
5.   A
6.   C
7.   A
8.   D
9.   D
10.   B
11.   D
12.   D
13.   B
14.   C
15.   C
16.   B
17.   B
18.   A
19.   B
20.   C
21.   D
22.   A
23.   C
24.   B
25.   D

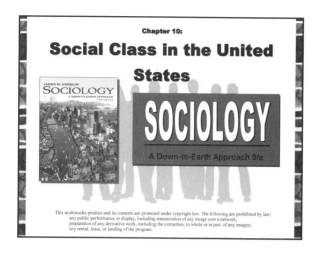

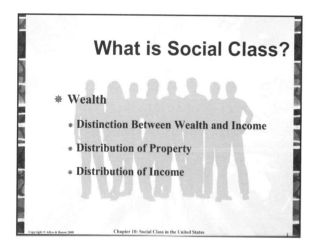

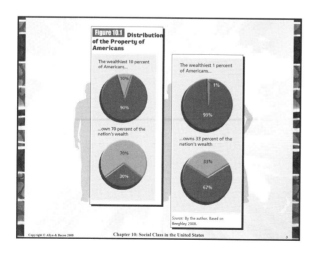

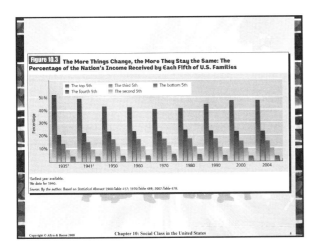

What is Social Class?

❋ **Wealth**

  ✳ **Distinction Between Wealth and Income**

  ✳ **Distribution of Property**

  ✳ **Distribution of Income**

❋ **Power**

Copyright © Allyn & Bacon 2008   Chapter 10: Social Class in the United States   7

Prestige

Occupations and Prestige

❋**They Pay More**

❋**They Require More Education**

❋**They Entail More Abstract Thought**

❋**They Offer Greater Autonomy**

❋**Displaying Prestige**

Copyright © Allyn & Bacon 2008   Chapter 10: Social Class in the United States   8

Status Inconsistency

❋ **Ordinarily Wealth, Power, and Prestige are Similar - Status Consistent**

❋ **When they Don't Match - Status Inconsistent**

Copyright © Allyn & Bacon 2008   Chapter 10: Social Class in the United States   9

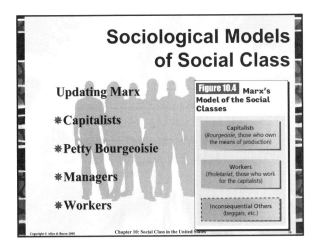

Sociological Models of Social Class

Updating Marx

* Capitalists

* Petty Bourgeoisie

* Managers

* Workers

Figure 10.4 Marx's Model of the Social Classes

Capitalists (*Bourgeoisie*, those who own the means of production)

Workers (*Proletariat*, those who work for the capitalists)

Inconsequential Others (beggars, etc.)

Copyright © Allyn & Bacon 2008   Chapter 10: Social Class in the United States

---

Sociological Models of Social Class

Updating Weber

* Capitalist Class

* The Upper Middle Class

* The Lower Middle Class

* The Working Class

* The Working Poor

* The Underclass

Copyright © Allyn & Bacon 2008   Chapter 10: Social Class in the United States

---

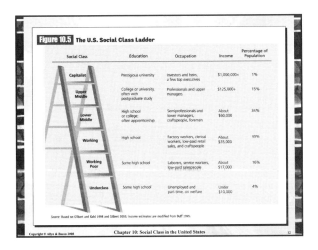

Figure 10.5 The U.S. Social Class Ladder

Social Class	Education	Occupation	Income	Percentage of Population
Capitalist	Prestigious university	Investors and heirs, a few top executives	$1,000,000+	1%
Upper Middle	College or university, often with postgraduate study	Professionals and upper managers	$125,000+	15%
Lower Middle	High school or college; often apprenticeship	Semiprofessionals and lower managers, craftspeople, foremen	About $60,000	34%
Working	High school	Factory workers, clerical workers, low-paid retail sales, and craftspeople	About $35,000	30%
Working Poor	Some high school	Laborers, service workers, low-paid salespeople	About $17,000	16%
Underclass	Some high school	Unemployed and part-time, on welfare	Under $10,000	4%

Source: Based on Gilbert and Kahl 1998 and Gilbert 2003; income estimates are modified from Duff 1995.

Copyright © Allyn & Bacon 2008   Chapter 10: Social Class in the United States

Social Class in the Auto Industry - Ford

* The Fords - Capitalist Class
* Ford Executives - Lower Capitalist Class
* Owner Ford Dealership - Upper Middle
* Ford Salesperson - Lower Middle Class
* Ford Mechanics - Working Class
* Ford Detailer - Working Poor
* Car Lot Cleaner - Underclass

Copyright © Allyn & Bacon 2008   Chapter 10: Social Class in the United States   13

Consequences of Social Class

* Physical Health

* Mental Health

Copyright © Allyn & Bacon 2008   Chapter 10: Social Class in the United States   14

Consequences of Social Class

Family Life

* Choices of Husbands and Wives

* Divorce

* Child Rearing

Copyright © Allyn & Bacon 2008   Chapter 10: Social Class in the United States   15

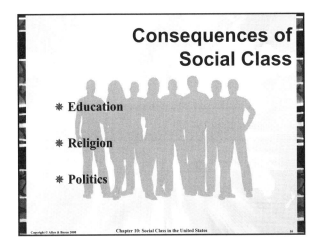

Consequences of Social Class

✱ Education

✱ Religion

✱ Politics

Copyright © Allyn & Bacon 2008 · Chapter 10: Social Class in the United States · 16

Consequences of Social Class

✱ Crime and the Judicial System

✱ Social Class and the Changing Economy

Copyright © Allyn & Bacon 2008 · Chapter 10: Social Class in the United States · 17

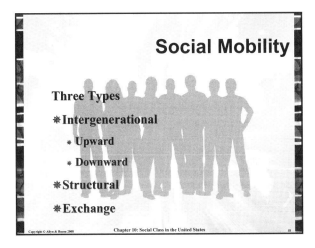

Social Mobility

Three Types
✱ Intergenerational
 ✱ Upward
 ✱ Downward
✱ Structural
✱ Exchange

Copyright © Allyn & Bacon 2008 · Chapter 10: Social Class in the United States · 18

Social Mobility

Women and Social Mobility

❈ **Studies of Boys**

❈ **More Recent Studies with Girls**

Copyright © Allyn & Bacon 2008   Chapter 10: Social Class in the United States   19

Interpreting Statistics on Social Mobility

❈ **Apple Doesn't Fall Far From Tree**

❈ **The Pain of Social Mobility**

Copyright © Allyn & Bacon 2008   Chapter 10: Social Class in the United States

Poverty

Who are Poor?

❈ **Drawing the Poverty Line**

❈ **Geography**

Copyright © Allyn & Bacon 2008   Chapter 10: Social Class in the United States   21

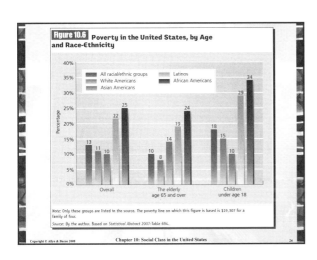

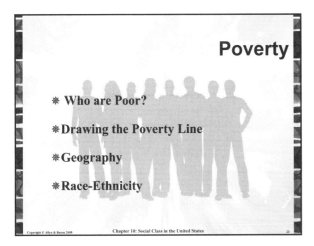

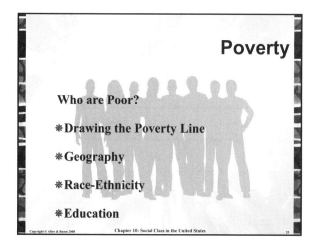

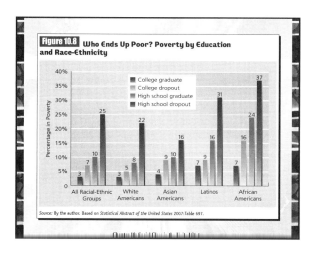

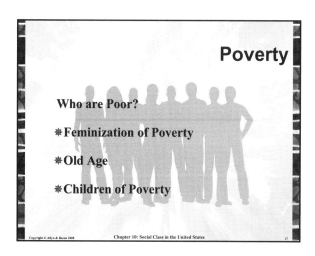

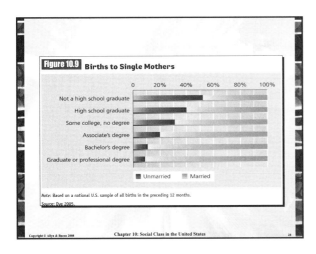

Figure 10.9 Births to Single Mothers

Note: Based on a national U.S. sample of all births in the preceding 12 months.

Source: Dye 2005.

Copyright © Allyn & Bacon 2008   Chapter 10: Social Class in the United States   28

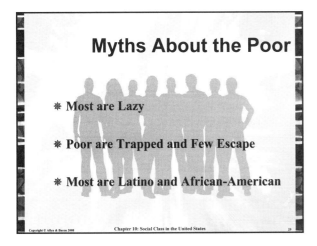

Myths About the Poor

✱ Most are Lazy

✱ Poor are Trapped and Few Escape

✱ Most are Latino and African-American

Copyright © Allyn & Bacon 2008   Chapter 10: Social Class in the United States   29

Myths About the Poor

✱ Most are Single Mothers and Kids

✱ Most Live in Inner City

✱ Most are on Welfare

Copyright © Allyn & Bacon 2008   Chapter 10: Social Class in the United States   30

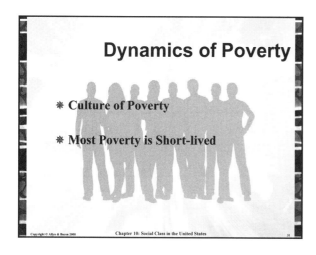

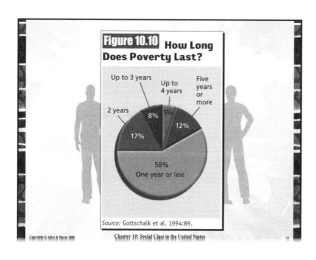

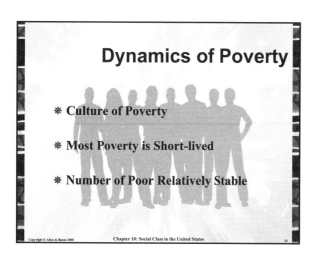

Why are People Poor?

❋ **Social Structure**

❋ **Features of Society**

❋ **Characteristics of Individuals**

Copyright © Allyn & Bacon 2008   Chapter 10: Social Class in the United States   34

Poverty

❋ **Welfare Reform**

  ＊ **Welfare Restructured in 1996**

❋ **Deferred Gratification**

Copyright © Allyn & Bacon 2008   Chapter 10: Social Class in the United States   35

Poverty

❋ **Where is Horatio Alger?**

❋ **Social Functions of a Myth**

Copyright © Allyn & Bacon 2008   Chapter 10: Social Class in the United States   36

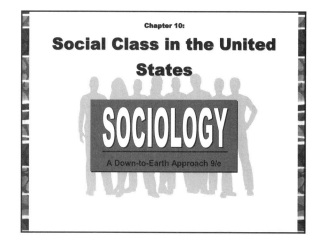

_____

_____

_____

_____

_____

_____

_____

CHAPTER SUMMARY

- Gender stratification refers to unequal access to power, property, and prestige on the basis of sex. Each society establishes a structure that, on the basis of sex and gender, opens and closes access to privileges. Sex refers to biological distinctions between males and females while gender is a social characteristic.

- In the "nature versus nurture" debate, most sociologists take the side of nurture. In recent years the door to biology has opened somewhat. Studies that have been done indicate that human behavior is a combination of nature and nurture.

- The dominant theory to explain the status of women as a minority group focuses on the physical limitations imposed by childbirth. Women assumed tasks associated with the home while men went out for periods of time to hunt large animals. Men were able to acquire possessions and gain prestige.

- George Murdock found a pattern of sex-typed activities among premodern societies, with greater prestige given to those performed by males. Patriarchy, or male dominance, appears to be universal.

- Gender discrimination also happens on a global level. The gender gaps occur in education, politics, pay, and violence against women.

- Feminist movements have gone through two major waves. A third wave is emerging which focuses more on the problems of women in the Least Industrialized Nations. Even though these movements in the United States have battled to eliminate some of the most blatant forms of gender discrimination, there are still many areas of inequality. Two indicators of gender inequality in everyday life are the general devaluation of femininity and the male dominance of conversation.

- In the workplace women's problems include discrimination in pay, the glass ceiling, being controlled along gender lines and sexual harassment.

- Traditional gender patterns still exist in regard to violent behavior. Female circumcision is a special case of violence against women.

- Women's traditional roles as homemakers and child care providers used to keep them out of politics, but today the trend is toward greater political equality.

- As females come to play a larger role in the decision-making processes of U.S. social institutions, stereotypes and role models will be broken. It is possible that a new appreciation of sexual differences will emerge that allows males and females to pursue their individual interests unfettered by gender.

LEARNING OBJECTIVES
After reading Chapter 11, you should be able to:

1. Define gender stratification and distinguish between sex and gender. (300)
2. Understand the controversy over what accounts most for gender differences in behavior, biology or culture; cite the evidence that best supports each side of the argument; and explain the dominant sociological position in the debate. (300-305)
3. Describe the global nature of gender inequality and discuss how females have become a minority group. (305-306)
4. Evaluate the different theories as to the origins of patriarchy. (307-308)
5. Describe how gender and work are related. (308-309)
6. In addition to work, discuss other aspects of global gender discrimination. (309-312)
7. Describe the three "waves" of the women's movement in the United States. (312-315)
8. Discuss and provide examples of gender inequality in healthcare and education. (315-318)
9. Talk about different forms of gender inequality in everyday life, including the general devaluation of femininity. (319)
10. Talk about gender relations in the workplace, including the pay gap, the cracking glass ceiling, the glass escalator, division of workers, and sexual harassment. (320-324)
11. Explain why and how violence against women continues to be a significant social problem in the United States. (324-328)
12. Discuss why women are underrepresented in American politics and what can, and is, being done about it. (328-329)
13. Describe future scenarios of gender definitions and relations in the United States. (329)

KEY TERMS

After studying the chapter, review the definition for each of the following terms.

feminism: the philosophy that men and women should be politically, economically, and socially equal; organized activities on behalf of this principle (312)

gender: the social characteristics that a society considers proper for its males and females; masculinity or femininity (300)

gender stratification: males' and females' unequal access to power, prestige, and property on the basis of their sex (2300)

glass ceiling: the mostly invisible barrier that keeps women from advancing to the top levels of work (323)

glass escalator: the mostly invisible accelerators that push men into higher-level positions, more desirable work assignments, and higher salaries (324)

matriarchy: a society in which women as a group dominate men as a group; authority is vested in females (303)

patriarchy: a society or group in which men dominate women; authority is vested in males (303)

sex: biological characteristics that distinguish females and males, consisting of primary and secondary sex characteristics (300)

sexual harassment: the abuse of one's position of authority to force unwanted sexual demands on someone (324)

KEY PEOPLE
Review the major theoretical contributions or findings of these people.

Janet Chafetz: Chafetz studied the second wave of feminism in the 1960s, noting that as large numbers of women began to work in the economy, they began to compare their working conditions with those of men. (314, 329)

Donna Eder: This sociologist discovered that junior high boys call one another "girl" when they don't hit each other hard enough during a football game. (319)

Frederick Engels: Engels was a colleague of Karl Marx and wrote a book about the origins of the family in which he argued that male dominance developed with the origin of private property. (308)

Cynthia Fuchs Epstein: Epstein is a proponent of the view that differences between males' and females' behavior is solely the result of social factors such as socialization and social control. (302)

Sue Fisher: She discovered that surgeons were recommending total hysterectomies to female patients when they were not necessary. (316)

Douglas Foley: This sociologist's study of sports lends support to the view that things feminine are generally devalued. (319)

Janet Giele and Judith Lorber: As stereotypes are broken, men and women will have more opportunities to express needs and emotions than was previously acceptable. (329)

Steven Goldberg: This sociologist's view is that the differences between males and females are not due to environment but to inborn differences that direct the emotions and behaviors of the two genders. (303)

Barbara Grosz: A professor at Harvard who experienced that female professors are not taken as seriously as male professors. (318-319)

Marvin Harris: This anthropologist suggested that male dominance grew out of the greater strength that men had which made them better suited for the hand-to-hand combat of tribal societies. (308)

Karen Horsfeld: Companies that divide their workers along gender lines find it easier to control their female workers. Females were less likely to file complaints when their bosses flirted with them. (324)

Alison Jaggar: As society changes, we may see a greater appreciation for sexual differences and gender equality can become a background condition for living in society rather than a goal to strive for. (329)

Gerda Lerner: While acknowledging that in all societies women—as a group—have never had decision-making power over men, Lerner suggested that patriarchy may have had different origins in different places around the globe. (305-306)

George Murdock: This anthropologist surveyed 324 premodern societies around the world and found that in all of them, activities were sex typed. (308)

Alice Rossi: This feminist sociologist has suggested that women are better prepared biologically for "mothering" than are men. (302-303)

Diana Scully: She learned that surgeons "sell" unnecessary female operations to women in order to keep themselves in business. (316)

Samuel Stouffer: In his classic study of combat soldiers during World War II, Stouffer noted the general devaluation of things associated with women. (319)

Larry Summers: President of Harvard university who suggested that women's inborn characteristics make them less qualified to succeed as engineers and scientists. (306)

Christine Williams: Williams found that men in nontraditional careers and occupations often experience a glass escalator—moving more quickly than women into desirable work assignments, higher-level positions, and larger salaries. (323)

PRACTICE TEST

1. Biological characteristics that distinguish females and males are referred to as: (300)
   a. cultural identification.
   b. gender markers.
   c. heredity.
   d. sex.

2. As opposed to the concept of sex, the concept of gender: (300)
   a. refers to primary sex characteristics.
   b. varies from one society to another.
   c. is defined to refer to the process of reproduction.
   d. verifies the biological model for explaining behavior by males and females.

3. Which of the following statements about gender stratification is *incorrect*? (300)
   a. It cuts across all aspects of social life.
   b. It cuts across all social classes.
   c. It refers to the unequal access to power, prestige, and property on the basis of sex.
   d. Unlike class stratification, it is not a structured feature of society.

4. Epstein argues that behavioral differences in males and females show that: (302)
   a. biology causes both differences in body structure and in human behavior.
   b. female crime rates are decreasing worldwide due to women's lack of aggression.
   c. biology, not social factors, influences the type of work men and women do.
   d. differences are the result of socialization and social control.

5. Which sociologist has suggested that women are better prepared biologically for "mothering" than men: (302)
   a. Alice Rossi
   b. Cynthia Graham
   c. Gerda Lerner
   d. Carol Gilligan

6. If biology is the principal factor in human behavior, what would we find around the world? (302)
   a. Things would be just like they are.
   b. Men and women would be much more like each other than they currently are.
   c. Women would be one sort of person and men another.
   d. None of the above.

7. Research on high testosterone levels in males is summarized by saying that: (304-305)
    a. the study of Vietnam veterans was correct in showing that high testosterone levels always leads to aggressive and illegal behavior.
    b. high testosterone increases aggression but not illegal behavior.
    c. increases in testosterone levels leads to conflict situations.
    d. such aggressive or illegal behaviors are related to social class.

8. According to Harvard President, Larry Summers: (306)
    a. women haven't received equal education to their male counterparts.
    b. there is discrimination against women in college engineering programs.
    c. few women are engineers and scientists because of their innate differences from men.
    d. none of the above.

9. The major theory of the origin of patriarchy points to: (307)
    a. the social consequences of human reproduction.
    b. men's greediness.
    c. women's willingness to give up power and control in return for protection.
    d. men's greater strength enabled them to overpower women.

10. When anthropologist George Murdock surveyed 324 premodern societies, which of the following was *not* one of his findings? (308)
    a. Activities were sex typed in all of them.
    b. Every society associates activities with one sex or the other.
    c. Biological requirements were the basis for men and women having different tasks.
    d. Activities considered "female" in one society may be considered "male" activities in another.

11. Around the world, what percent of women can't read? (309)
    a. 35%
    b.. 52%
    c. 66%
    d. 90%

12. Which statement concerning global discrimination is *incorrect*? (301)
    a. In most nations, women hold about 15 percent of the seats in parliament and congress
    b. The United States leads the world in the number of women who hold public office.
    c. Around the globe, women average less pay than men.
    d. A global human rights issue has become violence against women.

13. Feminism: (312)
     a.   is a view opposed to the policies held by suffragists.
     b.   has its historic roots in strongly radical, rather than conservative, views.
     c.   holds the view that biology is not destiny.
     d.   focuses on American society rather than Least Industrialized Nations.

14. Female circumcision: (313)
     a.   usually takes place when a girl reaches adolescence.
     b.   must be reversed to permit sexual intercourse by having the vagina narrowed.
     c.   is common in some parts of Muslim Africa, Malaysia, and Indonesia.
     d.   is supported by modern feminists as a symbol of dominance for women.

15. During which wave of the women's movement was raising women's pay a primary issue? (314)
     a.   first
     b   second
     c.   third
     d.   fourth

16. A possible "third wave" of feminism is now emerging. What is the focus of this wave? (314)
     a.   Widespread legal reforms to guarantee equality.
     b.   Greater compensation for victims of sexual harassment.
     c.   Broadening the values that underlie work and other social institutions.
     d.   Inclusion of women's contributions to our history.

17. Research has found that who is more likely to die after coronary bypass surgery? (315)
     a.   men
     b.   women
     c.   men and women have equal rates
     d.   researchers aren't sure since only men have been studied

18. Which statement reflects accurately gender inequality in education? (308-311)
     a.   Women have fallen behind in enrollment at the undergraduate level.
     b.   Significantly more males graduate from law school than females.
     c.   Women are less likely to become full professors.
     d.   Men and women enter graduate school in relatively equal numbers.

19.   Researchers who have studied conversation patterns between men and women conclude
      that: (319-320)
      a.   women talk more and interrupt men more frequently than the other way
      around.
      b.   men and women are social equals when it comes to everyday
      conversation.
      c.   even in everyday conversation, the talk between a man and a woman reflects
            social inequality.
      d.   men interrupt more in conversations, but women control the topics that are
            discussed.

20.   How many of America's top Fortune 500 corporations are headed by women? (323)
      a.   10
      b.   15
      c.   32
      d.   45

21.   The term "glass ceiling" can best be described as: (323)
      a.   the point after which males cannot progress.
      b.   the invisible barrier brought on by a worker's lack of education.
      c.   the invisible barrier that bars women from top business positions.
      d.   the point beyond which older workers cannot rise.

22.   Williams's notion of the "glass escalator" in the workplace refers to: (323)
      a.   men finding limited success in female-dominated fields.
      b.   men being given higher incomes than women in female-dominated fields.
      c.   men encountering unreasonable bias from co-workers.
      d.   men leaving jobs that are not in male-dominated fields.

23.   What is the age of the typical rape victim? (326)
      a.   12 to 34 years old
      b   18 to 25 years old
      c   17 to 40 years old
      d   16 to 30 years old

24.   Women who are convicted of killing another person: (327)
      a.   are generally given stiffer penalties than men.
      b.   usually have a history of interpersonal violence.
      c.   are more likely to be given probation than is a man.
      d.   are placed in minimum security prisons because they are not considered a risk to
            society

25.   Since our nation's first election in 1789 to the present: (328)
    a   about one-third of all U.S. senators have been women.
    b   it took until 1980 for an African American woman to be elected to the U.S. senate.
    c.   over 1800 men, but only 33 women have served in the U.S. senate.
    d.   over 1500 men and over 300 women have been elected to the U.S. senate.

Answer Key

1. D
2. B
3. D
4. D
5. A
6. C
7. D
8. C
9. A
10. C
11. C
12. B
13. C
14. C
15. B
16. C
17. B
18. C
19. C
20. A
21. C
22. B
23. A
24. C
25. C

Chapter 11:
Sex and Gender

SOCIOLOGY
A Down-to-Earth Approach 9/e

This multimedia product and its contents are protected under copyright law. The following are prohibited by law: any public performance or display, including transmission of any image over a network; preparation of any derivative work, including the extraction, in whole or in part, of any images; any rental, lease, or lending of the program.

What is Gender Stratification?

"males' and females' unequal access to property, power, and prestige."

Chapter 11: Sex and Gender

Issues of Sex and Gender

Sex - Biological Characteristics

　✳ **Female and Male**

　✳ **Primary and Secondary**

Sexual Characteristics

Copyright © Allyn & Bacon 2006 · Chapter 11: Sex and Gender · 3

Issues of Sex and Gender

Gender - Social Characteristics

✻ **Masculinity and Femininity**

✻ **Appropriate Behavior**

Copyright © Allyn & Bacon 2008   Chapter 11: Sex and Gender

Figure 11.1 **Teaching Gender**

By looking at the past, we get an idea of how far we have come. This illustration from a 1970s children's book shows the mind-set of the day. You can see how children who grew up during this period were taught to view gender and work.

Boys are pilots.   Girls are stewardesses.   Boys are presidents.   Girls are First Ladies.

Boys are doctors.   Girls are nurses.   Boys build houses.   Girls keep houses.

Source: From a 1970's children's book; in Cortese 2003.

Copyright © Allyn & Bacon 2008   Chapter 11: Sex and Gender

Gender Differences In Behavior
Biology or Culture?

Dominant Position in Sociology

✻ **Social Factors Primary, Not Biological**

✻ **If Biological Should Be Less Variation**

Copyright © Allyn & Bacon 2008   Chapter 11: Sex and Gender

Gender Differences In Behavior
Biology or Culture?

Opening the Door to Biology

❋ **Nature vs. Nurture**

❋ **A Medical Accident**

❋ **Vietnam Veteran Study**

Copyright © Allyn & Bacon 2008   Chapter 11: Sex and Gender   7

Gender and Inequality in Global Perspective

❋ **How Females became a Minority Group**

❋ **The Origins of Patriarchy**

❋ **Sex Typing of Work**

❋ **Gender and Prestige of Work**

Gender and Inequality in Global Perspective

Other Areas of Global Discrimination

❋ **Global Gap in Education**

❋ **Global Gap in Politics**

❋ **Global Gap in Pay**

❋ **Violence Against Women**

Copyright © Allyn & Bacon 2008   Chapter 11: Sex and Gender   9

Gender Inequality in the U.S.

Fighting Back: The Rise of Feminism

❋ **First Wave—Early 1900s**

❋ **Second Wave Began 1960s**

❋ **Third Wave Emerging Now**

Copyright © Allyn & Bacon 2008   Chapter 11: Sex and Gender   10

Gender Inequality in the U.S.

❋ **Gender Inequality in Health Care**

❋ **Gender Inequality in Education**

Copyright © Allyn & Bacon 2008   Chapter 11: Sex and Gender   11

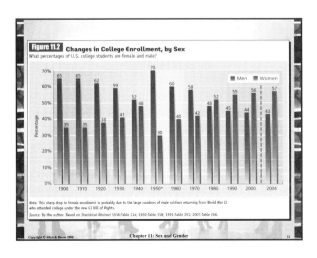

Figure 11.2 Changes in College Enrollment, by Sex

What percentages of U.S. college students are female and male?

Note: This sharp drop in female enrollment is probably due to the large numbers of male soldiers returning from World War II who attended college under the new GI Bill of Rights.

Source: By the author. Based on Statistical Abstract 1938:Table 114; 1959:Table 158; 1991:Table 261; 2007:Table 268.

Copyright © Allyn & Bacon 2008   Chapter 11: Sex and Gender   12

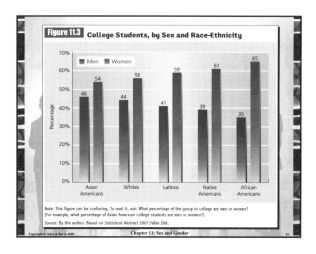

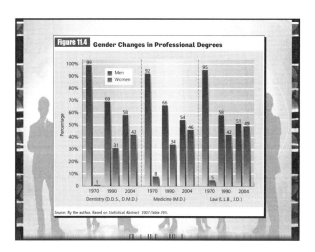

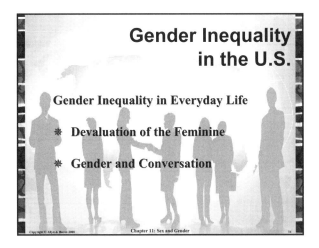

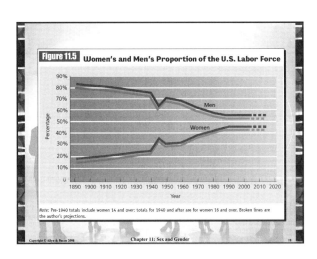

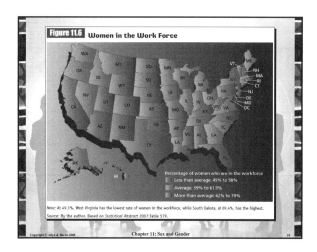

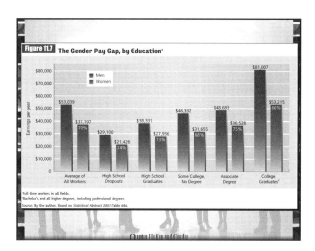

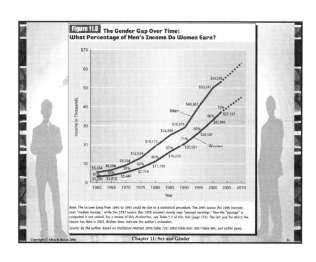

Gender Inequality in the Workplace

* **The Pay Gap**
* **Cracking the Glass Ceiling**
* **The Glass Escalator**

Copyright © Allyn & Bacon 2008   Chapter 11: Sex and Gender   22

_____

_____

_____

_____

_____

_____

_____

Gender Inequality in the Workplace

* **Gender and Control of Workers**

* **Sexual Harassment and Worse**

Copyright © Allyn & Bacon 2008   Chapter 11: Sex and Gender   23

_____

_____

_____

_____

_____

_____

_____

Gender and Violence

Violence Against Women

* **Forcible Rape**
* **Date (Acquaintance) Rape**
* **Murder**
* **Violence in the Home**
* **Women and Criminal Justice System**

Copyright © Allyn & Bacon 2008   Chapter 11: Sex and Gender   24

_____

_____

_____

_____

_____

_____

_____

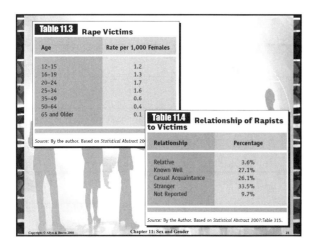

Table 11.3 Rape Victims	
Age	Rate per 1,000 Females
12–15	1.2
16–19	1.3
20–24	1.7
25–34	1.6
35–49	0.6
50–64	0.4
65 and Older	0.1

Source: By the author. Based on *Statistical Abstract 20[ ]*

Table 11.4 Relationship of Rapists to Victims	
Relationship	Percentage
Relative	3.6%
Known Well	27.1%
Casual Acquaintance	26.1%
Stranger	33.5%
Not Reported	9.7%

Source: By the Author. Based on *Statistical Abstract 2007*:Table 315.

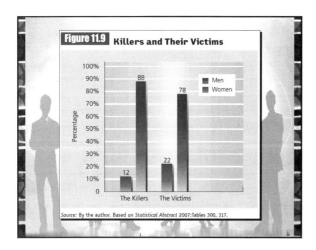

Figure 11.9 Killers and Their Victims

Source: By the author. Based on *Statistical Abstract 2007*:Tables 300, 317.

Gender and Violence

* Feminism and Gendered Violence
  * Symbolic Interactionists
    * Association of Strength, Virility, and Violence
  * Conflict Theory
    * Men Losing Power, Reassert Through Violence
* Solutions

Changing Face of Politics

❋ Women Majority in Population

❋ Women Underrepresented in Government

❋ Women Underrepresented in Law and Business Careers

Copyright © Allyn & Bacon 2008   Chapter 11: Sex and Gender   28

Table 11.6   U.S. Women in Political Office

	Percentage of Offices Held by Women	Number of Offices Held by Women
National Office		
U.S. Senate	16%	16
U.S. House of Representatives	16%	71
State Office		
Governors	18%	9
Lt. Governors	22%	11
Attorneys General	8%	4
Secretaries of State	24%	12
Treasurers	22%	11
State Auditors	12%	6
State Legislators	24%	1,734

Source: Center for American Women and Politics 2007.

Copyright © Allyn & Bacon 2008   Chapter 11: Sex and Gender   29

Glimpsing the Future - With Hope

❋ Barriers Coming Down

❋ Abandoning Stereotypes

❋ New Consciousness

Copyright © Allyn & Bacon 2008   Chapter 11: Sex and Gender   30

Chapter 11:
Sex and Gender

SOCIOLOGY

A Down-to-Earth Approach 9/e

CHAPTER 12
RACE AND ETHNICITY

CHAPTER SUMMARY

- Race is a complex and often misunderstood concept. Race is a reality in the sense that inherited physical characteristics distinguish one group from another. However, race is a myth in the sense of one race being superior to another and of there being pure races.

- Race is so arbitrary that scientists cannot agree upon how many races there are.   Race refers to inherited biological characteristics, while ethnicity refers to cultural ones.   .

- A minority group is defined as one singled out for unequal treatment by members of the dominant group. Both race and ethnicity can be a basis for unequal treatment. The extent of ethnic identification depends on the relative size of the group, its power, broad physical characteristics, and the amount of discrimination.

- Prejudice refers to an attitude and discrimination leading to unfair treatment. Individual discrimination is the negative treatment of one person by another, while institutional discrimination is discrimination built into society's social institutions. Prejudice can be learned based on the association with certain groups.

- Psychological theories explain the origin of prejudice in terms of frustration that gets directed toward scapegoats and in terms of those with authoritarian personalities. Functionalists emphasize how different social environments affect levels of prejudice. Conflict theorists look at the exploitation of racial-ethnic divisions by those in power, and symbolic interactionists stress how labels create selective perception and self-fulfilling prophecies.

- Throughout history in the U.S., and globally, dominant groups typically practice one of six policies toward minority groups: genocide, population transfer, internal colonialism, segregation, assimilation, or pluralism.

- The major ethnic groups in the United States, ranked from largest to smallest, are European Americans, Latinos, African Americans, Asian Americans, and Native Americans.

- Each minority group faces different issues. African Americans are increasingly divided into middle and lower classes, with very different experiences. Latinos are divided by country of origin. The well-being of Asian Americans varies by country of origin. For Native Americans, the issues are poverty, nationhood, and settling treaty obligations.

- The primary issues that dominate race-ethnic relations today are immigration, affirmative action, and how to develop a truly multicultural society.

LEARNING OBJECTIVES

After reading Chapter 12, you should be able to:

1. Explain how the concept of race is both a reality and a myth. (334-335)
2. Distinguish between race and ethnicity. (334-337)
3. Describe the characteristics of minority groups and dominant groups. (338-339)
4. Know what is meant by ethnic identity and the four factors that heighten or reduce it. (339)
5. Differentiate between prejudice and discrimination. (340)
6. Describe how prejudice can be learned through association with different groups and through the internalizing of dominant norms. (340-341)
7. Distinguish between individual discrimination and institutional discrimination. (341-342)
8. Understand the psychological and sociological theories of prejudice. (343-345)
9. List and provide examples of the six patterns of intergroup relations that develop between minority and dominant groups. (347-348)
10. Understand the racial breakdown of racial-ethnic groups in the United States. (350)
11. Compare and contrast the experiences of White Europeans, Latinos, African Americans, Asian Americans, and Native Americans in the United States. (351-364)
12. Talk about the major issues—and debates—currently dominating race and ethnic relations in the United States including immigration and affirmative action. (365-367)
13. State how the United States can move toward a multicultural society. (367)

KEY TERMS

After studying the chapter, review the definition for each of the following terms.

assimilation: the process of being absorbed into the mainstream culture (348)

authoritarian personality: Theodor Adorno's term for people who are prejudiced and rank high on scales of conformity, intolerance, insecurity, respect for authority, and submissiveness to superiors (343)

compartmentalize: to separate acts from feelings or attitudes (347)

discrimination: an act of unfair treatment directed against an individual or a group (340)

dominant group: the group with the most power, greatest privileges, and highest social status (338)

ethnic cleansing: a policy of population elimination, including forcible expulsion and genocide (348)

ethnic work: activities designed to discover, enhance, or maintain ethnic and racial identification (339)

ethnicity (and ethnic): having distinctive cultural characteristics (335)

individual discrimination: the negative treatment of one person by another on the basis of that person's perceived characteristics (341)

institutional discrimination: negative treatment of a minority group that is built into a society's institutions; also called *systemic discrimination* (341)

internal colonialism: the policy of economically exploiting minority groups (348)

melting pot: the view that Americans of various backgrounds would blend into a sort of ethnic stew (339)

minority group: people who are singled out for unequal treatment, and who regard themselves as objects of collective discrimination (338)

multiculturalism (also called pluralism): a philosophy or political policy that permits or encourages ethnic difference (348)

pan-Indianism: a movement that focuses on common elements in the cultures of Native Americans in order to develop a cross-tribal self-identity and to work toward the welfare of all Native Americans (364)

population transfer: forcing a minority group to move (347)

prejudice: an attitude or prejudging, usually in a negative way (340)

race: inherited physical characteristics that distinguish one group from another (334)

racism: prejudice and discrimination on the basis of race (340)

reserve labor force: the unemployed; unemployed workers who are thought of as being "in reserve"—capitalists take them "out of reserve" (put them back to work) during times of high production and then lay them off (put them back in reserve) when they are no longer needed (344)

rising expectations: the sense that better conditions are soon to follow, which, if unfilled, increases frustration (357)

scapegoat: an individual or group unfairly blamed for someone else's troubles (343)

segregation: the policy of keeping racial ethnic groups apart (348)

selective perception: seeing certain features of an object or situation, but remaining blind to others (345)

split-labor market: workers are split along racial, ethnic, gender, age or any other lines; this split is exploited by owners to weaken the bargaining power of workers (344)

WASP: a white Anglo-Saxon Protestant; narrowly, an American (351)
white ethnics: white immigrants to the United States whose culture differs from that of WASPs (351)

KEY PEOPLE

Review the major theoretical contributions or findings of these people.

Theodor Adorno: Adorno identified the authoritarian personality type. (343)

Kathleen Blee: She interviewed women who were members of the KKK and Aryan Nation. She found that their racism was not the cause of their joining, but the result of their membership in those groups. (340)

Ashley Doane: Doane identified four factors that affect an individual's sense of ethnic identity. (339) <NOTE:List the four factors here?>

John Dollard: This psychologist first suggested that prejudice is the result of frustration and scapegoats become the targets for their frustration. (343)

Rapheal Ezekiel: This sociologist did participant observation of neo-Nazis and the Ku Klux Klan in order to examine racism from inside racist organizations. (341)

Anthony Greenwald and Mahzarin Banaji: These psychologists created the "Implicit Association Test". They found that we learn the ethnic maps of our culture and a route to biased perception. (340-341)

Eugene Hartley: His study found that prejudice does not depend on negative experiences with others. Those who are prejudice against racial-ethnic groups are likely to be prejudice against others. (340)

Douglas Massey: This sociologists conducted research with students on race and the real estate industry. He found that white students' experiences were significantly different from those of African-American students. (360)

Peggy McIntosh: Being white is a taken-for-granted background assumption of U.S. society. (352)

Ashley Montagu: This physical anthropologist pointed out that some scientists have classified humans into only two races while others have identified as many as two thousand. (335)

Alejandro Portes and Rueben Rumbaut: These sociologists looked at the impact that immigration has had on our country, pointing out that there has always been an anti-immigrant sentiment present. (365)

Muzafer and Carolyn Sherif: The Sherifs researched the functions of prejudice and found that it builds in-group solidarity. (344)

W. I. and Dorothy Thomas: The Thomases observed that once people define a situation as real, it is real in its consequences. (335)

William Wilson: Wilson is known for his work on racial discrimination, in which he argues that class is a more important factor than race in explaining patterns of inequality. (359)

Louis Wirth: Wirth offered a sociological definition of minority group. (338)

PRACTICE TEST

1.   From a sociological perspective, which of the following statements concerning race is correct? (334)
     a.   Some races are, in fact, intellectually superior to others.
     b.   "Pure" race actually does exist.
     c.   No race is destined to establish a higher cultural and higher social order than any other race.
     d.   Genocide is often due to a sense of racial superiority.

2.   What does Tiger Woods call himself? (336)
     a.   Bonohispanio
     b.   Cablinasian
     c.   Filionese
     d.   none of the above

3.   What is a minority group? (338)
     a.   A group with a low population relative to other groups in an area.
     b.   A group that has migrated to an area.
     c.   A group that has been singled out for unequal treatment and regards itself as an object of collective discrimination.
     d.   A group with a low population worldwide.

4.   All of the following are true about minority groups *except* that: (338-339)
     a.   minority group status is ascribed rather than achieved.
     b.   their physical and cultural traits are held in low esteem by the dominant group.
     c.   members of a minority group feel little group solidarity.
     a.   minorities tend to marry within their own group.

5.   Which of the following factors affects a group's sense of ethnic identity? (339)
     a.   The amount of power the group has.
     b.   The size of the group.
     c.   The degree to which the group's physical appearance differs from the mainstream.
     d.   All of the above.

6.   Many people today are tracing their family lines. This is an example of: (339)
     a.   ethnic identity.
     b.   ethnic enclaves.
     c.   ethnic work.
     d.   ethnic pride.

7.	Discrimination is a (n) _____ and prejudice is a (n) _____. (340)
	a.	attitude, behavior
	b.	negative attitude, an action
	c.	behavior, attitude
	d.	preconceived attitude, internalized norm

8.	From her interviews with women in the KKK and Aryan Nation, what did, Kathleen Blee conclude: (340)
	a.	These women are basically ignorant people who want to stir up problems.
	b.	These women did extensive research on the group prior to membership.
	c.	These women joined because it matched their racist beliefs.
	d.	Racism was a result of membership in the group not the cause of joining the group

9.	Negative treatment on the basis of personal characteristics is: (341)
	a.	individual discrimination.
	b.	individual prejudice.
	c.	institutional discrimination.
	d.	institutional prejudice.

10.	What did the research on health care discover regarding treatment of different racial groups? (342)
	a.	Race does not matter when it comes to treatment in the health care system.
	b.	Whites are more likely to receive knee replacement operations.
	c.	African Americans are more likely to get cardiac catheterization.
	d.	African American doctors give better treatment to patients of the same race.

11.	The Federal Reserve Board study on the relationship between race and obtaining a mortgage loan found: (342)
	a.	that even if income levels were equal, African Americans were more likely than whites to be turned down for a loan.
	b.	there was no pattern of any institutionalized discrimination.
	c.	a significant decrease in African Americans receiving loans since 1970.
	d.	income was the only factor used as a basis for receiving a loan.

12.	According to Adorno, what type of personality is most likely to be prejudice?	(343)
	a.	democratic
	b.	authoritarian
	c.	authoritative
	d.	laissez-faire

13. According to John Dollard, what is the source of prejudice? (343)
    a. the authoritarian personality
    b. frustration
    c. a split-labor market
    d. selective perception

14. Why do functionalists consider prejudice functional for some groups? (344)
    a. It is a useful weapon in maintaining social divisions.
    b. It contributes to the creation of scapegoats.
    c. It helps to create solidarity within the group by fostering antagonisms directed against other groups.
    d. It affects how members of one group perceive members of other groups.

15. According to conflict theorists, prejudice: (344)
    a. benefits capitalists by splitting workers along racial or ethnic lines.
    b. contributes to the exploitation of workers, thus producing a split-labor market.
    c. keeps workers from demanding higher wages and better working conditions.
    d. all of the above.

16. Symbolic interactionists stress that prejudiced people: (345)
    a. are born that way.
    b. have certain types of personalities.
    c. learn their prejudices in interaction with others.
    d. none of the above.

17. Genocide: (347)
    a. occurred when Hitler attempted to destroy all Jews
    b. is the systematic annihilation of a race or ethnic group.
    c. often requires the cooperation of ordinary citizens.
    d. all of the above.

18. The process of being absorbed into the mainstream culture is called: (348)
    a. pluralism.
    b. colonialism.
    c. assimilation.
    d. segregation.

19. Who is the illegal travel guide? (354)
    a. Men who help Mexicans cross the border.
    b. Men who find jobs for illegal immigrants.
    c. Men who are involved in sex trafficking.
    d. Men who are involved in the drug trade.

20. How many states have passed laws making English their official language? (354)
   a. 26
   b. 31
   c. 43
   d. 47

21. In what year was the Civil Rights Act passed, making it illegal to discriminate in restaurants, theatres, and other public places? (357)
   a. 1971
   b. 1957
   c. 1977
   d. 1964

22. William Julius Wilson's central argument in his various books is that: (359)
   a. racism is no longer a dominant factor in American society.
   b. social class is more central to the African American experience than is race.
   c. race is more of a factor for Asian Americans than it is for African Americans.
   d. white Americans are experiencing a type of reverse racism from African Americans and Asian Americans.

23. Massey's study of those making phone calls to rental agents shows that: (360)
   a. callers were discriminated against on the basis of race, but not gender.
   b. stealth racism was a viable factor of discrimination.
   c. African Americans experienced less discrimination than did Asian Americans.
   d. social class was not a significant factor.

24. What is a difference between the wave of immigration at the turn of the last century and the current wave? (365)
   a. The current wave is much smaller.
   b. The current wave is more global in content.
   c. The current wave is experiencing a more welcoming environment.
   d. All of the above.

25. Which state recently passed Proposition 2, an amendment to the state constitution? (367)
   a. Rhode Island
   b. New York
   c. California
   d. Michigan

Answer Key

1. C
2. B
3. C
4. C
5. D
6. C
7. C
8. D
9. A
10. B
11. A
12. B
13. B
14. C
15. D
16. C
17. D
18. C
19. A
20. A
21. D
22. B
23. B
24. B
25. D

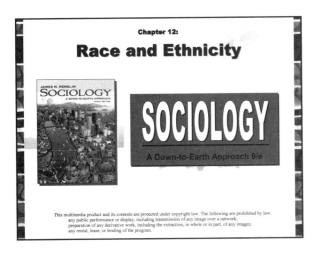

Chapter 12:
Race and Ethnicity

SOCIOLOGY
A Down-to-Earth Approach 9/e

This multimedia product and its contents are protected under copyright law. The following are prohibited by law: any public performance or display, including transmission of any image over a network; preparation of any derivative work, including the extraction, in whole or in part, of any images; any rental, lease, or lending of the program.

Race: Myth and Reality

* **Myth 1 - Idea That Any Race is Superior**
  * All Races Have Geniuses and Idiots
  * Genocide Still Around
* **Myth 2 - Idea that Any Race is Pure**
  * Human Characteristics Flow Endlessly Together

Copyright © Allyn & Bacon 2008   Chapter 12: Race and Ethnicity   2

Ethnic Groups

* **Race Refers to Biological Characteristics**
* **Ethnicity Refers to Cultural Characteristics**
  * Common Ancestry
  * Cultural Heritage
  * Nations of Origin

Copyright © Allyn & Bacon 2008   Chapter 12: Race and Ethnicity   3

Minority and Dominant Groups

* Minority Group - People Singled Out for Unequal Treatment

* Minority Group Not Necessarily Numerical Minority

Copyright © Allyn & Bacon 2008   Chapter 12: Race and Ethnicity

Minority and Dominant Groups

* Dominant Group - Group with Most...
  * Power
  * Privileges
  * Highest Social Status
* Dominant Group Does the Discriminating

Copyright © Allyn & Bacon 2008   Chapter 12: Race and Ethnicity

Emergence of Minority Groups

Minority Groups Occur Because of...

* Expansion of Political Boundaries

* Migration

Copyright © Allyn & Bacon 2008   Chapter 12: Race and Ethnicity

Constructing Racial-Ethnic Identity

* **Sense of Ethnicity**
  * **Relative Size**
  * **Power**
  * **Appearance**
  * **Discrimination**
* **Ethnic Work and the Melting Pot**

Copyright © Allyn & Bacon 2008   Chapter 12: Race and Ethnicity

_____

_____

_____

_____

_____

_____

_____

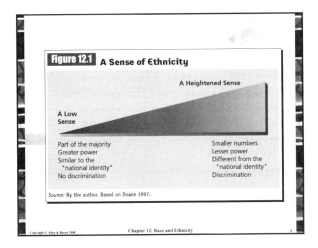

Figure 12.1 A Sense of Ethnicity

A Heightened Sense

A Low Sense

Part of the majority
Greater power
Similar to the
  "national identity"
No discrimination

Smaller numbers
Lesser power
Different from the
  "national identity"
Discrimination

Source: By the author. Based on Doane 1997.

Copyright © Allyn & Bacon 2008   Chapter 12: Race and Ethnicity

_____

_____

_____

_____

_____

Prejudice and Discrimination

* **Learning Prejudice**
  * **Prejudice vs. Discrimination**
* **Discrimination is Action**
* **Learning from Association**

Copyright © Allyn & Bacon 2008   Chapter 12: Race and Ethnicity

_____

_____

_____

_____

_____

_____

_____

Prejudice and Discrimination

❋ **Far-Reaching Nature of Prejudice**

❋ **Internalizing Dominant Norms**

  ❋ Media

  ❋ Group Membership

Copyright © Allyn & Bacon 2008 — Chapter 12: Race and Ethnicity

---

Individual and Institutional Discrimination

❋ **Health Care**

❋ **Home Mortgage and Car Loans**

Copyright © Allyn & Bacon 2008 — Chapter 12: Race and Ethnicity

---

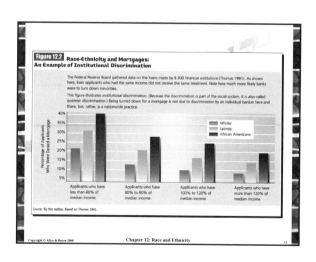

Figure 12.2 Race-Ethnicity and Mortgages: An Example of Institutional Discrimination

Copyright © Allyn & Bacon 2008 — Chapter 12: Race and Ethnicity

Theories of Prejudice

Psychological Perspectives

❋ **Frustration and Scapegoats**

❋ **The Authoritarian Personality**

Copyright © Allyn & Bacon 2008   Chapter 12: Race and Ethnicity   13

Theories of Prejudice

Sociological Perspectives

❋ **Functionalism**

❋ **Conflict Theory**

❋ **Symbolic Interactionism**

    ❋ **Labels Create Prejudice**

    ❋ **Self-Fulfilling Prophesy**

Copyright © Allyn & Bacon 2008   Chapter 12: Race and Ethnicity   14

Global Patterns of Intergroup Relations

❋ **Genocide**

❋ **Population Transfer**

❋ **Internal Colonialism**

Copyright © Allyn & Bacon 2008   Chapter 12: Race and Ethnicity   15

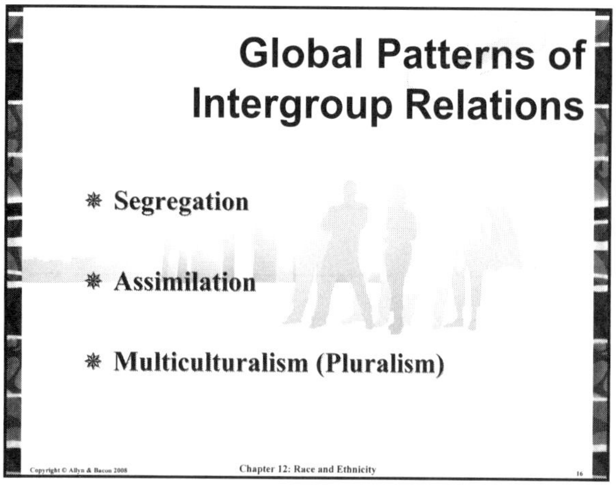

Global Patterns of Intergroup Relations
Segregation
Assimilation
Multiculturalism (Pluralism)
Copyright © Allyn & Bacon 2008
Chapter 12: Race and Ethnicity
16

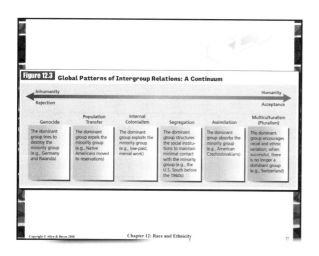

Figure 12.3 Global Patterns of Intergroup Relations: A Continuum
Inhumanity
Rejection
Humanity
Acceptance
Genocide
The dominant group tries to destroy the minority group (e.g., Germany and Rwanda)
Population Transfer
The dominant group expels the minority group (e.g., Native Americans moved to reservations)
Internal Colonialism
The dominant group exploits the minority group (e.g., low-paid, menial work)
Segregation
The dominant group structures the social institutions to maintain minimal contact with the minority group (e.g., the U.S. South before the 1960s)
Assimilation
The dominant group absorbs the minority group (e.g., American Czechoslovakians)
Multiculturalism (Pluralism)
The dominant group encourages racial and ethnic variation; when successful, there is no longer a dominant group (e.g., Switzerland)
Copyright © Allyn & Bacon 2008
Chapter 12: Race and Ethnicity
17

Race and Ethnic Relations in the United States
Figure 12.5 U.S. Racial-Ethnic Groups
Americans of European Descent
198,700,000
66.3%
German 16.0%
Irish 11.5%
English/British 9.9%
Italian 16,823,000 5.6%
French 11,730,000 3.9%
Scottish 11,075,000 3.7%
Polish 9,385,000 3.1%
Dutch 5,087,000 1.7%
Norwegian 4,585,000 1.5%
Swedish 4,326,000 1.4%
Russian 3,017,000 1.0%
Welsh 1,913,000 0.6%
Hungarian 1,527,000 0.5%
Danish 1,477,000 0.5%
Czech 1,462,000 0.5%
Portuguese 1,336,000 0.4%
Greek 1,310,000 0.4%
Swiss 1,033,000 0.3%
Others 11,000,000 3.3%
Americans of African, Asian, and North, Central, and South American Descent
96,146,000
32.1%
Latino 42,687,000 14.4%
African American
Asian American 12,687,000 4.3%
Native American 2,863,000 1.0%
Americans Who Claim Two or More Race-Ethnicities
1.5%
4,579,000 1.5%
0
4%
8%
12%
16%
Percentage of Americans
Overall Total: 299,608,000
Figure 12.4 Race-Ethnicity of the U.S. Population
African Americans 13%
Asian Americans 4%
Native Americans 1%
Claim two or more races 1.5%
Latinos 14%
Whites 66%
Source: By the author. See Figure 12.5.
The totals in this figure should be taken as broadly accurate only. The totals for groups and even for the U.S. population vary from table to table in the source. Because the total of the individual white ethnic groups listed in the source is 10 percent above the total of whites, I arbitrarily reduced each white ethnic group by 10 percent.
Interestingly, this total is six times higher than all the Irish who live in Ireland.
Includes French Canadian.
Includes "Scottish-Irish."
Most Latinos trace at least part of their ancestry to Europe.
In descending order, the largest groups of Asian Americans are from China, the Philippines, India, Korea, Vietnam, and Japan. See figure 12.10. Also includes those who identify themselves as Native Hawaiian or Pacific Islander.
Includes Native American, Inuit, and Aleut.
Source: By the author. Based on Statistical Abstract 2007:Table 50.
Copyright © Allyn & Bacon 2008
Chapter 12: Race and Ethnicity
18

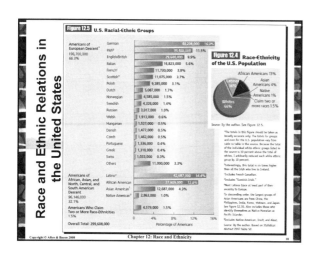

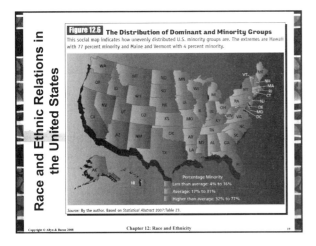

Figure 12.6 The Distribution of Dominant and Minority Groups
This social map indicates how unevenly distributed U.S. minority groups are. The extremes are Hawaii with 77 percent minority and Maine and Vermont with 4 percent minority.

Percentage Minority
Less than average: 4% to 16%
Average: 17% to 31%
Higher than average: 32% to 77%

Source: By the author. Based on *Statistical Abstract* 2007:Table 23.

Race and Ethnic Relations in the United States

Copyright © Allyn & Bacon 2008   Chapter 12: Race and Ethnicity   19

Race and Ethnic Relations in the United States
Europeans Americans

✳ Nation's Founders Included Only

   Those from England (WASPs)

✳ Other "White" Europeans Inferior

Copyright © Allyn & Bacon 2008   Chapter 12: Race and Ethnicity   20

Race and Ethnic Relations in the United States
Latinos (Hispanics)

✳ Numbers Origins, Location

Copyright © Allyn & Bacon 2008   Chapter 12: Race and Ethnicity   21

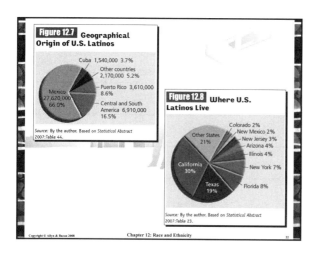

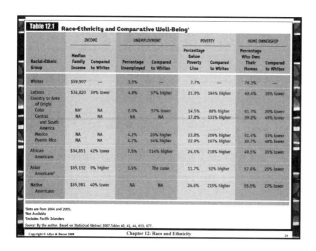

Table 12.2 Race-Ethnicity and Education

| Racial-Ethnic Group | EDUCATION COMPLETED | | | | DOCTORATES | | Percentage of U.S. Population |
	Less than High School	High School	Some College	College (BA or Higher)	Number Awarded	Percentage of all U.S. Doctorates[1]	
Whites	9.7%	33.4%	28.0%	28.9%	28,214	81.0%	66.3%
Latinos	41.1%	27.3%	19.6%	12.1%	1,662	4.7%	14.4%
Country or Area of Origin							
Cuba	26.5%	30.4%	18.4%	24.7%	NA	NA	
Puerto Rico	27.8%	33.7%	24.7%	13.8%	NA	NA	
Central and South America	37.6%	25.6%	18.3%	18.5%	NA	NA	
Mexico	47.7%	26.6%	17.4%	8.3%	NA	NA	
African Americans	19.4%	36.0%	27.0%	17.6%	2,900	8.1%	12.8%
Asian Americans	15.1%	17.2%	19.3%	48.2%	2,632	7.4%	4.3%
Native Americans	23.3%	31.3%	31.1%	14.1%	217	0.6%	1.0%

[1]Percentage after the doctorates awarded to nonresidents are deducted from the total.

Source: By the author. Based on *Statistical Abstract* 2007:Tables 41, 44, 289 and Figure 12.5 of this text.

Copyright © Allyn & Bacon 2008   Chapter 12: Race and Ethnicity   25

Race and Ethnic Relations in the United States
African-Americans

* **The Struggle for Civil Rights**

* **Rising Expectations and Civil Strife**

* **Continued Gains**

Copyright © Allyn & Bacon 2008   Chapter 12: Race and Ethnicity   26

Race and Ethnic Relations in the United States
African-Americans

* **Current Losses**

* **Race or Social Class?**

* **Racism as an Everyday Burden**

Copyright © Allyn & Bacon 2008   Chapter 12: Race and Ethnicity   27

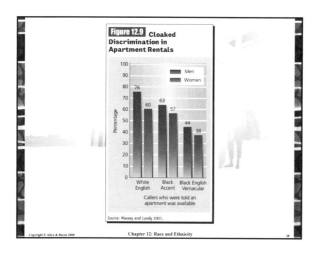

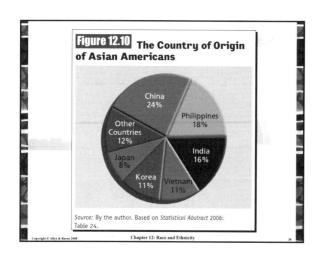

Race and Ethnic Relations in the United States
Native Americans

* Diversity of Groups
* From Treaties to Genocide and Population Transfer
* The Invisible Minority and Self-Determination
* Pan-Indianism

Copyright © Allyn & Bacon 2008   Chapter 12: Race and Ethnicity   31

Looking Towards the Future

* The Immigration Debate
* Affirmative Action
* Towards a True Multicultural Society

Copyright © Allyn & Bacon 2008   Chapter 12: Race and Ethnicity   32

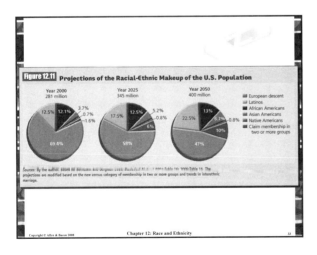

Figure 12.11 Projections of the Racial-Ethnic Makeup of the U.S. Population

Year 2000 281 million
Year 2025 345 million
Year 2050 400 million

European descent, Latinos, African Americans, Asian Americans, Native Americans, Claim membership in two or more groups

Copyright © Allyn & Bacon 2008   Chapter 12: Race and Ethnicity   33

Chapter 12:
Race and Ethnicity

SOCIOLOGY

A Down-to-Earth Approach 9/e

CHAPTER 13
THE ELDERLY

CHAPTER SUMMARY

- There are no universal attitudes, beliefs or policies regarding the aged; they range from exclusion and killing to integration and honor. Today there is a trend for people to live longer. Attitudes toward the elderly are rooted in society and differ from one social group to another.

- Industrialization is a worldwide trend. As countries industrialize, more of its people are able to live longer and reach old age. This is known as the graying of the globe.

- In the United States, the rising proportion of older people in the population is referred to as the "graying of America." Because of this trend, the cost of health care for the elderly has become a social issue, and sentiment about the elderly seems to be shifting.

- The symbolic interaction perspective identifies four factors that influence when people label themselves as "old": biological changes, biographical events, gender age, and cultural timetables. Culture is important in determining how individuals experience aging. Ageism is based on stereotypes that are influenced by the mass media.

- The functional perspective analyzes the withdrawal of the elderly from positions of responsibility. Disengagement, activity, and continuity theories are functional theories of how people adjust to growing old.

- Conflict theorists study the competition for scarce resources by rival interest groups (e.g., how different age cohorts may be on a collision course regarding Social Security, Medicare, and Medicaid).

- Elderly women are most likely to be alone and to be poor. About 5 percent of the elderly live in nursing homes. Problems of dependency for the elderly include inadequate and understaffed nursing homes, elder abuse, and poverty. Poverty in old age has been greatly reduced through government programs.

- Industrialization has changed the individual's experience with death. The process of dying involves denial, anger, negotiation, depression, and acceptance. Hospices, a recent cultural device, are intended to provide dignity in death, to reduce the emotional and physical burden on relatives, and to reduce costs. Suicide increases with age and shows sharply different patterns by sex and race.

- With technological advances, it may be possible to increase the human life span. It is possible that as body parts wear out, they will simply be replaced. There are many questions that could be asked regarding what society would be like if citizens lived to 150 or 200 years old.

LEARNING OBJECTIVES
After reading Chapter 13, you should be able to:

1. Understand what is meant by the "social construction of aging" and how it affects the way societies define and treat their elderly members. (372)
2. Explain the effects of industrialization on life expectancy, population demographics, and the distribution of resources on a global level. (372-373)
3. Describe and illustrate the "graying of America." (374)
4. Understand the regional, gender, racial, and ethnic differences of aging in the United States. (375-376)
5. Understand the global perspective of life expectancy in various countries of the world. (375)
6. Describe the various components of the symbolic interactionist perspective on aging, how it has changed over time, and the influence that the mass media plays. (376-379)
7. Describe the functionalist perspective on aging and the theories put forth about people's adjustment to aging, which include disengagement theory, activity theory, and continuity theory. (380-382)
8. Describe the conflict perspective on aging and some of the controversy surrounding these issues, including social security and health care costs. (382-387)
9. Discuss the major organizations in the United States that protect and promote the political interests of the elderly. (387)
10. Describe and discuss some of the problems that many elderly people in the United States encounter in nursing homes, including understaffing, dehumanization, and death. (388-390)
11. Describe the role that technology can play in nursing homes. (390)
12. Understand elder abuse and poverty among the elderly, including the role of gender and ethnicity. (391-393)
13. Know how industrialization and medical advances have affecting the sociology of death and dying in the United States. (392)
14. Identify the five stages of death that people go through when dying. (392-393)
15. Talk about the role that hospices play in humanizing the processes of death and dying. (393-394)
16. Describe some of the social factors that may affect elderly suicide rates in the United States. (394)
17. Describe how adjustment to death is different for expected vs. unexpected deaths. (394)
18. Discuss the affect of technological breakthroughs on increasing the life span of humans. (394-395)

KEY TERMS

After studying the chapter, review the definition for each of the following terms.

activity theory: the view that satisfaction during old age is related to a person's amount and quality of activity (381)

age cohort: people born at roughly the same time who pass through the life course together (380)

ageism: prejudice, discrimination, and hostility directed against people because of their age; can be directed against any age group, including youth (377)

continuity theory: the focus on this theory is how people adjust to retirement by continuing aspects of their earlier lives (382)

dependency ratio: the number of workers required to support one dependent person age 15 and younger or age 65 and older (385)

disengagement theory: the view that society prevents disruption by having the elderly vacate (or disengage from) their positions of responsibility so that the younger generation can step into their shoes (381)

gender age: the relative value placed on men's and women's ages (377)

graying of America: refers to the growing percentage of older people in the U.S. population (374)

hospice: a place (or services brought into someone's home) for the purpose of giving comfort and dignity to a dying person (393)

life expectancy: the number of years that an average person at any age, including newborns, can expect to live (374)

life span: the maximum length of life of a species; for human, the longest that a human has lived (376)

KEY PEOPLE
Review the major theoretical contributions or findings of these people.

Robert Butler: Butler coined the term "ageism" to refer to prejudice, discrimination, and hostility directed against people because of their age. (377)

Elaine Cumming and William Henry: These two developed disengagement theory to explain how society prevents disruption when the elderly vacate their positions of responsibility. (381)

Charles Hart: This anthropology graduate student carried out research on the Tiwi, a gerontocracy. (371-372)

Elisabeth Kübler-Ross: This psychologist found that coming face-to-face with one's own death sets in motion a five-stage process. (392)

Margaret Kuhn: Founded the Gray Panthers in 1970. This organization encourages all people to work for the welfare of the young and old. (387)

Meredith Minkler and Ann Robertson: Conflict sociologists who believe that the costs for services for the elderly do not have to come at the expense of children. The government can support both of these groups to relieve poverty. (387)

Karl Pillemer and Jill Suitor: These sociologists interviewed more than 200 caregivers of Alzheimer patients and found that the precipitating cause of elder abuse is stress from caring for a person who is dependent, demanding, and even violent. (391)

Alan Simpson: A Senator who called the elderly "greedy geezers" who demand government hand-outs while they "tee off near their second homes in Florida". (384)

Lars Tornstam: A Swedish sociologist who developed the theory of gerotranscendance, explaining that the elderly undergo a self-transformation and begin to feel more united with the universe. (378)

PRACTICE TEST

1. Which of the following most accurately describes what is meant by the term "social construction of aging?" (3372)
    a. Attitudes toward aging are determined by biological factors.
    b. Attitudes toward aging are independently set by each individual.
    c. Attitudes toward aging are set by the culture in which people live.
    d. Attitudes toward aging are set by historical precedent.

2. What is life expectancy? (374)
    a. The maximum length of life of a species.
    b. The number of years a person can expect to live.
    c. The type of life a person born into a certain social class is likely to live.
    d. The exact number of years that a particular individual can expect to live.

3. The term "graying of America" can be explained by the fact that: (374)
    a. today there are over 7 million more elderly Americans than there are teenagers.
    b. the average 65-year-old can expect to live 40 years longer than in 1900.
    c. the median age of Americans has remained relatively stable since 1850 but the percent of elderly has gone up dramatically.
    d. Americans rank first in the world regarding life expectancy.

4. Which of the following groups of countries represents the correct ordering for life expectancy, from longest to shortest? (375)
    a. Hong Kong, Japan, Greece, United States
    b. United States, Hong Kong, Italy, Germany
    c. United States, Germany, Great Britain, Switzerland
    d. Switzerland, United States, Italy, Japan

5. The racial/ethnic group with the higher percentage of those who are 85 years of age and over is: (375)
    a. African Americans.
    b. white Americans.
    c. Asian Americans.
    d. Latino Americans.

6. The relative value that a culture places on men's and women's ages is: (377)
    a. cultural aging.
    b. ageism.
    c. gender age.
    d. relative age.

7. Factors that may push people to apply the label of old to themselves include: (367)
    a. personal history or biography.
    b. cultural signals about when a person is old.
    c. biological factors.
    d. all of the above.

8. What is ageism? (377)
    a. The withdrawal of the elderly from society.
    b. Prejudice and discrimination against the elderly.
    c. The power gained by the elderly in a society.
    d. A government policy directed against the elderly.

9. Gerotranscendence is: (368)
    a. when the elderly undergo a self-transformation and are more at one with the universe.
    b. when the elderly move from being active to a more sedentary lifestyle.
    c. when the elderly accept death and transcend this life.
    d. when the elderly stop working and volunteer in their community.

10. What is an age cohort? (380)
    a. People within a society who are born at roughly the same time and who pass through the life course together.
    b. The total number of elderly in a society.
    c. Those in a society involved in ageism.
    d. Two groups of people born ten years apart.

11. The mass media: (380)
    a. communicate messages that reflect the currently devalued status of the elderly.
    b. tell us what people over 65 should be like.
    c. often treat the elderly in discourteous and unflattering terms.
    d. all of the above.

12. What is one of the main criticisms of disengagement theory? (381)
    a. It assumes that the elderly want to stay active.
    b. It doesn't take into account forced retirement.
    c. It doesn't take into account the individual's perspective.
    d. It contains implicit bias against older people.

13. Activity theory in research of the elderly: (381)
    a. does not sufficiently take into account what activities actually mean to a person.
    b. shows that formal activities are less important than informal ones.
    c. assumes that greater levels of activity lead to lower levels of life satisfaction.
    d. shows that solitary activities are significantly more important than group activities.

14. Conflict theorists believe that retirement benefits are the result of: (382)
    a. generous hearts in Congress.
    b. a struggle between competing interest groups.
    c. many years of hard work by elderly Americans.
    d. none of the above.

15. Which aspect of the original Social Security legislation was challenged by the elderly for many years following its passage in 1934? (382-383)
    a. mandatory retirement at age 65
    b. survivor payments to orphaned children
    c. lack of coverage for nonworking spouses
    d. payments tied to income

16. Which of the following statements is true about the elderly? (384)
    a. Participation in the electoral process will decline because older citizens are less likely to vote.
    b. The poverty rate for the elderly is less than the national average.
    c. Most of the elderly could not live without Social Security.
    d. None of the above.

17. Which of the following is *not* a problem associated with Social Security today? (384-385)
    a. The cash payments senior citizens receive are not tied to the money they invested in the fund.
    b. The money collected from workers for Social Security is used by the government to cover general operating expenses.
    c. The number of workers who pay into Social Security is shrinking while the number of retired who collect from Social Security is growing.
    d. Low payments have contributed to an increase in elderly poverty.

18. Which organization for the elderly is considered too powerful? (387)
    a. Gray Panthers
    b. AARP
    c. Black Panthers
    d. Elder Brigade

19. The correct relationship between isolation and gender is illustrated by the fact that: (388)
    a. feelings of loss and isolation in widowhood are more likely to be experienced by men than by women.
    b. elderly men experience a higher rate of widowhood than do elderly women.
    c. less than half of elderly women live with their husbands.
    d. less than half of elderly men live with their wives.

20. Research on the elderly in nursing homes shows that: (388-389)
    a. currently, more than 25 percent of the elderly are living in a nursing home.
    b. only about 10 percent of the elderly spend any time in a nursing home.
    c. elderly with similar conditions who remain in the community are less likely to get sick and are more likely to live longer than those in nursing homes.
    d. most elderly in nursing homes are under the age of 85.

21. When an elderly person is abused, their abuser is most likely: (391)
    a. their son.
    b. their daughter.
    c. a nurse or other professional caregiver.
    d. their spouse.

22. What is the term to describe a form of existence that is neither life nor death—the brain is dead but the body lives on. (392)
    a. institutional death
    b. technological life
    c. technological fix
    d. living death

23. In preindustrial societies, the sick: (392)
    a. were taken care of at home.
    b. were taken care of in hospitals.
    c. were taken care of in hospices.
    d. did not live long enough to have to be taken care of by anyone.

24. According to Kubler-Ross, the first stage one experiences after finding out that they are terminally ill is: (393)
    a. acceptance.
    b. anger.
    c. depression.
    d. denial.

25.   Creative aging is: (395)
    a.   promoting opportunities for the elderly to learn and use their creative abilities.
    b.   letting the elderly surround themselves with beautiful items in their home.
    c.   encouraging the elderly to get a creative pet to care for.
    d.   encouraging the elderly to volunteer in day care centers.

Answer Key

1.	C
2.	B
3.	A
4.	A
5.	B
6.	C
7.	D
8.	B
9.	A
10.	A
11.	D
12.	C
13.	A
14.	B
15.	A
16.	B
17.	D
18.	B
19.	C
20.	C
21.	D
22.	B
23.	A
24.	D
25.	A

Chapter 13:

The Elderly

SOCIOLOGY

A Down-to-Earth Approach 9/e

This multimedia product and its contents are protected under copyright law. The following are prohibited by law: any public performance or display, including transmission of any image over a network; preparation of any derivative work, including the extraction, in whole or in part, of any images; any rental, lease, or lending of the program.

Aging in Global Perspective

* **Social Construction of Aging**
  * Tiwi vs. Abkhasians
* **Industrialization and Graying of the Globe**
  * 2/3 of All People Who Have Ever Passed 50 are Alive Today

Copyright © Allyn & Bacon 2008   Chapter 13: The Elderly   2

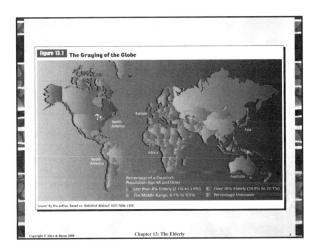

Figure 13.1 The Graying of the Globe

Percentage of a Country's Population Age 65 and Older
Less than 4% Elderly (2.1% to 3.9%)   Over 10% Elderly (10.9% to 22.1%)
The Middle Range, 4.1% to 9.9%   Percentage Unknown

Source: By the author. Based on *Statistical Abstract 2007*: Table 1300.

Copyright © Allyn & Bacon 2008   Chapter 13: The Elderly   3

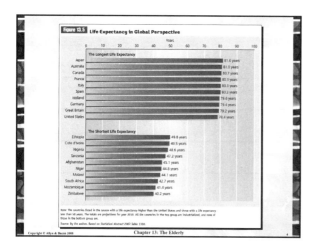

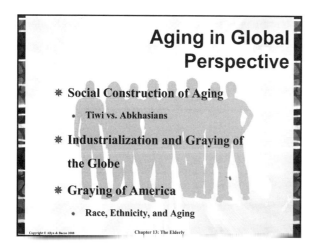

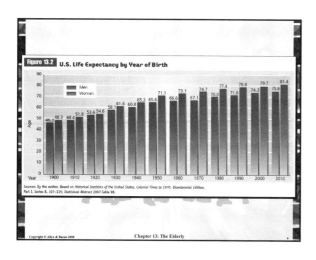

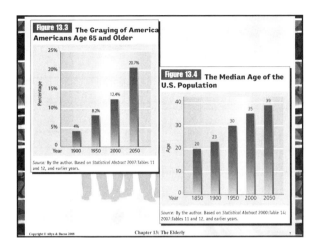

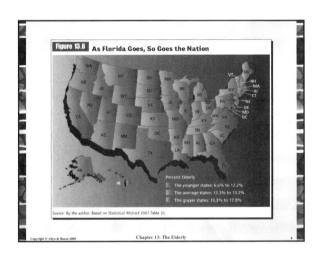

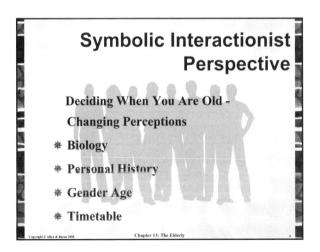

Changing Perceptions of the Elderly

* Agism

* Shifting Meanings

* Gerotranscendence Theory

* Influence of Mass Media

Copyright © Allyn & Bacon 2008 — Chapter 13: The Elderly — 10

Functionalist Perspective

* Disengagement Theory
  * Evaluation
* Activity Theory
  * Evaluation
* Continuity Theory
  * Evaluation

Copyright © Allyn & Bacon 2008 — Chapter 13: The Elderly — 11

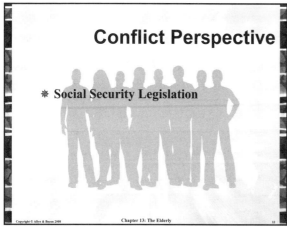

Conflict Perspective

* Social Security Legislation

Copyright © Allyn & Bacon 2008 — Chapter 13: The Elderly — 12

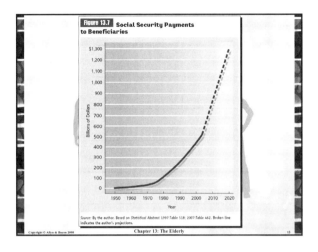

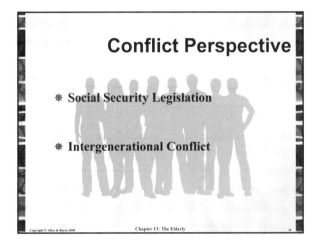

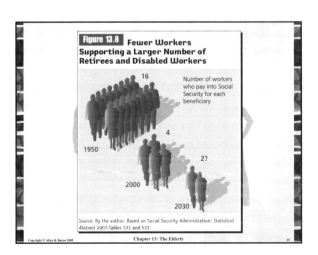

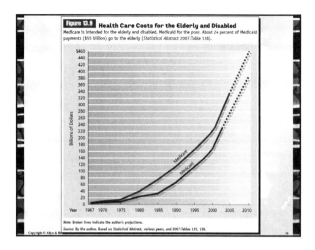

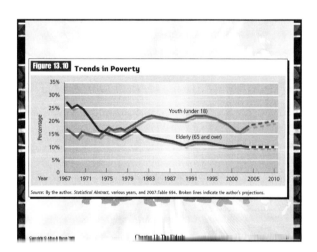

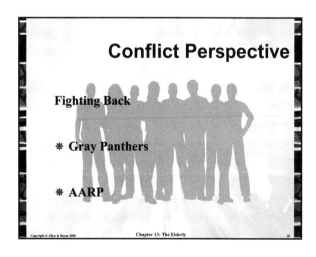

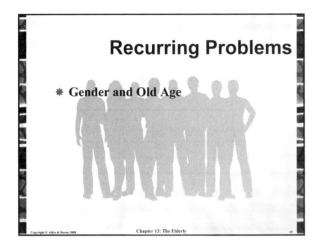

Recurring Problems

❋ Gender and Old Age

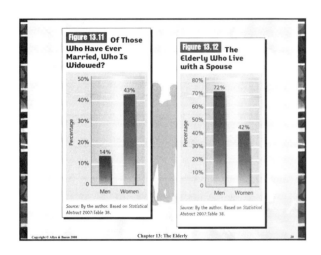

Figure 13.11 Of Those Who Have Ever Married, Who Is Widowed?

Source: By the author. Based on Statistical Abstract 2007:Table 38.

Figure 13.12 The Elderly Who Live with a Spouse

Source: By the author. Based on Statistical Abstract 2007:Table 38.

Problems of Dependency

❋ Gender and Old Age

❋ Nursing Homes

• Understaffing, Dehumanization, and Death

• Technology and Nursing Homes

• A New Model

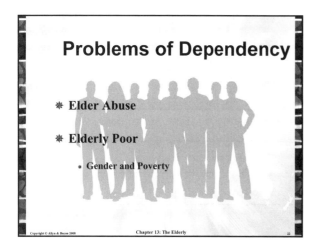

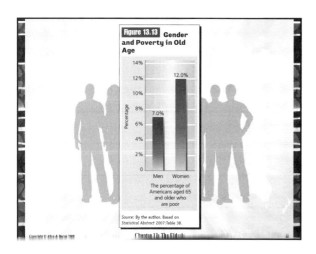

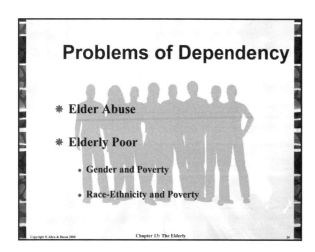

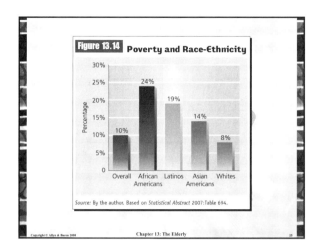

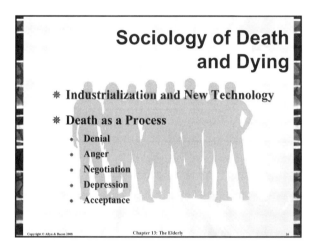

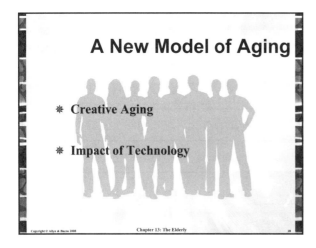

CHAPTER 14
THE ECONOMY

CHAPTER SUMMARY

- The earliest hunting and gathering societies were characterized by subsistence economies; economic systems became more complex as people discovered first how to domesticate and cultivate (horticultural and pastoral societies), then to farm (agricultural societies) and finally to manufacture (industrial societies). Currently we are in a postindustrial society and with the merger of biology and economics we may be on the verge of the emergence of biotech societies.

- In the least complex societies, people exchanged goods and services through barter. As societies and economies evolved, certain items were assigned uniform value and became the medium of exchange. Today we rely increasingly on electronic transfer of funds with credit, debit cards, and e-cash.

- The two major economic systems are capitalism, in which the means of production are privately owned, and socialism, in which the means of production are state owned. There are different forms of both capitalism (laissez-faire capitalism and welfare capitalism) and socialism (democratic socialism). Each is critical of the other; however, in recent years each system has adopted features of the other.

- Functionalists state that work is a fundamental source of social solidarity; preindustrial societies foster mechanical solidarity while industrial societies are characterized by organic solidarity. This process has continued and we are now developing a global division of labor.

- Conflict theorists focus on power, noting how global capitalism affects workers and owners. Corporations dominate modern capitalism; an inner circle makes certain that corporate capitalism is protected. The sociological significance of global capitalism is that the interests of the inner circle extend beyond national boundaries. Workers lose jobs, while the inner circle maintains its power and profits.

- Almost everyone today works in service jobs. A quiet revolution has occurred due to the dramatic increase in the number of married women who work for pay. An underground economy exists that includes economic activity that is not reported to the government. Inflation has whittled away worker's paychecks and today, workers in the U.S. work more hours per week than do workers of any industrialized nation.

- Work will continue to be restructured as a result of downsizing, new technologies, and the expansion of global capitalism. Increased economic inequality between the rich and poor nations is possible. Lower level workers may face challenges as a result of downsizing and restructuring.

269

LEARNING OBJECTIVES
After reading Chapter 14, you should be able to:

1. Trace the transformation of economic systems through the evolutionary history of human society and, for each society, discuss the different levels of and reasons for social inequality. (400-401)
2. Discuss how the industrialization of society into its modern form impacts an individual's life. (401)
3. Know what is meant by the "medium of exchange;" and describe its evolution along with economic systems. (403-405)
4. Describe the basic components of capitalism; differentiate between laissez-faire capitalism and welfare capitalism; and understand how and why welfare capitalism developed in the United States. (405-406)
5. Identify the basic components of socialism and discuss why some countries have developed democratic socialism in response to some of its shortcomings. (406-407)
6. Describe the ideologies, criticisms, and convergence of capitalism and socialism. (407-409)
7. Know the functionalist view of the globalization of capitalism, including the global division of labor and the ownership and management of corporations. (409-412)
8. Discuss the conflict perspective view of the inner circle of corporate capitalism, interlocking directorates, and global investing. (413-418)
9. Discuss how the composition of the American work force has changed significantly over the past one hundred years including the increase in the numbers of women in the work force. (418-421)
10. Know what is meant by the underground economy in the United States. (422)
11. Talk about recent changes in the U.S. economy related to patterns of work and leisure, including the effects of industrialization, trends in leisure, and teleworking. (423-424)
12. Discuss the implications for the future of global capitalism including global trade and the impact of new technologies. (424-425)

KEY TERMS
After studying the chapter, review the definition for each of the following terms.

barter: the direct exchange of one item for another (403)

capitalism: an economic system characterized by the private ownership of the means of production, market competition, and the pursuit of profit (405)

conspicuous consumption: Thorstein Veblen's term for a change from the Protestant ethic to an eagerness to show off wealth by the elaborate consumption of goods (401)

convergence theory: the view that as capitalist and socialist economic systems each adopt features of the other, a hybrid (or mixed) economic system will emerge (409)

corporate capitalism: the domination of the economic system by giant corporations (412)

corporation: the joint ownership of a business enterprise, whose liabilities and obligations are separate from those of the owners (412)

credit card: a device that allows its owner to purchase goods and to be billed later (404)

currency: paper money (403)

debit card: a device that allows its owner to charge purchases against his or her bank account (404)

democratic socialism: a hybrid economic system in which capitalism is mixed with state ownership (407)

deposit receipts: a receipt stating that a certain amount of goods is on deposit in a warehouse or bank; the receipt is used as a form of money (403)

e-cash: digital money that is stored on computers (404)

economy: a system of distribution of goods and services (400)

fiat money: currency issued by a government that is not backed by stored value (403)

gold standard: paper money backed by gold (403)

gross domestic product (GDP): the amount of goods and services produced by a nation (403)

inflation: an increase in prices (403)

interlocking directorates: the same people serving on the board of directors of several companies (416)

laissez-faire capitalism: unrestrained manufacture and trade (literally, "hands off" capitalism) (405)

leisure: time not taken up by work or necessary activities (423)

market forces: the law of supply and demand (406)

market restraints: laws and regulations that limit the capacity to manufacture and sell products (405)

mechanical solidarity: Durkheim's term for the unity (or a shared consciousness) that people feel as a result of performing the same or similar tasks (410)

medium of exchange: the means by which people value goods and services in order to make an exchange, for example, currency, gold, and silver (403)

money: any item (from sea shells to gold) that serves as a medium of exchange; today, currency is the most common form (403)

monopoly: the control of an entire industry by a single company (406)

multinational corporation: companies that operate across national boundaries; also called *transnational corporations* (413)

oligopoly: the control of an entire industry by several large companies (413)

organic solidarity: Durkheim's term for the interdependence that results from the division of labor; people depending on others to fulfill their jobs (411)

quiet revolution: the fundamental changes in society that occurred as a result of vast numbers of women entering the workforce (421)

socialism: an economic system characterized by the public ownership of the means of production, central planning, and the distribution of goods without a profit motive (406)

stockholders' revolt: the refusal of a corporation's stockholders to rubber-stamp decisions made by its managers (412)

stored value: the goods that are stored and held in reserve to back up or provide the value for a currency (403)

subsistence economy: a type of economy in which human groups live off the land with little or no surplus (400)

underground economy: exchanges of goods and services that are not reported to the government and thereby escape taxation (410)

welfare (or state) capitalism: an economic system in which individuals own the means of production but the state regulates many economic activities for the welfare of the population (405)

KEY PEOPLE

Review the major theoretical contributions or findings of these people.

Daniel Bell: Bell identified six characteristics of the postindustrial society. (401)

Emile Durkheim: Durkheim contributed the concepts of mechanical and organic solidarity to our understanding of social cohesion. (410-411)

Karl Marx: Marx was an outspoken critic of capitalism who wrote about the basis for profits under capitalism. (407)

Michael Useem: Using a conflict perspective, Useem studied the activities of the "inner circle" of corporate executives. (413)

Thorstein Veblen: Veblen created the term "conspicuous consumption" to refer to the eagerness to show off one's wealth through the elaborate consumption of material goods. (401)

PRACTICE TEST

1. What is a subsistence economy? (400)
    a. An economy which provides for all individuals with a reasonable surplus.
    b. An economy where individuals live off the land with little or no surplus.
    c. An economy where only services are traded.
    d. An economy where there is an established standard currency.

2. Which of the following is *not* a feature of industrial economies? (401)
    a. Machines are powered by fuels.
    b. A surplus unlike anything the world had seen is created.
    c. The steam engine was invented and became the basis for the economy.
    d. A service sector developed and employed the majority of workers.

3. What did Veblen label the lavishly wasteful spending of goods designed to enhance social prestige? (401)
    a. prestigious consumption
    b. wasteful consumption
    c. conspicuous prestige
    d. conspicuous consumption

4. Which of the following is *not* a defining characteristic of postindustrial economies? (401)
    a. a large surplus of goods
    b. extensive trade among nations
    c. machines powered by fuels
    d. a "global village"

5. The author of your text suggests that a new type of society may be emerging. What two forces have combined to produce this new society? (401)
    a. biology and politics
    b. politics and economics
    c. biology and economics
    d. biology and religion

6. Currency issued by a government that is not backed by stored value is known as: (403)
    a. money.
    b. medium of exchange.
    c. fiat money.
    d. standard.

7.   Digital money stored on computers is: (404)
      a.   gold standard.
      b.   fiat money.
      c.   electronic medium.
      d.   e-cash.

8.   The current economic system in the United States is: (405)
      a.   laissez-faire capitalism.
      b.   unrestrained capitalism.
      c.   welfare capitalism.
      d.   market capitalism.

9.   Which of the following is a characteristic of a socialist economy? (406)
      a.   central planning
      b.   pursuit of profits
      c.   monopolistic goals for private corporations
      d.   private ownership

10.   Karl Marx believed profit was: (407)
      a.   excess value withheld from workers.
      b.   necessary to ensure the reliable supply of goods.
      c.   not usually high enough to ensure a fair return for factory workers.
      d.   necessary to properly compensate workers.

11.   An example of convergence theory in the Unites States is exemplified by: (409)
      a.   subsidized housing.
      b.   the employer, not the government, determining the level of a minimum wage.
      c.   limiting Social Security benefits to the amount one has paid into the system over their lifetime.
      d.   the prohibition of ownership of property by the Federal Government.

12.   Which country has had to stop lots of riots as it enters a new system of capitalism?   (410)
      a.   China
      b.   Russia
      c.   Egypt
      d.   India

13.   Corporations involve the idea that: (412)
      a.   there is control of wealth by ownership.
      b.   ownership is separate from management.
      c.   ownership is synonymous with management.
      d.   shareholders control ownership and daily management.

14. A stockholders' revolt occurs when: (412)
    a. major stockholders dump their holdings in the open market.
    b. stockholders lead workers in a protest against company policies.
    c. stockholders refuse to rubber-stamp the recommendations made by management.
    d. people boycott the stocks of certain companies that are socially irresponsible.

15. The control of an entire industry by several large companies is called: (413)
    a. a welfare market.
    b. a monopoly.
    c. an oligopoly.
    d. market restraint.

16. Which of the following is the world's largest corporation? (413)
    a. General Electric
    b. Citigroup
    c. Bank of America
    d. Sears

17. Which of the following statements about Michael Useem's inner circle is *incorrect*? (413)
    a. Members of the inner circle are united by a mutual interest in preserving capitalism.
    b. Relationships among members of the inner circle are always cooperative rather than competitive.
    c. Within their own country, they have close ties with political leaders who stand firmly for the private ownership of property.
    d. Globally, they promote the ideology of capitalism.

18. Which perspective believes that the wealthy expand their power through serving on the board of directors of several companies? (416)
    a. functional-symbolism
    b. symbolic interaction
    c. conflict
    d. functionalist

19. In the 1800's, a typical American farmer produced enough food to feed five people. Today he or she now feeds about how many people? (418)
    a. 80
    b. 60
    c. 40
    d. 20

20. The gender pattern of the percentage of women in the American work force shows that: (419)
   a. the current percentage is actually equal to that of the mid-nineteenth century.
   b. Canada has a higher percentage of women in the workforce than the U.S.
   c. Sweden has a higher percentage of women in the work force than the U.S.
   d. almost one of two U.S. workers is a woman.

21. What term is used to describe the fundamental changes in society that follow the movement of vast numbers of women from the home to the work force? (421)
   a. the feminization of work
   b. the "mommy movement"
   c. the quiet revolution
   d. the backlash

22. The underground economy is characterized by economic activities that are: (422)
   a. always illegal.
   b. always legal.
   c. always reported to the government, but are not governed by official tax rules.
   d. are both legal and illegal economic activities.

23. Which of the following statements about wages is *correct*? (422-423)
   a. The buying power of today's wages is greater than any time in the last 30 years.
   b. In current dollars, workers today are paid less than they were 30 years ago.
   c. The buying power of today's wages is actually less than it was 30 years ago.
   d. Both the buying power and current value of wages are greater today than they were 30 years ago.

24. When compared with workers in Western Europe, U.S. workers have _____ leisure time. (423)
   a. more
   b. less
   c. the same
   d. two hours more of

25. Which of the statements about telework is *incorrect?* (424)
   a. Corporations have been able to save office space.
   b. Managers feel a loss of control over their workers.
   c. Teleworkers love working at home so they don't have to interact with their coworkers.
   d. Some workers go on a 24/7 work binge.

Answer Key

1. B
2. D
3. D
4. C
5. C
6. C
7. D
8. C
9. A
10. A
11. A
12. A
13. B
14. C
15. C
16. B
17. B
18. C
19. A
20. D
21. C
22. D
23. C
24. B
25. C

The Transformation of Economic Systems

❋ **Preindustrial Societies: Birth of Inequality**
  ❋ Hunting and Gathering Societies
  ❋ Pastoral and Horticultural Societies
  ❋ Agricultural Societies

❋ **Increasing Social and Economic Inequalities**

Copyright © Allyn & Bacon 2008   Chapter 14: The Economy

The Transformation of Economic Systems

❋ **Industrial Societies: Birth of the Machine**

  ❋ Brought Previously Unseen Surpluses

  ❋ More Efficient Machines Led to Conspicuous Consumption

Copyright © Allyn & Bacon 2008   Chapter 14: The Economy

The Transformation of Economic Systems

Postindustrial Societies: Birth of Information Age

* Service Sector
* Vast Surplus of Goods
* Extensive Trade Among Nations
* Wider Variety and Quantity of Goods
* Information Explosion
* Global Village

Copyright © Allyn & Bacon 2008   Chapter 14: The Economy   4

The Transformation of Economic Systems

Bioeconomic Societies: Merger of Biology and Economics

* We May Be On the Verge of New Type of Society
* Likely to Lead to Even Greater Inequalities
* Implications for Your Life

The Transformation of the Medium of Exchange

* Earliest Mediums of Exchange
* Medium of Exchange in Agricultural Societies
* Medium of Exchange in Industrial Societies
  * Gold Standard and Paper Money
  * Fiat Money
  * Gross Domestic Product

Copyright © Allyn & Bacon 2008   Chapter 14: The Economy   6

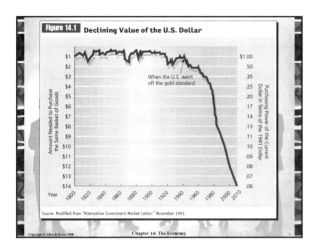

Figure 14.1 Declining Value of the U.S. Dollar

When the U.S. went off the gold standard

Source: Modified from "Alternative Investment Market Letter," November 1991.

Copyright © Allyn & Bacon 2008   Chapter 14: The Economy

The Transformation of the Medium of Exchange

* **Earliest Mediums of Exchange**
* **Medium of Exchange in Agricultural Societies**
* **Medium of Exchange in Industrial Societies**
* **Medium of Exchange in Postindustrial Societies**

Copyright © Allyn & Bacon 2008   Chapter 14: The Economy

World Economic Systems

* **Capitalism**
  * Private Ownership of Means of Production
  * Market Competition
  * Pursuit of Profit
* **Laissez-Faire Capitalism**
* **Welfare or State Capitalism**

Copyright © Allyn & Bacon 2008   Chapter 14: The Economy

World Economic Systems

* **Socialism**
    * Public Ownership of Means of Production
    * Central Planning
    * Distribution of Goods Without Profit Motive

* **Democratic Socialism**

Copyright © Allyn & Bacon 2008   Chapter 14: The Economy

_____
_____
_____
_____
_____
_____
_____
_____

Ideologies of Capitalism and Socialism

Capitalists

* Market Prices Should Determine
  Products and Prices

* Profit is Good

Copyright © Allyn & Bacon 2008   Chapter 14: The Economy

_____
_____
_____
_____
_____
_____
_____

Ideologies of Capitalism and Socialism

Socialists

* Profit is Immoral
* Item's Value Based on the
  Work that Went Into It
* Government Protects
  Workers from Exploitation

Copyright © Allyn & Bacon 2008   Chapter 14: The Economy

_____
_____
_____
_____
_____
_____
_____
_____

Criticisms of Capitalism and Socialism

Capitalism

* Leads to Social Inequality

* Tiny Top Layer Exploits Vast Bottom Layer

* Few Who Own the Means of Production Reap Huge Profits

Copyright © Allyn & Bacon 2008   Chapter 14: The Economy   13

Criticisms of Capitalism and Socialism

Socialism

* Does Not Respect Individual Rights

* Others Control People's Lives

* Give Everyone an Equal Chance to be Poor

Copyright © Allyn & Bacon 2008   Chapter 14: The Economy   14

Convergence of Capitalism and Socialism

* Convergence Theory

* Hybrid or Mixed Economy

* Changes in China and Russia

* Changes in America

Copyright © Allyn & Bacon 2008   Chapter 14: The Economy   15

Functionalist View of the Globalization of Capitalism

* New Global Division of Labor
  * Mechanical Solidarity
  * Organic Solidarity
* Now We Depend on Workers Around the Globe

Copyright © Allyn & Bacon 2008   Chapter 14: The Economy   16

_____
_____
_____
_____
_____
_____
_____

Ownership and Management of Corporations

* Corporate Capitalism
* Separation of Ownership and Management
* Stockholders' Revolt

Copyright © Allyn & Bacon 2008   Chapter 14: The Economy   17

_____
_____
_____
_____
_____
_____
_____

Functions on a Global Scale

* Three Major Trading Blocks
  * North and South America
  * Europe
  * Asia
* Greater Productivity and Standard of Living

Copyright © Allyn & Bacon 2008   Chapter 14: The Economy   18

_____
_____
_____
_____
_____
_____
_____

Dysfunctions on a Global Scale

* Loss of Jobs in Industrialized Nations
* Rust Belts in U.S.
* Challenges to Small Towns

Chapter 14: The Economy

Conflict View of Globalization of Capitalism

* Inner Circle of Corporate Capitalism
  * Multinational Corporations
  * Oligopoly
* Interlocking Directorates
* Global Investing

Chapter 14: The Economy

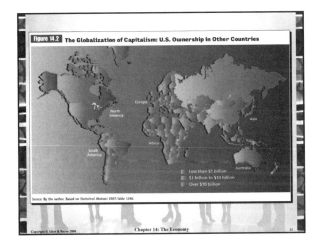

Figure 14.2 The Globalization of Capitalism: U.S. Ownership in Other Countries

Source: By the author. Based on Statistical Abstract 2007:Table 1788.

Chapter 14: The Economy

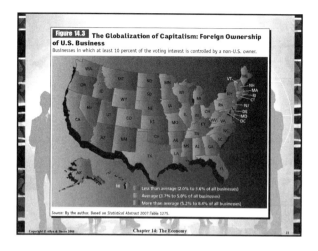

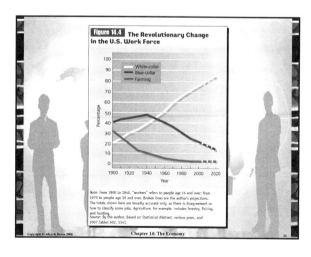

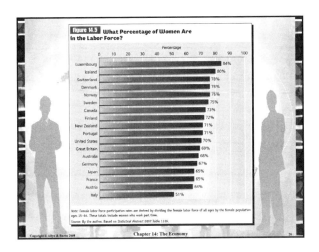

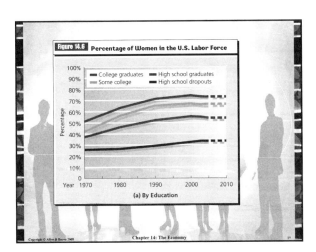

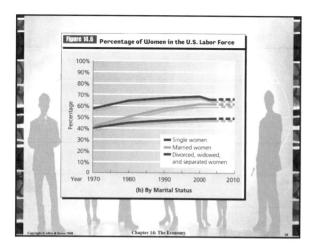

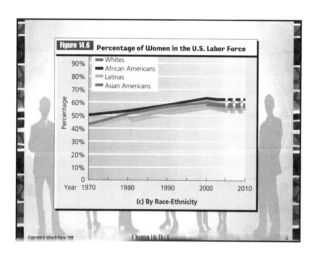

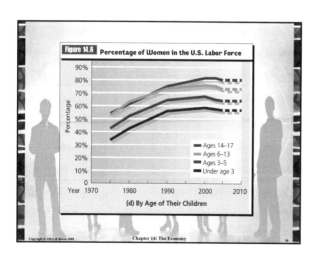

Work in U.S. Society

* Transition to Postindustrial Society
* Women and Work
* Underground Economy
* Stagnant and Shrinking Paychecks

Copyright © Allyn & Bacon 2008 — Chapter 14: The Economy — 31

_____
_____
_____
_____
_____
_____
_____

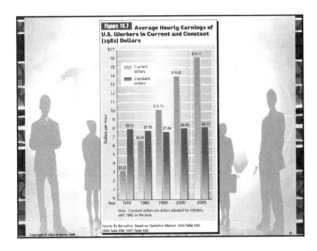

Figure 14.7 Average Hourly Earnings of U.S. Workers in Current and Constant (1982) Dollars

_____
_____
_____
_____
_____
_____
_____
_____

Work in U.S. Society

Patterns of Work and Leisure

* Effects of Industrialization

* Trends in Leisure

Copyright © Allyn & Bacon 2008 — Chapter 14: The Economy — 33

_____
_____
_____
_____
_____
_____
_____

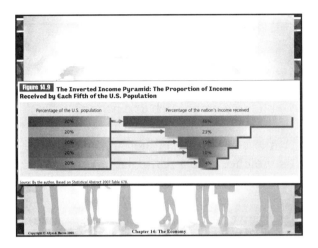

Figure 14.9 The Inverted Income Pyramid: The Proportion of Income Received by Each Fifth of the U.S. Population

CHAPTER 15
POLITICS

CHAPTER SUMMARY

- The essential nature of politics is power. Every group is political. This chapter focuses on macropolitics which refers to large-scale power over a large group such as a nation.

- Authority refers to the legitimate use of power, while coercion is its illegitimate use. The state is a political entity that claims a monopoly on violence over a particular territory. Max Weber identified three types of authority: traditional, rational-legal, and charismatic.

- The three forms of government are monarchies (power is based on hereditary rule); democracies (power is given by the citizens); and dictatorships and oligarchies (power is seized by an individual or a small group).

- In the United States, with its winner-takes-all electoral system, political parties must appeal to the center, and minority parties make little headway. In contrast, many democracies in Europe have a system of proportional representation that encourages the formation of coalitional government.

- Voting patterns in the United States consistently demonstrate that whites, the elderly, the rich, the employed, and the highly educated are most likely to vote. The more people are socially integrated and have a stake in the political system, the more likely they are to vote. Special interest groups, with their lobbyists and PACs, play a significant role in U.S. politics.

- Functionalists and conflict theorists have very different views on who rules the United States. According to the functionalists, no one group holds power; the outcome is that the competing interest groups balance one another (pluralism). According to conflict theorists, the United States is governed by a ruling class made up of members drawn from the elite (power elite).

- War is not an option for all human groups but despite the massive costs in lives and property, war continues to be an option to pursue political objectives. Even though terrorism has been common through history, it is now a fact of life for Americans. The effect of war and exposure to brutality and killing often causes dehumanization of the enemy.

- The global expansion of communication, transportation, and trade, the widespread adoption of capitalism and the retreat of socialism, as well as the trend toward larger political unions suggest that a new international world order may be in the process of emerging. It is possible that this group could help bring about global peace. However, the resurgence of nationalism poses a roadblock to this new world order.

LEARNING OBJECTIVES

After reading Chapter 15, you should be able to:

1. Understand the relationship between power, politics, and the state. (432-433)
2. Know the difference between authority and coercion, and explain why and how the state is able to claim a monopoly on the legitimate use of violence. (433)
3. Describe the three ideal types of authority identified by Max Weber. (433-435)
4. Discuss how and why the transfer of authority from one leader to another is crucial for social stability. (435)
5. Identify the characteristics of monarchies, democracies, dictatorships, and oligarchies. (436-439)
6. Discuss how the two major political parties in the United States are different from and similar to one another. (439-440)
7. Compare and contrast the democratic systems of the United States and Europe, and explain how these differences affect the role of minor political parties in each system. (440-441)
8. Identify the major voting patterns in the United States and discuss the reasons for voter alienation and voter apathy. (441-444)
9. Talk about the role that money plays in American politics and how lobbyists and special interest groups influence the political process. (444-446)
10. Compare and evaluate the competing views of functionalists and conflict theorists on the distribution of power in American politics. (446-447-436)
11. Discuss the causes, costs, and ramifications of war throughout human history. (447-448)
12. Discuss the essential conditions of war as well as the "fuels" identified by Timasheff. (448)
13. Discuss war and its dehumanizing affect and identify the four characteristics of dehumanization. (449-450)
14. Discuss terrorism and the how it has become a part of life, as well as how advanced weaponry and future alliances can sow the seeds for future conflict. (450-455)
15. Evaluate the possibilities for—and the potential ramifications of—a new world order characterized by global political and economic unity. (455-458)

KEY TERMS

After studying the chapter, review the definition for each of the following terms.

anarchy: a condition of lawlessness or political disorder caused by the absence or collapse of governmental authority (446)

authority: power that people consider legitimate, as rightly exercised over them; also called *legitimate power* (432)

centrist party: a political party that represents the center of political opinion (440)

charismatic authority: authority based on an individual's outstanding traits, which attract followers (434)

checks and balances: the separation of powers among the three branches of U.S. government—legislative, executive and judicial—so that each is able to nullify the actions of the other two, thus preventing the domination by any single branch (446)

citizenship: the concept that birth (and residence) in a country impart basic rights (437)

city-state: an independent city whose power radiates outward, bringing the adjacent area under its rule (436)

coalition government: a government in which a country's largest party aligns itself with one or more smaller parties (441)

coercion: power that people do not accept as rightly exercised over them; also called *illegitimate power* (432)

dehumanization: the act or process of reducing people to objects that do not deserve the treatment accorded humans (449)

democracy: a system of government in which authority derives from the people; the term comes from two Greek words that translate literally as "power to the people" (436)

dictatorship: a form of government in which power is seized by an individual (437)

direct democracy: a form of democracy in which the eligible voters meet together to discuss issues and make their decisions (437)

lobbyists: people who influence legislation on behalf of their clients (444)

macropolitics: the exercise of large-scale power, the government being the most common example (432)

micropolitics: the exercise of politics in everyday life, such as deciding who is going to do the housework or use the remote control (432)

monarchy: a form of government headed by a king or queen (436)

nationalism: a strong identity with a nation, accompanied by the desire for the nation to be dominant (456)

noncentrist party: a political party that represents less central (or popular) ideas (440)

oligarchy: a form of government in which power is held by a small group of individuals; the rule of the many by the few (438)

pluralism: the diffusion of power among many interest groups, preventing any single group from gaining control of the government (446)

political action committee (PAC): an organization formed by one or more special-interest groups to solicit and spend funds for the purpose of influencing legislation (445)

politics: the exercise of power and attempts to maintain or to change power relations (432)

power: the ability to carry out your will, even over the resistance of others (432)

power elite: C. Wright Mills's term for the top people in U.S. corporations, military, and politics who make the nation's major decisions (446)

proportional representation: an electoral system in which seats in a legislature are divided according to the proportion of votes each political party receives (440)

rational-legal authority: authority based on law or written rules and regulations; also called *bureaucratic authority* (434)

representative democracy: a form of democracy in which voters elect representatives to meet together to discuss issues and make decisions on their behalf (437)

revolution: armed resistance designed to overthrow and replace a government (433)

routinization of charisma: the transfer of authority from a charismatic figure to either a traditional or a rational-legal form of authority (436)

ruling class: another term for the power elite (447)

special-interest group: a group of people who have a particular issue in common and who can be mobilized for political action (444)

state: a political entity that claims a monopoly on the use of violence in some particular territory; commonly known as a country (433)

terrorism: the use of violence or the threat of violence to produce fear in order to attain political objectives (450)

totalitarianism: a form of government that exerts almost total control over the people (438)

traditional authority: authority based on custom (433)

universal citizenship: the idea that everyone has the same basic rights by virtue of being born in a country (or by immigrating and becoming a naturalized citizen) (437)

voter apathy: indifference and inaction on the part of individuals or groups with respect to the political process (441)

war: armed conflict between nations or politically distinct groups (447)

KEY PEOPLE

Review the major theoretical contributions or findings of these people.

Peter Berger: Berger argued that violence is the ultimate foundation of any political order. (432-433)

William Domhoff: Domhoff uses the term ruling class to refer to the power elite. He focused on the top one percent of Americans who belong to the super rich. (446)

Martha Huggins: She interviewed Brazilian police who use torture and sometimes blame the victim as a technique of neutralization. (450)

C. Wright Mills: Mills suggested that power resides in the hands of an elite group made up of the top leaders of the largest corporations, the most powerful generals of the armed forces, and certain elite politicians. (446)

Alejandro Portes and Ruben Rumbaut: These sociologists studied the process of assimilation of immigrants into American society, observing that the first step in the process is the group's political organization to protect their ethnic interests. (442)

Tamotsu Shibutani: Shibutani noted that the process of dehumanization is helped along by the tendency for prolonged conflicts to be transformed into a struggle between good and evil. (450)

Pitirim Sorokin: Sorokin studied wars from 500 B.C. to A.D. 1925 and found that war was a fairly common experience. There had been 967 wars during this time span, for an average of a war every two or three years. (448)

Nicholas S. Timasheff: Timasheff identified three essential conditions of societies going to war. He also identified seven "fuels" that may heat the antagonistic situation to a point of thinking about war to actually waging it. (448)

Max Weber: Weber noted that we perceive power as either legitimate or illegitimate. He also identified three different types of authority: traditional, rational-legal, and charismatic. (432-435)

PRACTICE TEST

1. Power that people accept as rightly exercised over them is referred to as: (432)
    a.   coercion.
    b.   authority.
    c.   revolution.
    d.   the state.

2. According to Max Weber, the government holds a monopoly on: (433)
    a.   the ability to tax its citizens.
    b.   the right to govern.
    c.   the ability to legitimately use force or violence within its territory.
    d.   the ability to make rules for society.

3. The President of the United States rules by: (434)
    a.   charismatic authority.
    b.   political authority.
    c.   rational-legal authority.
    d.   traditional authority.

4. Joan of Arc is an example of which type of authority? (434)
    a.   coercive
    b.   traditional
    c.   charismatic
    d.   rational-legal

5. John F. Kennedy is one of those few leaders who combined which two types of authority? (435)
    a.   coercion, legal-rational
    b.   legal-rational, charismatic
    c.   charismatic, traditional
    d.   illegitimate, legal-rational

6. Representative democracy: (437)
    a.   is a form of democracy in which elected officials represent citizens' interests.
    b.   is perhaps the greatest gift the United States has given the world.
    c.   was considered revolutionary when it was first conceived.
    d.   all of the above.

7. The idea that everyone has the same rights by virtue of being born in a country is: (437)
    a.   direct democracy.
    b.   universal citizenship.
    c.   state citizenship.
    d.   an ideal that has rarely been realized.

8.   Which type of government exerts almost total control over people? (438)
      a.   totalitarianism
      b.   a monarchy
      c.   an oligarchy
      d.   socialism

9.   Since 1900, political parties in the United States are such that: (439-440)
      a.   third parties can win Presidential elections.
      b.   the third party, called the Reform Party, eventually became the Republican
      Party.
      c.   Democrats and Republicans are in direct opposition regarding free public
            education, a strong military, and capitalism.
      d.   Democrats and Republicans represent different slices of the center.

10.   The United States has: (440)
      a.   centrist parties.
      b.   noncentrist parties.
      c.   proportional representation.
      d.   none of the above.

11.   Which electoral system can be found in most European countries? (440)
      a.   a winner-take-all system
      b.   a proportional representation system
      c.   direct democracy
      d.   representative democracy

12.   What do studies of voting patterns in the United States show? (441-443)
      a.   Voting patterns are too inconsistent to draw meaningful conclusions.
      b.   Voting varies by age, race/ethnicity, education, employment, income, and
      gender.
      c.   Younger people are more likely to vote than older individuals.
      d.   All of the above.

13.   In the 2004 Presidential election, what percent of Americans voted? (443)
      a.   14
      b.   26
      c.   58
      d.   70

14.   The political gender gap in American Presidential elections refers to: (443)
      a.   African American females tending to vote for a Republican.
      b.   white males being more likely to vote Republican.
      c.   a majority of both African American males and white males being more likely to
            vote Republican.
      d.   both white men and women voting for a Republican over a Democrat.

15. What does an average candidate for the Senate spend on a campaign? (445)
   a. $1 million
   b. $2.3 million
   c. $3.6 million
   d. $5 million

16. Functionalists see that _____ prevents groups from having total government control. (446)
   a. the existence of a powerful elite
   b. the presence of checks and balances
   c. the presence of many PACs to which politicians owe allegiance
   d. all of the above

17. Which perspective suggests that the power elite determines the economic and political conditions under which the country operates? (447)
   a. functionalists
   b. conflict theorists
   c. symbolic interactionists
   d. political sociologists

18. According to C. Wright Mills, which group of the "power elite" is the most powerful? (447)
   a. political leaders
   b. corporate leaders
   c. military leaders
   d. lobbyists

19. War is: (448)
   a. armed conflict between nations or politically distinct groups.
   b. universal.
   c. chosen for dealing with disagreements by all societies at one time or another.
   d. all of the above.

20. Which of the following is *not* one of the essential conditions of war identified by Nicholas Timasheff? (448)
   a. The existence of a strong, well-armed military force.
   b. A cultural tradition of war.
   c. An antagonistic situation in which two or more states confront incompatible objectives.
   d. The presence of a "fuel" that heats the antagonistic situation to a boiling point.

21.   According to Martha Huggins which technique of neutralization did Brazilian   police use? (450)
   a. emotional distance
   b. emphasis on following orders
   c. blame the victim
   d. inability to resist pressures

22.   Which of the Most Industrialized Nations does the most business selling arms to other nations, and thereby sowing the seeds of possible future wars? (452)
   a. Sweden
   b. Great Britain
   c. France
   d. the United States

23.   What is the estimated number of children who are used as child soldiers   worldwide? (455)
   a. 125,000
   b. 250,000
   c. 300,000
   d. 430,000

24.   The European Union, known as the EU: (456)
   a. has adopted a common cross-national currency, but each nation has maintained its own internal currency.
   b. applies only to political coalitions without reference to the use of the military.
   c. has avoided even the semblance of drafting a single constitution.
   d. has adopted a cross-national currency.

25.   Which organization is striving to be the legislative body of the world? (456)
   a. CAFTA
   b. European United
   c. United Nations
   d. NAFTA

Answer Key

1. B
2. C
3. C
4. C
5. B
6. D (all of the above)
7. B
8. A
9. D
10. A
11. B
12. B
13. C
14. B
15. D
16. B
17. A
18. B
19. A
20. A
21. C
22. D
23. C
24. D
25. C

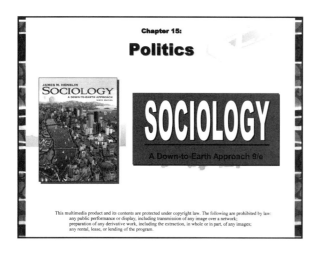

Chapter 15:
Politics

SOCIOLOGY
A Down-to-Earth Approach 9/e

This multimedia product and its contents are protected under copyright law. The following are prohibited by law:
any public performance or display, including transmission of any image over a network;
preparation of any derivative work, including the extraction, in whole or in part, of any images;
any rental, lease, or lending of the program.

What is Politics?

"Power relations wherever they exist."

Micro and Macro Politics

❋ **Micropolitics**

　　✳ **Exercise of Power in Everyday Life**

❋ **Macropolitics**

　　✳ **Exercise of Power Over a Large Group**

Power, Authority, and Violence

❋ **Authority is Legitimate Power**
  • Illegitimate Power is Coercion

❋ **Authority and Legitimate Violence**
  • Governments Have Exclusive Rights to Violence

❋ **The Collapse of Authority**
  • Revolution

Copyright © Allyn & Bacon 2008   Chapter 15: Politics

Power, Authority, and Violence

❋ **Traditional Authority**
  • Authority Based on Tradition

❋ **Rational-Legal Authority**
  • Authority Based on Written Rules

❋ **Charismatic Authority**
  • Authority Freely and Graciously Given
  • Threat Posed by Charismatic Leaders

Copyright © Allyn & Bacon 2008   Chapter 15: Politics

Power, Authority, and Violence

❋ **Authority as an Ideal Type**
  • Traditional, Rational-Legal, Charismatic
  • Not Ideal or Desirable Necessarily

❋ **Transfer of Authority**
  • Orderly from One Leader to Another

Copyright © Allyn & Bacon 2008   Chapter 15: Politics

Types of Governments

* Monarchies
* Democracies
  * Direct
  * Representative
  * Universal Citizenship
* Dictatorships and Oligarchies
  * Totalitarianism

Copyright © Allyn & Bacon 2008   Chapter 15: Politics

U.S. Political System

Political Parties and Elections

* Democrats, Republicans, and Third Parties
* Primaries and Elections
* Centrism and Extremes

Copyright © Allyn & Bacon 2008   Chapter 15: Politics

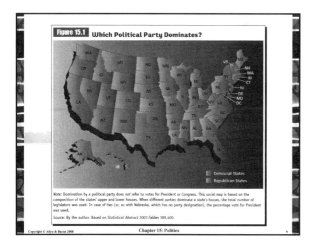

Figure 15.1 Which Political Party Dominates?

Note: Domination by a political party does not refer to votes for President or Congress. This social map is based on the composition of the states' upper and lower houses. When different parties dominate a state's houses, the total number of legislators was used. In case of ties (or, as with Nebraska, which has no party designation), the percentage vote for President was used.

Source: By the author. Based on Statistical Abstract 2007:Tables 389,400.

Copyright © Allyn & Bacon 2008   Chapter 15: Politics

Democratic Systems in Europe

✳ **Elections are Not Winner-Take-All**

✳ **Based on System of Proportional Representation**

✳ **Encourages Non-Centrist Parties**

✳ **Coalition Governments**

Copyright © Allyn & Bacon 2008   Chapter 15: Politics   10

Voting Patterns

✳ **Non-Hispanic Whites Most Likely to Vote**

✳ **African-Americans Next Most Likely**

✳ **Latinos Least Likely to Vote**

Copyright © Allyn & Bacon 2008   Chapter 15: Politics   11

Voting Patterns

✳ **Social Integration**

✳ **Alienation and Apathy**

✳ **Gender and Racial-Ethnic Gap in Voting**

Copyright © Allyn & Bacon 2008   Chapter 15: Politics   12

Table 15.2 How the Two-Party Presidential Vote Is Split

	1988	1992	1996	2000	2004
Women					
Democrat	50%	61%	65%	56%	53%
Republican	50%	39%	35%	44%	47%
Men					
Democrat	44%	55%	51%	47%	46%
Republican	56%	45%	49%	53%	54%
African Americans					
Democrat	92%	94%	99%	92%	90%
Republican	8%	6%	1%	8%	10%
Whites					
Democrat	41%	53%	54%	46%	42%
Republican	59%	47%	46%	54%	58%
Latinos					
Democrat	NA	NA	NA	61%	58%
Republican	NA	NA	NA	39%	42%
Asian Americans					
Democrat	NA	NA	NA	62%	77%
Republican	NA	NA	NA	38%	23%

Sources: Statistical Abstract 1999:Table 464; 2002:Table 372; 2007:Table 387.

Copyright © Allyn & Bacon 2008   Chapter 15: Politics   13

Lobbyists and Special Interests

❋ **Special Interest Groups are People Who Think Alike on a Particular Issue and Mobilize for Political Action**

❋ **Lobbyists are People Paid to Influence Legislation**

Copyright © Allyn & Bacon 2008   Chapter 15: Politics   14

PACs in U.S. Elections

❋ **Elections are Expensive**

　✳ **Senate Campaign about $5,000,000**

　✳ **House Campaign about $1,000,000**

❋ **PACs Contribute and are Owed**

❋ **Criticisms of Lobbyists and PACs**

Copyright © Allyn & Bacon 2008   Chapter 15: Politics   15

Who Rules the U.S.?

Functionalist Perspective: Pluralism

❋ Diffusion of Power Among Many

❋ Checks and Balances

Copyright © Allyn & Bacon 2008   Chapter 15: Politics   16

Who Rules the U.S.?

Conflict Perspective: The Power Elite

❋ Top Business, Political, and
   Military Leaders

❋ Ruling Class

❋ Not a Secret Group, Just Similar
   Backgrounds and Orientations

Copyright © Allyn & Bacon 2008   Chapter 15: Politics   17

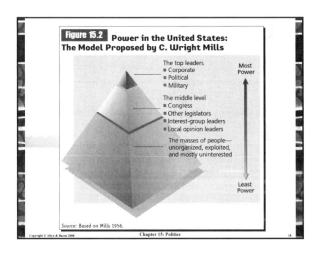

Figure 15.2 Power in the United States: The Model Proposed by C. Wright Mills

The top leaders
■ Corporate
■ Political
■ Military

Most Power

The middle level
■ Congress
■ Other legislators
■ Interest-group leaders
■ Local opinion leaders

The masses of people—unorganized, exploited, and mostly uninterested

Least Power

Source: Based on Mills 1956.

Copyright © Allyn & Bacon 2008   Chapter 15: Politics   18

War and Terrorism

❋ **Is War Universal?**

* Human Aggression and Killing, Yes

* War, No

❋ **How Common is War?**

* Humans Long for Peace but Glorify War

* War is Very Common and Frequent

Copyright © Allyn & Bacon 2008   Chapter 15: Politics   19

War and Terrorism

❋ **Why do Nations go to War?**

* Revenge
* Power
* Prestige
* Unity
* Positions
* Ethnicity
* Beliefs

War and Terrorism

❋ **Cost of War**

❋ **Toll in Lives**

❋ **Toll in Dollars**

Copyright © Allyn & Bacon 2008   Chapter 15: Politics   21

Dehumanization

* Increased Emotional Distance

* Emphasis on Following Orders

* Inability to Resist Pressures

* Diminished Sense of Responsibility

Dehumanization

* Blaming the Victim

* Struggle Between Good and Evil

* Success and Failure of

  Dehumanization

War and Terrorism

* Terrorism

  * "The use of violence to create fear in an effort to bring about political objectives."

* Suicide Terrorism

Sowing the Seeds

＊ **Selling War Technology**

＊ **Making Alignments**

＊ **Protecting Interests**

＊ **Child Soldiers**

Copyright © Allyn & Bacon 2008   Chapter 15: Politics   25

New World Order?

＊ **Major Trends**

＊ **Obstacles to Unity**

＊ **Domination by the Elite**

Chapter 15:

Politics

SOCIOLOGY

A Down-to-Earth Approach 9/e

CHAPTER 16
THE FAMILY

CHAPTER SUMMARY

- Family can be broadly defined as two or more people who consider themselves related by blood, marriage, or adoption. Marriage and family patterns vary remarkably across cultures, but four universal themes in marriage are mate selection, descent, inheritance, and authority.

- According to the functionalist perspective, the family is universal because it serves six essential functions: economic production, socialization of children, care of the sick and aged, recreation, sexual control, and reproduction. Conversely, isolation and emotional overload are the dysfunctions that result from the changes in the nuclear family. The conflict theorists focus on how marriage and the family help perpetuate inequalities. Symbolic interactionists focus on the contrasting experiences and perspectives of men and women that are played out in marriage.

- The family life cycle consists of various stages beginning with the love and courtship stage. This is followed by marriage, childbirth, child rearing, and the family in later life. Within the United States, marriage follows predictable patterns of age, social class, race and religion, while childbirth and childbearing vary by social class.

- Family diversity is represented by various racial and ethnic differences and the variety of family structures. One-parent families, childless families, blended families, and gay families represent some of the different types of families today.

- Trends in American families include postponement of first marriage and childbirth, unmarried mothers, cohabitation, grandparents as parents, the "sandwich generation" and concern about elder care.

- Various studies have focused on problems in measuring divorce, children of divorce, ex-spouses, and remarriage. While time seems to heal most children's wounds over the divorce of their parents, research suggests that a minority carry the scars of divorce into adulthood. Men and women experience divorce differently: for men, this event often results in a weakening of their relationships with children; for women, it means a decline in their standard of living. Although most divorced people remarry, their rate of remarriage has slowed considerably.

- Violence and abuse—including child abuse, battering, marital rape, and incest—are the "dark side" of family life.

- Researchers have identified variables that help marriages and families last and be happy.

- The trends for the future include a continued increase in cohabitation, births to unmarried mothers, postponement of marriage, and parenting by grandparents. The continuing growth in the numbers of working wives will impact the marital balance of power.

LEARNING OBJECTIVES

After reading Chapter 16, you should be able to:

1. Explain why it is difficult to define the term "family" and discuss some of the different ways that family systems can be organized and classified. (462)

2. Identify the common cultural themes that run through marriage and the family. (463-464

3. Explain why the family is universal and list the basic societal needs that it fulfills. (464-465)

4. Contrast the functionalists, conflict, and symbolic interaction perspectives regarding marriage and family and provide examples that illustrate each of the perspectives. (464-468)

5. Identify the major elements of the family life cycle and discuss how each of these elements may be affected by age, education, social class, race and ethnicity, sex, and/or religion. (468-474)

6. Describe the distinctive characteristics of family life in African American, Latino, Asian American, and Native American families, and discuss the role that social class and culture play. (474-477)

7. Discuss the characteristics and challenges that one-parent, childless, blended, gay and lesbian families in the United States may face. (478-480)

8. Identify the general patterns and trends in the following areas: postponing marriage and childbirth, cohabitation, single motherhood, grandparents as parents, the sandwich generation, and elder care. (481-485)

9. Talk about the different measures of divorce rates, the effects of divorce on children, grandchildren of divorce, the absent father, and remarriage. (485-491)

10. Describe the "dark side" of family life as it relates to battering, child abuse, marital rape, and incest. (491-493)

11. Identify the characteristics that most contribute to happy marriages and happy families. (493-494)

12. Talk about future patterns and trends in marriage and family life in the United States. (494)

KEY TERMS
After studying the chapter, review the definition for each of the following terms.

bilineal (system of descent): a system of reckoning descent that counts both the mother's and the father's side (464)

blended family: a family whose members were once part of other families (480)

cohabitation: unmarried couples living together in a sexual relationship (481)

egalitarian: authority more or less equally divided between people or groups, in this instance between husband and wife (464)

endogamy: the practice of marrying within one's own group (463)

exogamy: the practice of marrying outside one's group (464)

extended family: a nuclear family plus other relatives, such as grandparents, uncles and aunts (462)

family: two or more people who consider themselves related by blood, marriage, or adoption (462)

family of orientation: the family in which a person grows up (462)

family of procreation: the family formed when a couple's first child is born (462)

homogamy: the tendency of people with similar characteristics to marry one another (470)

household: people who occupy the same housing unit (462)

incest: sexual relations between specified relatives, such as brothers and sisters or parents and children (493)

incest taboo: the rule that prohibits sex and marriage among designated relatives (464)

machismo: an emphasis on male strength and dominance (476)

marriage: a group's approved mating arrangements, usually marked by a ritual of some sort (463)

matriarchy: a society in which women as a group dominate men as a group (464)

matrilineal (system of descent): a system of reckoning descent that counts only the mother's side (464)

nuclear family: a family consisting of a husband, wife, and child(ren) (462)

patriarchy: a society or group in which men dominate women; authority is vested in males (464)

patrilineal (system of descent): a system of reckoning descent that counts only the father's side (464)

polyandry: a form of marriage in which women have more than one husband (462)

polygyny: a form of marriage in which men have more than one wife (462) y

romantic love: feelings of erotic attraction accompanied by an idealization of the other (468)

serial fatherhood: a pattern of parenting in which a father, after divorce, reduces contact with his own children, acts as a father to the children of the woman he marries or lives with, then ignores these children, too, after moving in with or marrying another woman (490)

system of descent: how kinship is traced over the generations (464)

KEY PEOPLE
Review the major theoretical contributions or findings of these people.

Paul Amato and Jacob Cheadle: These sociologists were the first to study the grandchildren of divorced parents. They found that the effects of divorce continue across generations. (489)

Philip Blumstein and Pepper Schwartz: These sociologists interviewed same sex couples and found that they face the same problems as heterosexual couples. (480)

Urie Bronfenbrenner: This sociologist studied the impact of divorce on children and found that children adjust better if there is a second adult who can be counted on for support. (489)

Andrew Cherlin: Cherlin notes that our society has not yet developed adequate norms for remarriage. (491)

Donald Dutton and Arthur Aron: These researchers compared the sexual arousal levels of men who were in dangerous situations with men in safe situations. They found that the former were more sexually aroused than the latter. (470)

David Finkelhor and Kersti Yllo: These sociologists interviewed 10 percent of a representative sample of women from Boston who reported that their husbands used physical force to compel them to have sex. (493)

Lori Girshick: She interviewed lesbians who had been sexually assaulted by their partners. (493)

Ann Goetting: She interviewed women who had been in abusive relationships to understand the factors that allowed them to leave. (492)

Mavis Hetherington: A psychologist who's research shows that 75-80 percent of children of divorce function as well as children who are reared by both parents. (488-489)

Arlie Hochschild: Hochschild conducted research on families in which both parents are employed full-time in order to find out how household tasks are divided up. She found that women do more of the housework than their husbands, resulting in women putting in a *second shift* at home after their workday has ended. (495)

William Jankowiak and Edward Fischer: These anthropologists surveyed data on 166 societies and found that the majority of them contained the ideal of romantic love. (468)

Melvin Kohn: Kohn found that the type of work that parents do has an impact on how they rear their children. (473)

Jeanette & Robert Lauer: These sociologists interviewed 351 couples who had been married fifteen years or longer in order to find out what makes a marriage successful. (493)

Elizabeth Marquardt: She wrote the book, *Between Two Worlds*, which chronicles the experiences of children of divorce. (488)

Diana Russell: Russell found that incest victims who experience the most difficulty are those who have been victimized the most often over longer periods of time and whose incest was "more intrusive." (493)

William Sayres: He believes that they term family is so difficult to define because cultures organize members of family differently. (462)

Nicholas Stinnett: Stinnett studied 660 families from all regions of the United States and parts of South America in order to find out what are characteristics of happy families. (494)

Murray Straus: This sociologist has studied domestic violence and found that, while husbands and wives are equally likely to attack one another, men inflict more damage on women than the reverse. (491)

Bob Suzuki: This sociologist studied Chinese and Japanese American families and identified several distinctive characteristics of this type of family. (477)

Judith Wallerstein: A psychologist who claims that divorce has detrimental, long term effects on children. (488)

PRACTICE TEST

1. Which of the following refers to the marriage of one man to several women? (462)
    a. polygyny
    b. monogamy
    c. polyandry
    d. bigamy

2. The family of orientation is: (462)
    a. the family formed when a couple's first child is born.
    b. the same thing as an extended family.
    c. the same as the family of procreation.
    d. a family in which a person grows up.

3. Endogamy is a part of which common cultural theme: (463)
    a. descent.
    b. mate selection.
    c. inheritance.
    d. authority.

4. In a matrilineal system: (464)
    a. descent is figured only on the mother's side.
    b. children are not considered related to their mother's relatives.
    c. descent is traced on both the mother's and the father's side.
    d. descent is figured only on the father's side.

5. What is the newest dating idea? (465)
    a. using a matchmaker.
    b. having parents select potential dates.
    c. dating on demand using your TV.
    d. using an online dating service.

6. According to recent data, which of the following statements is true? (467)
    a. Over time, husbands have decreased the amount of housework that they do.
    b. Both husbands and wives are spending more time in childcare.
    c. Over time, women have increased the amount of childcare that they do.
    d. Children are getting less attention from their parents than they used to.

7. About what percent of Americans marry someone from their own racial background? (470)
    a. 93%
    b. 84%
    c. 73%
    d. 65%

8. The best predictors for children receiving quality day care are: (472)
    a.   the age of the staff versus the age of the children under care.
    b.   the region of the country and the race of the staff.
    c.   the training of the staff regarding childhood development and the income of the parents.
    d.   the amount of early childhood development training by the staff and a small number of children assigned to each day care worker.

9. In the U.S., about what percent of 24-to-29-year-olds live with their parents? (474)
    a.   61%
    b.   42%
    c.   30%
    d.   9%

10. Which racial/ethnic group is most likely to have households headed by women? (463)
    a.   African-American
    b.   Asian-American
    c.   Hispanic-American
    d.   non-Hispanic White American

11. In what ways do Native American families differ from most U.S. families? (474-475)
    a.   There are more single parent families.
    b.   There is less nonmarital childbirth.
    c.   Elders play a more active role in their children's families.
    d.   They have higher rates of divorce and marital instability.

12. Since 1970, the number of children in the United States who live with both parents has: (478)
    a.   remained stable.
    b.   dropped.
    c.   increased.
    d.   has gone down and is now up again

13. Children from one-parent families are more likely to: (478)
    a.   drop out of school.
    b.   become delinquent.
    c.   be poor as adults.
    d.   all of the above.

14.   Which racial-ethnic group has the highest percentage of childless women? (478)
       a.   African Americans.
       b.   mixed family.
       c.   Asians
       d.   Latinas.

15.   What country became the first to legalize same-sex marriages? (480)
       a.   Nigeria
       b.   United States
       c.   Denmark
       d.   Canada

16.   Cohabitation: (481-482)
       a.   is the condition of living together as an unmarried couple.
       b.   has increased ten times in the past 30 years.
       c.   has occurred before about half of all couples marry.
       d.   all of the above.

17.   All Industrialized Nations show sharp increases in births to single women *except*: (484)
       a.   Sweden.
       b.   Denmark.
       c.   France.
       d.   Japan.

18.   Which of the following factors reduce someone's chance of divorce during the first 10 years of marriage? (487)
       a.   getting married over the age of 25
       b.   waiting to have a baby 7 months or longer after marriage
       c.   having parents who are not divorced
       d.   all of the above reduce risk of divorce

19.   What did the author of a recent book about the children and divorce discover? (488)
       a.   That the affect of divorce is less severe than other researchers have shown.
       b.   That most children really transition well within the first year of divorce.
       c.   That children feel that they are caught between two worlds.
       d.   That it is was a relief to them that their parents divorced.

20.   A sociological conclusion regarding spousal abuse is that: (491)
       a.   women and men are equally as likely to inflict injuries on their spouses.
       b.   about 40 percent of all injuries in spousal abuse are experienced by men.
       c.   violence against women is related to the sexist structure of society.
       d.   both males and females are equally socialized in American society in terms of resorting to violence to handle frustration and disagreements.

21.	All of the following explain why some women leave abusive spousal situations *except*: (492)
	a.	a woman's having a positive self-concept.
	b.	a woman's obtaining adequate finances.
	c.	a woman's having supportive family and friends.
	d.	a woman's fostering and keeping traditional values.

22.	According to Diana Russell, what percent of married women report that their husbands have raped them? (493)
	a.	5%
	b.	10%
	c.	14%
	d.	34%

23.	Of those marriages found to be "unhappy" but in which the couples were staying together, all of the following were reasons, according to Lauer, *except*: (493)
	a.	thinking of their spouse as their best friend.
	b.	religious reasons.
	c.	family tradition reasons.
	d.	for the sake of the children.

24.	According to research by Diana Russell, who is most likely to be the offender in incest? (493)
	a.	brothers
	b.	fathers/stepfathers
	c.	first cousins
	d.	uncles

25.	According to the author, what trend(s) are likely to continue into the next century? (494)
	a.	increase in cohabitation
	b.	increase in age at first marriage
	c.	more equality in the husband-wife relationship
	d.	all of the above

Answer Key

1. A
2. D
3. B
4. A
5. C
6. B
7. A
8. D
9. B
10. A
11. C
12. B
13. D
14. C
15. C
16. D
17. D
18. D
19. C
20. A
21. D
22. C
23. A
24. D
25. D

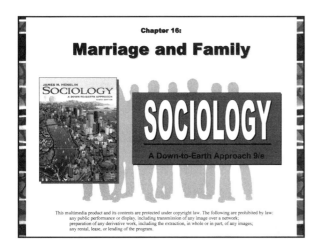

Chapter 16:
Marriage and Family

SOCIOLOGY
A Down-to-Earth Approach 9/e

This multimedia product and its contents are protected under copyright law. The following are prohibited by law: any public performance or display, including transmission of any image over a network; preparation of any derivative work, including the extraction, in whole or in part, of any images; any rental, lease, or lending of the program.

What is a Family?

✳ In U.S. - One Woman, Man, and Children

✳ Other Cultures Polygamy and Polyandry

✳ Approved Group into which a Child is Born?

Copyright © Allyn & Bacon 2008   Chapter 16: Marriage and Family

---

Family Defined

"A family consists of people who consider themselves related by blood, marriage, or adoption."

Copyright © Allyn & Bacon 2008   Chapter 16: Marriage and Family

Family Can Be...

✳ Nuclear

✳ Extended

✳ Family of Orientation

✳ Family of Procreation

Copyright © Allyn & Bacon 2008   Chapter 16: Marriage and Family   4

What is Marriage?

✳ Until Recently...Taken for Granted

✳ Acceptance of Same-Sex Marriages

✳ Must be Alive?

Copyright © Allyn & Bacon 2008   Chapter 16: Marriage and Family   5

What is Marriage?

"Marriage is a group's approved mating arrangement...usually marked by a ritual."

Copyright © Allyn & Bacon 2008   Chapter 16: Marriage and Family   6

Common Cultural Themes

Families Establish Patterns of…

✳ **Mate Selection**

✳ **Descent**

✳ **Inheritance**

✳ **Authority**

  ✳ **Patriarchy**

  ✳ **Matriarchy**

  ✳ **Egalitarian**

Copyright © Allyn & Bacon 2008   Chapter 16: Marriage and Family   7

Marriage and Family in Theoretical Perspective

Functionalist

✳ **Economic Production**

✳ **Socialization of Children**

✳ **Care of Sick and Aged**

Copyright © Allyn & Bacon 2008   Chapter 16: Marriage and Family   8

Marriage and Family in Theoretical Perspective

Functionalist

✳ **Recreation**

✳ **Sexual Control**

✳ **Reproduction**

Copyright © Allyn & Bacon 2008   Chapter 16: Marriage and Family   9

Marriage and Family in Theoretical Perspective
Functionalist

❋ **Functions of the Incest Taboo**

❋ **Isolation and Emotional Overload**

Copyright © Allyn & Bacon 2008   Chapter 16: Marriage and Family   10

Marriage and Family in Theoretical Perspective
Conflict

❋ **Struggles between Wives and Husbands**
❋ **Power Struggle over…**
  ✽ **Housework**
  ✽ **Child Care**
  ✽ **Money**
  ✽ **Attention**
  ✽ **Respect**
  ✽ **Sex**

Copyright © Allyn & Bacon 2008   Chapter 16: Marriage and Family   11

Marriage and Family in Theoretical Perspective
Symbolic Interaction

❋ **Gender, Housework, and Child Care**

❋ **Gender Division of Labor**

Copyright © Allyn & Bacon 2008   Chapter 16: Marriage and Family   12

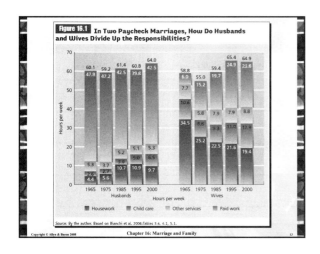

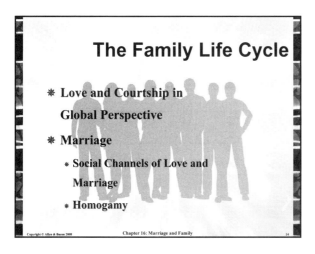

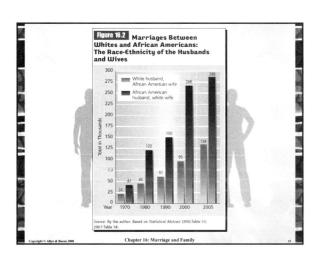

The Family Life Cycle

Childbirth

❋ Marital Satisfaction Decreases

❋ Additional Complications

Copyright © Allyn & Bacon 2008   Chapter 16: Marriage and Family

---

The Family Life Cycle

Child Rearing

❋ Married Couples and Single Mothers

❋ Day Care

❋ Nannies

❋ Social Class

Copyright © Allyn & Bacon 2008   Chapter 16: Marriage and Family

---

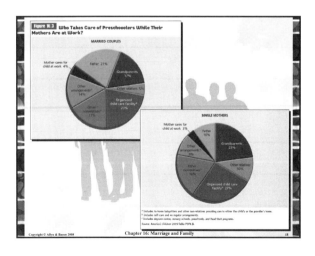

Copyright © Allyn & Bacon 2008   Chapter 16: Marriage and Family

The Family Life Cycle

Family Transitions

❋ **Adultolescents and the Not-**

So-Empty Nest

❋ **Widowhood**

Copyright © Allyn & Bacon 2008   Chapter 16: Marriage and Family   19

Diversity in U.S. Families

❋ **African-American Families**

❋ **Latino Families**

❋ **Asian Families**

❋ **Native American Families**

Copyright © Allyn & Bacon 2008   Chapter 16: Marriage and Family   20

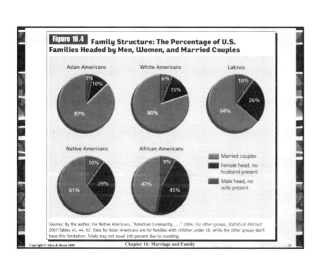

Figure 16.4 Family Structure: The Percentage of U.S. Families Headed by Men, Women, and Married Couples

Asian Americans — 3%, 10%, 87%
White Americans — 6%, 15%, 80%
Latinos — 10%, 26%, 64%
Native Americans — 10%, 29%, 61%
African Americans — 9%, 45%, 47%

Married couples
Female head, no husband present
Male head, no wife present

Sources: By the author. For Native Americans, "American Community . . ." 2004. For other groups, *Statistical Abstract* 2007:Tables 41, 44, 62. Data for Asian Americans are for families with children under 18, while the other groups don't have this limitation. Totals may not equal 100 percent due to rounding.

Copyright © Allyn & Bacon 2008   Chapter 16: Marriage and Family   21

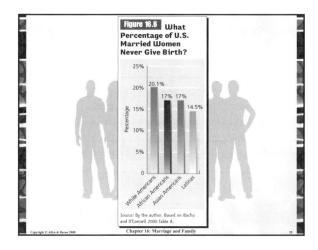

Figure 16.6 What Percentage of U.S. Married Women Never Give Birth?

Diversity in U.S. Families

✳ **One-Parent Families**

✳ **Families Without Children**

✳ **Blended Families**

✳ **Gay and Lesbian Families**

Trends in U.S. Families

✳ **Postponing Marriage and Childbirth**

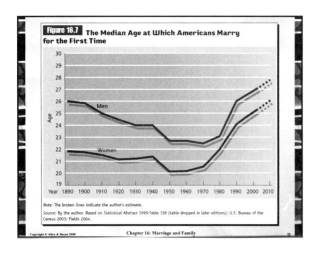

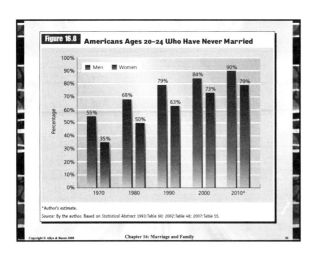

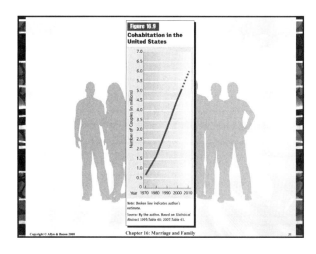

Trends in U.S. Families

❋ **Postponing Marriage and Childbirth**

❋ **Cohabitation**

❋ **Unmarried Mothers**

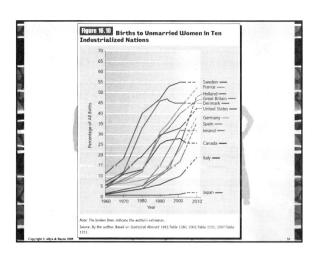

Trends in U.S. Families

* Postponing Marriage and Childbirth
* Cohabitation
* Unmarried Mothers
* Grandparents as Parents
* The Sandwich Generation & Elder Care

Copyright © Allyn & Bacon 2008   Chapter 16: Marriage and Family   34

Divorce and Remarriage

* Problems in Measuring Divorce

Copyright © Allyn & Bacon 2008   Chapter 16: Marriage and Family   35

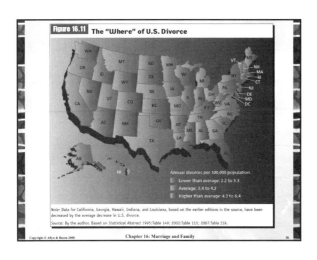

Figure 16.11 The "Where" of U.S. Divorce

Annual divorces per 100,000 population
Lower than average: 2.2 to 3.3
Average: 3.4 to 4.2
Higher than average: 4.3 to 6.4

Note: Data for California, Georgia, Hawaii, Indiana, and Louisiana, based on the earlier editions in the source, have been decreased by the average decrease in U.S. divorce.

Source: By the author. Based on Statistical Abstract 1995:Table 149; 2002:Table 111; 2007:Table 119.

Copyright © Allyn & Bacon 2008   Chapter 16: Marriage and Family   36

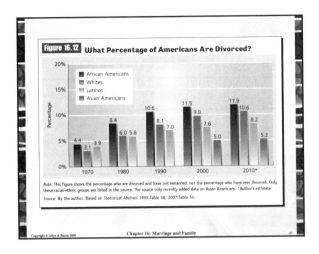

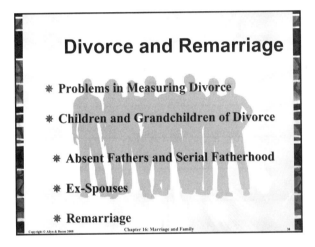

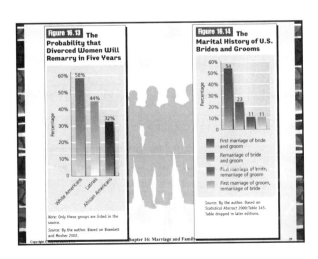

Two Sides of Family Life

The Dark Side

* Spouse Battering

* Child Abuse

* Marital or Intimacy Rape

* Incest

Copyright © Allyn & Bacon 2008   Chapter 16: Marriage and Family

---

Two Sides of Family Life

The Bright Side—Successful Marriages

* Spouse is Best Friend

* Like Spouse as Person

* Think Marriage is Long-Term Commitment

* Believe Marriage is Sacred

Two Sides of Family Life

The Bright Side—Successful Marriages

* Agree with Spouse Aims and Goals

* Believe Spouse Grown More Interesting

* Want Relationship to Succeed

* Laugh Together

Copyright © Allyn & Bacon 2008   Chapter 16: Marriage and Family

Happy Families

❋ Spend a Lot of Time Together

❋ Are Quick to Express Appreciation

❋ Committed to Promoting Mutual Welfare

❋ Talk and Listen a Lot

❋ Are Religious

❋ Deal with Crises Positively

Chapter 16: Marriage and Family

Symbolic Interactionism and Misuse of Statistics

❋ Divorce Statistics Explained

❋ People are Individuals

❋ We Create our Own World

Chapter 16: Marriage and Family

The Future of Marriage and Family

❋ No Danger of Becoming a Relic

❋ Cohabitation, Single Mothers, Age at Marriage, Grandparents as Parents will Increase

❋ Continued Distorted Images of Marriage and Family

Chapter 16: Marriage and Family

CHAPTER 17
EDUCATION

CHAPTER SUMMARY

- In earlier societies, education consisted of informal learning and was synonymous with acculturation. Today, education refers to a group's formal system of teaching knowledge, values, and skills.

- In general, formal education reflects a nation's economy. It is more extensive in the most industrialized nations, such as Japan, and very spotty in the least industrialized nations, such as Egypt.

- Functionalists emphasize the functions of education, including teaching knowledge and skills, transmitting cultural values, social integration, gatekeeping, and promoting personal and social change and mainstreaming. They note that education has replaced some traditional family functions and provides a host of other functions as well.

- Conflict theorists view education as a mechanism for maintaining social inequality and reproducing the social class system. Accordingly, they stress such matters as the way in which education reflects the social structure of society (the correspondence principle); unequal funding of schools; culturally biased IQ tests; the hidden curriculum; and the advantage of family background regardless of students' personal abilities.

- Symbolic interactionists examine classroom interaction. They study how teacher expectations cause a self-fulfilling prophecy, producing the very behavior that the teacher is expecting.

- Problems facing the current U.S. educational system include falling Scholastic Aptitude Test (SAT) scores, grade inflation, social promotion, functional illiteracy, and violence in schools.

- Suggestions for school reform include implementing and maintaining a secure and safe learning environment and having higher standards for students and teachers.

LEARNING OBJECTIVES

After reading Chapter 17, you should be able to:

1. Summarize the development of modern education and discuss the links between democracy, industrialization, and universal education. (500-502)
2. Compare the education systems of Japan, Russia, and Egypt, and examine how they represent the differences in education between Most Industrialized, Industrializing, and Least Industrialized Nations. (502-504)

3. From the functionalist perspective, identify and discuss the functions of education including: teaching knowledge and skills; cultural transmission of values; social integration; and gatekeeping. (505-507)

4. Discuss the family and other functions that have been replaced or fulfilled by the education system. (507-508)

5. From the conflict perspective, explain and discuss the different ways the education system reinforces basic social inequalities. This includes the hidden curriculum, use of IQ tests, funding of schools, the correspondence principle, and the effect of family background. (508-513)

6. From the symbolic interactionist perspective, cite the research into—and talk about the implications of—the effects of teachers' expectations on student performance. (513-515)

7. Identify the major problems that exist within the United States educational system and evaluate some of the potential solutions. (515-521)

KEY TERMS

After studying the chapter, review the definition for each of the following terms.

correspondence principle: the sociological principle that schools correspond to (or reflect) the social structure of society (511)

credential society: the use of diplomas and degrees to determine who is eligible for jobs, even though the diploma or degree may be irrelevant to the actual work (506)

cultural transmission: in reference to education, the ways in which schools transmit a society's culture, especially its core values (506)

education: a formal system of teaching knowledge, values, and skills (500)

functional illiterate: a high school graduate who has difficulty with basic reading and math (518)

gatekeeping: the process by which education opens and closes doors of opportunity; another term for the social placement function of education (507)

grade inflation: higher grades given for the same work; a general rise in student grades without a corresponding increase in learning or test scores (518)

hidden curriculum: the unwritten goals of schools, such as obedience to authority and conformity to cultural norms (508)

latent functions: unintended beneficial consequences of people's actions (505)

mainstreaming: helping people to become part of the mainstream of society (507)

mandatory education laws: laws that require all children to attend school until a specified age or until they complete a minimum grade in school (501)

manifest functions: intended beneficial consequences of people's actions (505)

self-fulfilling prophecy: Robert Merton's term for an originally false assertion that becomes true simply because it was predicted (514)

social placement: a function of education—funneling people into a society's various positions (507)

social promotion: passing students to the next grade even though they have not mastered basic materials (518)

tracking: the sorting of students into different educational programs on the basis of real or perceived abilities (507)

KEY PEOPLE
Review the major theoretical contributions or findings of these people.

Samuel Bowles and Herbert Gintis: Bowles and Gintis used the term *correspondence principle* to refer to the ways in which schools reflect the social structure of society. Bowles also compared college attendance among the brightest and weakest students. Of the intellectually weakest students, 26% from affluent homes went to college compared to 6% from poorer homes. (511-512)

Anthony Carnevale and Stephen Rose: They confirmed the research conducted by Bowles. They found that regardless of personal abilities—children from more well-to-do families are not only more likely to go to college, but to attend the more elite schools. (512)

James Coleman and Thomas Hoffer: A study of students in Catholic and public high schools by these two sociologists demonstrated that performance was based on setting higher standards for students rather than on individual ability. (521)

Randall Collins: Collins studied the credential society. (506)

Kingsley Davis and Wilbert Moore: They pioneered a view known as social placement. People are funneled into a societies various positions; rewards of high income and prestige are offered to motivate capable people to postpone gratification and to put up with years of rigorous education. (507)

Adrian Dove: A social worker in Watts who believes that the IQ test has bias so that children from certain social backgrounds will perform better than others. (511)

George Farkas: Farkas and a team of researchers investigated how teacher expectations affect student grades. They found that students signal teachers that they are good students by being eager, cooperative and working hard. (514-515)

Harry Gracey: Gracey conducted a participant observation study of kindergarten and concluded that the purpose of kindergarten is to socialize students into the student role. He referred to kindergarten as a boot camp. (510)

Horace Mann: An educator from Massachusetts who proposed that "common schools," supported through taxes, be established throughout his state. (501)

Robert Merton: He coined the term, self-fulfilling prophecy. This is a false assumption of something that is going to happen, but then comes true simply because it was predicted. (514)

Talcott Parsons: Another functionalist who suggested that a function of schools is to funnel people into social positions. (507)

Ray Rist: This sociologist's classic study of an African American grade school uncovered some of the dynamics of educational tracking. (513)

Robert Rosenthal and Lenore Jacobson: These social psychologists conducted a study of teacher expectations and student performance and found that a self-fulfilling prophecy had taken place—when teachers were led to believe certain students were smart, they came to expect more of them, and the students gave more in return. (514)

PRACTICE TEST

1. In earlier societies: (500)
   a. there was no separate social institution called education.
   b. education was synonymous with acculturation.
   c. persons who already possessed certain skills taught them to others.
   d. all of the above

2. "Common schools," supported through taxes, were proposed by: (500)
   a. Thomas Jefferson.
   b. Noah Webster.
   c. Horace Mann.
   d. John Dewey.

3. Laws requiring school attendance up to a specified age or a minimum grade are: (501)
   a. credential laws.
   b. mandatory education laws.
   c. compulsory education laws.
   d. none of the above.

4. All of the following are true about Japan *except*: (503)
   a. competition is discouraged among individuals.
   b. children in grade school work as a group.
   c. children all use the same textbook.
   d. any student is eligible to attend college.

5. Which of the following statements about education in Egypt is *incorrect*? (503-   504)
   a. Because education is free at all levels, the most talented children attend, regardless of parents' economic resources.
   b. The Egyptian constitution guarantees five years of free grade school for all children.
   c. The educational system consists of five years of grade school, three years of preparatory school, and three years of high school.
   d. Only 39 percent of women and 64 percent of men are literate.

6. Sociologist Randall Collins defined *credential society* as: (506)
   a. a society that uses degrees and diplomas to determine who gets jobs.
   b. a society that has established formal means of passing on cultural values.
   c. a society that relies on informal means of passing on culture.
   d. a society that uses only accredited school boards.

7. Which of the following is a latent function of education? (508)
   a. Students are tracked throughout their entire education experience.
   b. People who go father in school live longer.
   c. Income is similar between high school and college graduates.
   d. It is the process of transmitting mainstream cultural values.

8.   According to conflict theorists, what is the purpose of the educational system?   (508)
     a.   transmitting skills and information
     b.   ensuring dominance of the controlling class
     c.   building social networks
     d.   promoting equality between the rich and the poor

9.   The best estimate regarding the current number of U.S. home schooled children is: (509)
     a.   250,000.
     b.   500,000.
     c.   1,000,000.
     d.   5,000,000.

10.   Harry Gracey's study showed that lessons taught in kindergarten classes: (510)
     a.   were not relative to situations outside of the classroom.
     b.   could never apply to any eventual routines of the actual work world.
     c.   had a strong hidden curriculum.
     d.   such as "show and tell" are no longer used in schools.

11.   IQ tests have been criticized because: (511)
     a.   they are difficult to score.
     b.   they are expensive to administer.
     c.   they are often administered at the wrong point in a child's intellectual development.
     d.   they are culturally biased

12.   Public schools are largely supported by: (511)
     a.   state funding.
     b.   federal funding.
     c.   local property taxes.
     d.   none of the above.

13.   The ways in which schools correspond to, or reflect, the social structure of society is: (511-512)
     a.   the reproduction of social class.
     b.   the correspondence principle.
     c.   the status quo quotient.
     d.   the status maintenance process.

14. Research by Samuel Bowles on the connection between social class and college attendance showed that: (512)
   a.   regardless of ability, students from affluent homes were more likely to go to college than students from poor homes.
   b.   regardless of the family's social class, students with ability went on to college.
   c.   among the brightest students, family background made no difference in terms of the student's decision to attend college.
   d.   there are no social class differences among the weakest students in terms of their decision to go on to college.

15. All of the following examples are ways in which schools correspond to the needs of society *except* for which one? (512)
   a.   encourage cooperation
   b.   unequal funding of schools
   c.   enforce punctuality in attendance and homework
   d.   promote patriotism

16. Which two groups are the least likely to attend 4 year colleges? (513)
   a.   Asian Americans and African Americans
   b.   Asian Americans and white Americans
   c.   African Americans and Native Americans
   d.   Latinos and Native Americans

17. Rist's study of an African American grade school showed that students at table   one: (513)
   a.   were closest to the teacher, yet not treated any better than tables farther away.
   b.   were not given any more attention by the teacher than those at other tables.
   c.   were treated better by the teacher but the children had no perception of this.
   d.   were seated there because of their social class.

18. The Rosenthal and Jacobson experiment regarding teachers' perceptions and IQ scores was especially compelling because those designated as "spurters" were: (514)
   a.   actually randomly chosen.
   b.   those who actually had very low IQ scores.
   c.   those who actually had very high IQ scores.
   d.   those who went against the notion of a self-fulfilling prophecy.

19. Farka's research showed which of the following groupings as being the best at displaying signals that teachers would perceive as being positive ones, thereby giving them higher grades? (514-515)
   a.   white boys and white girls
   b.   boys and African Americans
   c.   African American girls and white boys
   d.   girls and Asian Americans

20. When compared to scores of twenty to thirty years ago, today's student scores on tests such as the SAT: (516)
    a. are higher.
    b. are lower.
    c. have remained about the same.
    d. none of the above.

21. The sociological implications of the examples of the University of Phoenix and Cardean University regarding their M.B.A. programs show that: (517)
    a. distance learning is a great equalizer for people of all social classes.
    b. distance learning is an example of the globalization of capitalism.
    c. prestigious schools would not lend their stature and legitimacy to distance learning.
    d. prestigious universities had to charge the same tuition as Cardean University.

22. Grade inflation and social promotion has resulted in: (518)
    a. age-based promotion.
    b. functional illiteracy.
    c. higher standards for students.
    d. academic excellence.

23. Shooting deaths and other homicides in schools have: (520)
    a. been consistently increasing since 1992.
    b. increased for shooting deaths, but not other homicides since 1992.
    c. stayed about the same from 1992 to the present.
    d. decreased since 1992.

24. Coleman and Hoffer concluded that test scores for students in Roman Catholic schools were higher than students' scores in public schools because: (521)
    a. students in parochial schools were more intelligent than public school students.
    b. more money is spent per student in parochial schools.
    c. expectations and standards are higher in parochial schools.
    d. attendance is better in parochial schools.

25. What does Jaime Escalante's approach to education emphasize? (522)
    a. The importance of adequate funding to effective teaching.
    b. The importance of student readiness.
    c. The importance of creating a system that inspires hope.
    d. The importance of traditional formal education.

Answer Key

1.	A
2.	C
3.	B
4.	D
5.	A
6.	A
7.	B
8.	B
9.	C
10.	C
11.	D
12.	C
13.	B
14.	A
15.	C
16.	D
17.	D
18.	A
19.	D
20.	B
21.	B
22.	B
23.	D
24.	C
25.	C

Chapter 17:
Education

SOCIOLOGY
A Down-to-Earth Approach 9/e

This multimedia product and its contents are protected under copyright law. The following are prohibited by law: any public performance or display, including transmission of any image over a network; preparation of any derivative work, including the extraction, in whole or in part, of any images; any rental, lease, or lending of the program.

The Development of Modern Education

Education in Earlier Societies

✳ **Education Consisted of Informal Learning**

✳ **Education was Equivalent to Acculturation**

The Development of Modern Education

Industrialization and Universal Education

✳ **In U.S. Jefferson and Webster Proposed Universal Schooling**

✳ **Uniform National Culture Through Education**

✳ **Rich Educated, Poor Not**

Copyright © Allyn & Bacon 2008   Chapter 17: Education

The Development of Modern Education

Industrialization and Universal Education

❋ **Horace Mann Proposed "Common Schools" Supported by Taxes**

❋ **By 1918, All States had Mandatory Education**

Copyright © Allyn & Bacon 2008   Chapter 17: Education

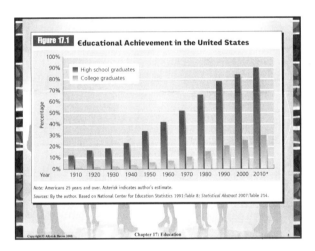

Figure 17.1 Educational Achievement in the United States

Note: Americans 25 years and over. Asterisk indicates author's estimate.
Sources: By the author. Based on National Center for Education Statistics 1991:Table 8; *Statistical Abstract* 2007:Table 214.

Copyright © Allyn & Bacon 2008   Chapter 17: Education

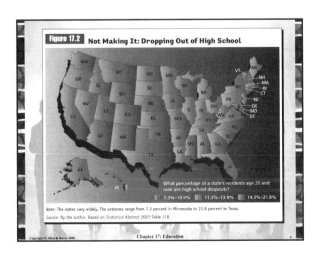

Figure 17.2 Not Making It: Dropping Out of High School

What percentage of a state's residents age 25 and over are high school dropouts?
7.3%–10.9%   11.3%–13.9%   14.3%–21.8%

Note: The states vary widely. The extremes range from 7.3 percent in Minnesota to 21.8 percent in Texas.
Source: By the author. Based on *Statistical Abstract* 2007:Table 218.

Copyright © Allyn & Bacon 2008   Chapter 17: Education

The Development of Modern Education

* **Education in Japan**
  * Emphasis on Solidarity Within Group
  * Discourages Competition among Individuals
* **Education in Russia**
  * Education, including College, was Free
  * Post-Soviet Russia is Reinventing Education

Copyright © Allyn & Bacon 2008   Chapter 17: Education   7

The Development of Modern Education

Education in Egypt

* Most People Work so Find Little Need for Education
* Most Cannot Afford Education
* Mandatory Attendance Laws that Exist are Not Enforced

Chapter 17: Education   8

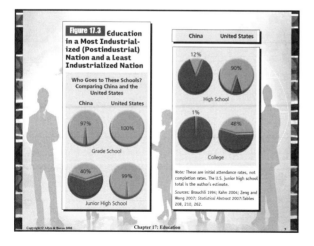

Figure 17.3 Education in a Most Industrialized (Postindustrial) Nation and a Least Industrialized Nation

Who Goes to These Schools? Comparing China and the United States

China   United States

China   United States

Grade School: China 97%, United States 100%

Junior High School: 40%, 99%

High School: China 12%, United States 90%

College: China 1%, United States 48%

Note: These are initial attendance rates, not completion rates. The U.S. junior high school total is the author's estimate.

Sources: Brauchli 1994; Kahn 2004; Zeng and Wang 2007; Statistical Abstract 2007:Tables 208, 210, 262.

Copyright © Allyn & Bacon 2008   Chapter 17: Education   9

Functionalist Perspective:
Providing Social Benefits

✳ Teaching Knowledge and Skills

✳ Cultural Transmission of Values

✳ Social Integration

Copyright © Allyn & Bacon 2008 · Chapter 17: Education

Functionalist Perspective:
Providing Social Benefits

✳ Gatekeeping

✳ Replacing Family Functions

✳ Other Functions

✳ Surprising Latent Functions

Copyright © Allyn & Bacon 2008 · Chapter 17: Education

Conflict Perspective:
Perpetuating Social Inequality

✳ The Hidden Curriculum

✳ Tilting the Tests: Discrimination by IQ

✳ Stacking the Deck: Unequal Funding

Copyright © Allyn & Bacon 2008 · Chapter 17: Education

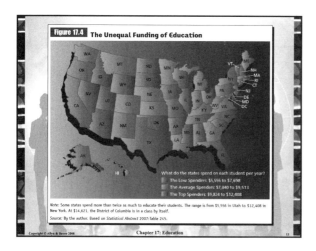

The Hidden Curriculum

Tilting the Tests: Discrimination by IQ

Stacking the Deck: Unequal Funding

Correspondence Principle

Family Background

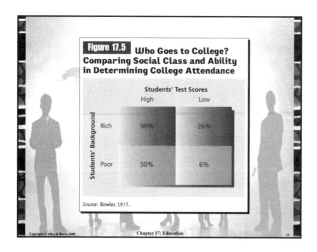

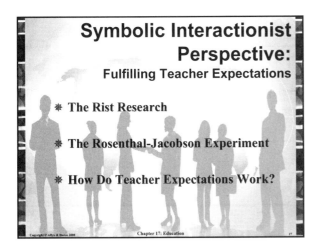

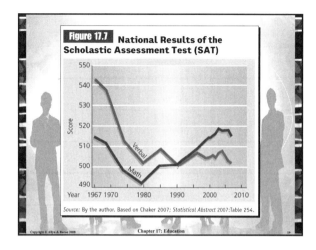

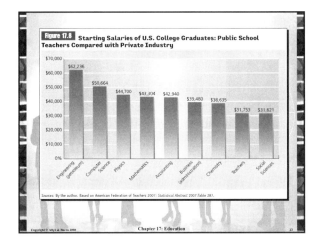

CHAPTER 18
RELIGION

CHAPTER SUMMARY

- The sociological study of religion involves the analysis of the relationship between society and religion to gain insight into the role of religion in people's lives. For Durkheim, the key elements of religion are beliefs separating the profane from the sacred, rituals, and a moral community.

- According to functionalists, religion meets basic human needs such as answering questions about ultimate meaning, providing emotional comfort, social solidarity, guidelines for everyday life, social control, adaptation, support for the government, and social change. Functional equivalents are groups or activities other than religion that provide these same functions. Functionalists also believe religion has two main dysfunctions: religious persecution and war and terrorism.

- Symbolic interactionists focus on how religious symbols communicate meaning and how ritual and beliefs unite people into a community.

- Conflict theorists see religion as a conservative force that serves the needs of the ruling class by reflecting and reinforcing social inequality.

- Unlike Marx, who asserted that religion impedes social change by encouraging people to focus on the afterlife, Weber saw religion as a powerful force for social change. He analyzed how Protestantism gave rise to an ethic that stimulated "the spirit of capitalism." The result was capitalism, which transformed society.

- The world's major religions include Judaism, Christianity, Islam, Hinduism, Buddhism, and Confucianism. As different religions have distinct teachings and practices, different groups within a religion contrast sharply with one another.

- Sociologists have identified cults, sects, churches, and ecclesia as distinct types of religious organizations. All religions began as cults; although most ultimately fail; those that survive become sects. Both cults and sects represent belief systems that are at odds with the prevailing beliefs and values of the broader society. If a sect grows, and its members make peace with the rest of society, it changes into a church. Ecclesiae, or state religions, are rare.

- Membership in religions in the United States varies by region, social class, and race-ethnicity. Religion in the United States is characterized by diversity, pluralism and freedom, competition and recruitment, commitment, tolerance, a fundamentalist revival, and the electronic church.

- The secularization of religion, a shift from spiritual concerns to concerns of "this world," is the force behind the dynamics of religious organization. As a cult or sect evolves into a church, its teachings are adapted to reflect the changing social status of its members; dissatisfied members break away to form new cults or sects.

- Even in countries where a concerted effort was made to eliminate it, religion has continued to thrive. Religion apparently will continue to exist as long as humanity does since science is unable to answer some key questions such as the whether God exists or not, the purpose of life, if there is an afterlife, and morality.

LEARNING OBJECTIVES
After reading Chapter 18, you should be able to:

1. Define religion and explain its essential elements. (526)
2. Describe the functions and dysfunctions of religion from the functionalist perspective. (527-530)
3. Know what is meant by functional equivalents of religion and provide examples. (529-530)
4. Describe the dysfunctions of religion and provide examples. (530
5. Apply the symbolic interactions perspective to religious symbols, rituals, beliefs, and religious experience, and discuss how each of these help to establish and/or maintain communities of like-minded people. (530-533)
6. From the conflict perspective, discuss how religion supports the status quo, as well as reflects, reinforces, and legitimates social inequality. (533-534)
7. Summarize Max Weber's analysis of religion and the spirit of capitalism and explain its significance. (535-536)
8. Identify the major characteristics and key figures in founding the world's major religions. (536-541)
9. Define cult, sect, church, and ecclesia and describe the process by which some groups move from one category to another. (541-545)
10. Describe the three major patterns of adaptation that occur when religion and culture conflict with one another. (544-545)
11. Know how religious membership varies by social class (family income, education, occupational prestige) and race-ethnicity. (545-549)
12. Describe and discuss the major features of religious groups in the United States including diversity, pluralism and freedom, competition and recruitment, commitment, toleration, fundamentalist revival, and the electronic church. (45-549)
13. Define secularization and distinguish between the secularization of religion and the secularization of culture. (549-551)
14. Discuss the future of religion and the questions that science cannot answer. (552)

KEY TERMS

After studying the chapter, review the definition for each of the following terms.

animism: the belief that all objects in the world have spirits, some of which are dangerous and must be outwitted (537)

anti-Semitism: prejudice, discrimination, and persecution directed against Jews (537)

born again: a term describing Christians who have undergone a life-transforming religious experience so radical that they feel they have become new persons (532)

charisma: literally, an extraordinary gift from God; more commonly, an outstanding, "magnetic" personality (542)

charismatic leader: literally, someone to whom God has given a gift; more commonly, someone who exerts extraordinary appeal to a group of followers (542)

church: according to Durkheim, one of the three essential elements of religion—a moral community of believers (p.526) a second definition is the type of religious organization described on page 543, a large, highly organized group with formal, sedate worship services and little emphasis on personal conversion (526)

civil religion: Robert Bellah's term for religion that is such an established feature of a country's life that its history and social institutions become sanctified by being associated with God (5529)

cosmology: teachings or ideas that provide a unified picture of the world (532)

cult: a new religion with few followers, whose teachings and practices put it at odds with the dominant culture and religion (542)

denomination: a "brand name" within a major religion, for example, Methodist or Baptist (543)

ecclesia: a religious group so integrated into the dominant culture that it is difficult to tell where the one begins and the other leaves off; also called a *state religion* (543)

evangelism: an attempt to win converts (543)

functional equivalent: in this context, a substitute that serves the same functions (or meets the same needs) as religion, for example, psychotherapy (529)

fundamentalism: the belief that true religion is threatened by modernism and that the faith as it was originally practiced should be restored (538)

modernization: the transformation of traditional societies into industrial societies (535)

monotheism: the belief that there is only one God (537)

polytheism: the belief that there are many gods (537)

profane: Durkheim's term for common elements of everyday life (526)

Protestant ethic: Weber's term to describe the ideal of a self-denying, highly moral life, accompanied by hard work and frugality (535)

reincarnation: in Hinduism and Buddhism, the return of the soul (or self) after death in a different form (540)

religion: according to Durkheim, beliefs and practices that separate the profane from the sacred and unite its adherents into a moral community (526)

religious experience: a sudden awareness of the supernatural or a feeling of coming in contact with God (532)

rituals: ceremonies or repetitive practices; in this context, religious observances, or rites, often intended to evoke a sense of awe of the sacred (532)

sacred: Durkheim's term for things set apart or forbidden, that inspire fear, awe, reverence, or deep respect (526)

sect: a group larger than a cult that still feels substantial hostility from and toward society (543)

secular: belonging to the world and its affairs (549)

secularization of culture: the process by which a culture becomes less influenced by religion (550)

secularization of religion: the replacement of a religion's "otherworldly" concerns with concerns about "this world" (551)

spirit of capitalism: Weber's term for the desire to accumulate capital as a duty—not to spend it, but as an end in itself—and to constantly reinvest it (535)

state religion: a government-sponsored religion; also called ecclesia (529)

KEY PEOPLE
Review the major theoretical contributions or findings of these people.

Emile Durkheim: Durkheim investigated world religions and identified elements that are common to all religions, such as separation of sacred from profane, beliefs about what is sacred, practices surrounding the sacred, and a moral community. (526)

John Hostetler: Hostetler is known for his research and writings on the Amish. (533)

Benton Johnson: Johnson analyzed types of religious groups, such as cults, sects, churches, and ecclesia. (542)

William Kephart and William Zellner: These sociologists also investigated the Amish religion and the practice of shunning. (533)

Karl Marx: Marx was critical of religion, calling it the opium of the masses. (533)

Richard Niebuhr: He noted that there are many ways to solve doctrinal disputes besides splintering off and forming other religious organizations. (549)

Liston Pope: Another sociologist who studied types of religious groups. (542)

Lynda Powell: An epidemiologist that evaluated the research done on the effects of religion on health. (528)

Stanley Presser and Linda Stinson: They examined written reports of how people spent their Sundays. They concluded that about 30 percent attend church weekly. (547)

Ian Robertson: Robertson noted that there is a fundamental distinction between a religion and its functional equivalent; unlike the latter, the activities of a religion are directed toward God, gods, or some supernatural being. (530)

Ernst Troeltsch: Yet another sociologist who is associated with types of religious groups from cults to ecclesia. (542)

Anthony Wallace: This anthropologist predicted that religion would eventually die out as a result of the increasing diffusion of scientific knowledge. (552)

Max Weber: Weber studied the link between Protestantism and the rise of capitalism and found that the ethic associated with Protestant denominations was compatible with the early needs of capitalism. (535-536)

PRACTICE TEST

1.   Emile Durkheim used the term *profane* to describe: (526)
      a.   common elements of everyday life.
      b.   a group united by their religious beliefs.
      c.   things set apart which inspire fear, awe, and reverence.
      d.   things declared immoral by a religion.

2.   All of the following are usually a function of religion *except*: (527-529)
      a.   social solidarity.
      b.   social control.
      c.   support for the government.
      d.   legitimization of social stratification.

3.   What did researchers discover about the effects of religion on health? (528)
      a.   They discovered that there was little relationship.
      b.   Prayer (or meditation) changes people's brain activity and improves their immune
            response.
      c.   People who were hospitalized were more religious than the doctors
      realized.
      d.   Regular prayer can cure many diseases.

4.   The idea of the functional equivalent of religion is illustrated by: (529)
      a.   such diverse groups as Alcoholics Anonymous and political parties.
      b.   activities of even non-religious groups being directed towards God.
      c.   groups that have no sacred writings or rituals.
      d.   none of the above.

5.   The Inquisition is an example of: (530)
      a.   manifest functions of religion.
      b.   latent functions of religion.
      c.   dysfunctions of religion.
      d.   functional equivalents of religion.

6.   Religious terrorists have all of the following in common *except:* (531)
      a.   they are convinced that God wants the evil destroyed.
      b.   they have a leader who they feel they must obey.
      c.   they are convinced that God has chosen them for this task.
      d.   they are nurtured by a community in which they find identity.

7.   What are Protestants referring to when they use the term *born again*? (532)
      a.   rcincarnation
      b.   Christ's rebirth after his crucifixion
      c.   a personal life-transforming religious experience
      d.   finding salvation in the afterlife

8.   A general conclusion about the role of ritual in religion is that rituals: (532)
     a.   involve ceremonies that are unique, non-repetitive practices.
     b.   do not include everyday practices such as singing in a church.
     c.   are found in Christian churches but not those of other religions.
     d.   can serve as a means of uniting people into a moral community.

9.   Sociologists studied the practice of shunning in which community? (533)
     a.   the Muslims
     b.   the Mennonites
     c.   the Jews
     d.   the Amish

10. What was Weber's view on the function of religion? (535)
     a.   Religion is the key to modernization of capitalist industrial societies.
     b.   Religion prevents the working class from realizing their exploitation.
     c.   Religion unites like-minded people in a moral community.
     d.   Religion is an expression of society's basic morality.

11. Calvinists believed that: (535)
     a.   no one is predestined by God to go to heaven.
     b.   church members must live as if they are predestined for heaven.
     c.   no one is predestined by God to go to hell.
     d.   church membership assures that one is going to heaven.

12. Which religion was the first one to be based in monotheism? (537)
     a.   Hinduism
     b.   Buddhism
     c.   Judaism
     d.   Christianity

13. The belief that all objects in the world have spirits is: (537)
     a.   a central belief of Islam.
     b.   referred to as animism.
     c.   no longer accepted by people around the world.
     d.   the same as monotheism.

14. What was an unanticipated outcome of the Reformation? (538)
     a.   the splintering of Christianity
     b.   the reunification of the Catholic Church
     c.   the elimination of corruption in the Church
     d.   the downgrading of women's status in the Church hierarchy

15. Which branch of Islam is more conservative and inclined to fundamentalism? (538)
    a. orthodox
    b. Sunni
    c. Shi'ite
    d. black Muslim

16. The religion with no specific founder is: (539)
    a. Islam.
    b. Hinduism.
    c. Buddhism.
    d. Confucianism.

17. A central belief in karma is a part of what religion? (540)
    a. Confucianism
    b. Islam
    c. Hinduism
    d. Buddhism

18. Which religious group emphasizes the need to reject society? (541)
    a. sect
    b. church
    c. cult
    d. ecclesia

19. What did the court rule in the case of the Santeros who sacrificed animals? (542)
    a. The court ruled in their favor that they were being discriminated against.
    b. The court ruled in favor of the city officials who passed a law prohibiting the sacrifice of animals.
    c. The court ruled that only small animals could be sacrificed.
    d. The court is still in the process of making a decision.

20. Churches: (543)
    a. are highly bureaucratized.
    b. have more sedate worship services.
    c. gain new members from within, from children born to existing members.
    d. all of the above.

21. "Brand names" within a religion are known as: (544)
    a. sects.
    b. splinter groups.
    c. denominations.
    d. status seekers.

22.   What time has been called "the most segregated hour in the United States"? (546)
      a.   5:00-6:00 pm on a Saturday
      b.   10:00-11:00 am on a Sunday
      c.   11:00-12:00 pm on a Thursday
      d.   3:00-4:00 pm on a Sunday

23.   Hispanic immigrants are adopting which religion? (548)
      a.   Lutheranism
      b.   Baptists
      c.   Pentecostalism
      d.   Catholicism

24.   The idea of the secularization of religion refers to: (550)
      a.   a culture that was once heavily influence by a religion is no longer influenced as much by that religion.
      b.   the notion that religion shifts its focus from spiritual matters to affairs of the world.
      c.   some "mainstream" religions, such as Methodists, that have never gone through this secularization process.
      d.   religions that have maintained a strong continuity of seeing a wide variety of acts as sinful.

25.   Questions that science cannot answer include: (552)
      a.   "is there a God?"
      b.   "what is the purpose of life?"
      c.   "what happens when a person dies?"
      d.   all of the above.

Answer Key

1. A
2. D
3. B
4. A
5. C
6. B
7. C
8. D
9. D
10. A
11. B
12. C
13. B
14. A
15. C
16. B
17. C
18. C
19. A
20. D
21. C
22. B
23. C
24. A
25. D

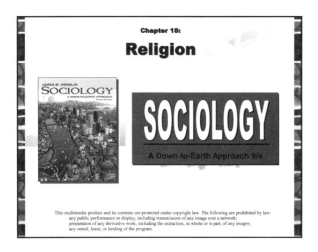

Chapter 18:

Religion

SOCIOLOGY

A Down-to-Earth Approach 9/e

This multimedia product and its contents are protected under copyright law. The following are prohibited by law: any public performance or display, including transmission of any image over a network; preparation of any derivative work, including the extraction, in whole or in part, of any images; any rental, lease, or lending of the program.

What is Religion?

Emile Durkheim said, "A religion is a unified system of beliefs and practices relative to sacred things."

Copyright © Allyn & Bacon 2008   Chapter 18: Religion   2

Three Elements of Religion

❋ Beliefs that Some Things are Sacred

❋ Practices Centering on Things Considered Sacred

❋ A Moral Community Resulting from a Group's Beliefs and Practices

Copyright © Allyn & Bacon 2008   Chapter 18: Religion   3

The Functionalist Perspective

* Questions about Ultimate Meaning

* Emotional Comfort

* Social Solidarity

* Guidelines for Everyday Life

Copyright © Allyn & Bacon 2008   Chapter 18: Religion

The Functionalist Perspective

* Social Control

* Adaptation

* Support for the Government

* Social Change

Copyright © Allyn & Bacon 2008   Chapter 18: Religion

Functional Equivalents of Religion

* Organizations Like Alcoholics Anonymous

* Psychotherapy

* Humanism

* Transcendental Meditation

* Political Parties

Copyright © Allyn & Bacon 2008   Chapter 18: Religion

Dysfunctions of Religion

✳ **Religion as Justification for Persecution**

✳ **War and Terrorism**

Copyright © Allyn & Bacon 2008   Chapter 18: Religion

Symbolic Interactionist Perspective

✳ **Religious Symbols**

✳ **Rituals**

✳ **Beliefs**

✳ **Religious Experience**

✳ **Community**

Copyright © Allyn & Bacon 2008   Chapter 18: Religion

Conflict Perspective

✳ **Marx's Opium of the People**

✳ **Legitimization of Social Inequalities**

  • **Social Arrangements Represent God's Desires**

  • **Divine Rights of Kings**

  • **Pharaoh as God**

  • **Hindu Cast System**

Copyright © Allyn & Bacon 2008   Chapter 18: Religion

Religion and the Spirit of Capitalism - Weber

❋ Source of Profound Social Change

❋ Religion Held the Key to Modernization

Copyright © Allyn & Bacon 2008   Chapter 18: Religion   10

Protestant Ethic and the Spirit of Capitalism

❋ Accumulation of Capital

❋ Move to Thrift and Investment

❋ Predestination

❋ Salvation through Good Works

❋ Self-denying Approach to Life

❋ Luxury Seen as Sinful

❋ Investment and Reinvestment

Copyright © Allyn & Bacon 2008   Chapter 18: Religion   11

The World's Major Religions

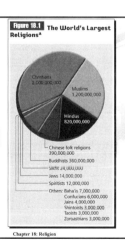

Figure 18.1 The World's Largest Religions[a]

Christians 2,000,000,000
Muslims 1,200,000,000
Hindus 820,000,000
Chinese folk religions 390,000,000
Buddhists 360,000,000
Sikhs 24,000,000
Jews 14,000,000
Spiritists 12,000,000
Others: Baha'is 7,000,000
Confucians 6,000,000
Jains 4,000,000
Shintoists 3,000,000
Taoists 3,000,000
Zoroastrians 3,000,000

Copyright © Allyn & Bacon 2008   Chapter 18: Religion   12

The World's Major Religions

Judaism

* Originated 4,000 Years Ago
* Originated in Mesopotamia
* God's Chosen People Through Covenant with Abraham
* Fundamental Change in Religion to Monotheism
* Contemporary—Orthodox, Reform, Conservative

Copyright © Allyn & Bacon 2008 — Chapter 18: Religion — 13

The World's Major Religions

Christianity

* Also Monotheistic
* Believe Jesus Christ is Messiah
* Born in Poverty to a Virgin
* At about 30 Jesus Began Teaching

Copyright © Allyn & Bacon 2008 — Chapter 18: Religion — 14

The World's Major Religions

Christianity

* 12 Main Followers—Apostles
* Belief in Christ's Resurrection
* Split to Greek Orthodoxy in 11th Century, Reformation in 16th Century
* Currently about 2 Billion Adherents

Copyright © Allyn & Bacon 2008 — Chapter 18: Religion — 15

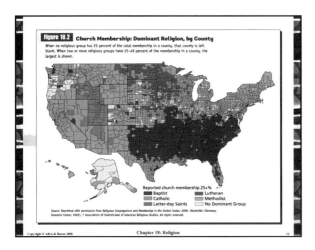

Figure 18.2 **Church Membership: Dominant Religion, by County**

When no religious group has 25 percent of the total membership in a county, that county is left blank. When two or more religious groups have 25–49 percent of the membership in a county, the largest is shown.

Reported church membership 25+%
- Baptist
- Catholic
- Latter-day Saints
- Lutheran
- Methodist
- No Dominant Group

Source: Reprinted with permission from *Religious Congregations and Membership in the United States: 2000.* (Nashville: Glenmary Research Center, 2002), © Association of Statisticians of American Religious Bodies. All rights reserved.

Copyright © Allyn & Bacon 2008   Chapter 18: Religion

The World's Major Religions

Islam

✳ World's Third Monotheistic Religion

✳ Founded by Muhammad (Born in Mecca)

✳ About Age 40 had Visions from God

✳ Visions and Teachings Written in Koran

Copyright © Allyn & Bacon 2008   Chapter 18: Religion

The World's Major Religions

Islam

✳ Muhammad Founded a Theocracy in Median

✳ Two Main Branches—Sunni and Shiite

✳ Shiites More Conservative and Fundamentalist

✳ Consider Bible Sacred but Koran Final Word

Copyright © Allyn & Bacon 2008   Chapter 18: Religion

The World's Major Religions

Hinduism

* No Specific Founder

* Chief Religion in India for 4,000 Years

* No Canonical Scripture

* Brahmanas, Bhagavad-Gita, and
  Upanishads Expound Moral Virtues

Copyright © Allyn & Bacon 2008   Chapter 18: Religion   19

_____

_____

_____

_____

_____

_____

The World's Major Religions

Hinduism

* People Make Sacrifices to gods

* Polytheistic—Many gods

* Central Belief is Karma—Spiritual
  Progress

* No Final Judgment—Reincarnation

* Spiritual Perfection Results in Nirvana

Copyright © Allyn & Bacon 2008   Chapter 18: Religion   20

_____

_____

_____

_____

_____

_____

The World's Major Religions

Buddhism

* Siddhartha Gautama Founded in
  about 600 B.C.

* Four Noble Truths
  * Existence is Suffering
  * Origin of Suffering is Desire
  * Suffering Ceases when Desire Ceases
  * Follow "Noble Eightfold Path" to End Desire

Copyright © Allyn & Bacon 2008   Chapter 18: Religion   21

_____

_____

_____

_____

_____

_____

The World's Major Religions

Buddhism—Eightfold Path

* Right Belief   * Right Occupation or Living

* Right Resolve   * Right Effort

* Right Speech   * Right-Mindedness

* Right Conduct * Right Ecstasy

Copyright © Allyn & Bacon 2008   Chapter 18: Religion   22

The World's Major Religions

Confucianism

* K'ung Fu-tsu Born in China 551 B.C.

* Public Official Distressed by Corruption in Government

* Urged Social Reform

* Developed System of Morality Based on Peace, Justice, Universal Order

Copyright © Allyn & Bacon 2008   Chapter 18: Religion   23

The World's Major Religions

Confucianism

* Teaching Written in the *Analects*
* Basic Moral Principle—Jen
* Loyalty and Morality above Self-Interest
* Confucian Golden Rule
* Taught the "Middle Way"
* Originally Atheistic, Gods Added along the Way

Copyright © Allyn & Bacon 2008   Chapter 18: Religion   24

Types of Religious Groups

* Cults
  * Begin with Charismatic Leader
  * Most Popular Religions Started this Way
  * Most Cults Fail
* Sects
  * Loosely Organized and Fairly Small
  * Emphasize Personal Salvation

Copyright © Allyn & Bacon 2008   Chapter 18: Religion   25

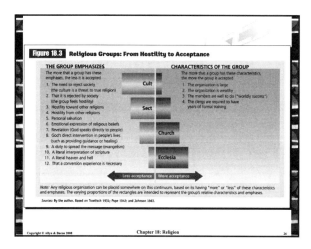

Figure 18.3 Religious Groups: From Hostility to Acceptance

THE GROUP EMPHASIZES

The more that a group has these emphases, the less it is accepted

1. The need to reject society (the culture is a threat to true religion)
2. That it is rejected by society (the group feels hostility)
3. Hostility toward other religions
4. Hostility from other religions
5. Personal salvation
6. Emotional expression of religious beliefs
7. Revelation (God speaks directly to people)
8. God's direct intervention in people's lives (such as providing guidance or healing)
9. A duty to spread the message (evangelism)
10. A literal interpretation of scripture
11. A literal heaven and hell
12. That a conversion experience is necessary

CHARACTERISTICS OF THE GROUP

The more that a group has these characteristics, the more the group is accepted

1. The organization is large
2. The organization is wealthy
3. The members are well to do ("worldly success")
4. The clergy are required to have years of formal training

Cult — Sect — Church — Ecclesia

Less acceptance ← → More acceptance

Note: Any religious organization can be placed somewhere on this continuum, based on its having "more" or "less" of these characteristics and emphases. The varying proportions of the rectangles are intended to represent the group's relative characteristics and emphases.

Sources: By the author. Based on Troeltsch 1931; Pope 1942; and Johnson 1963.

Copyright © Allyn & Bacon 2008   Chapter 18: Religion   26

Types of Religious Groups

* Churches
  * Highly Bureaucratized
  * National and International
  * Relationship with God Less Intense
* Ecclesia
  * State Religions
  * Part of Cultural Identification
* Variations in Patterns

Copyright © Allyn & Bacon 2008   Chapter 18: Religion   27

When Religion and Culture Conflict

✴ **Members Reject Dominant Culture**

✴ **Members Reject Specific Elements of a Culture**

✴ **Society Rejects Religious Group**

Copyright © Allyn & Bacon 2008   Chapter 18: Religion   28

Religion in the U.S.

Characteristics of Members

✴ **Social Class**

Copyright © Allyn & Bacon 2008   Chapter 18: Religion   29

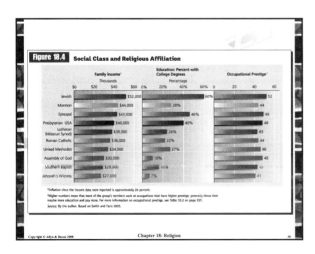

Figure 18.4 Social Class and Religious Affiliation

Copyright © Allyn & Bacon 2008   Chapter 18: Religion   30

Religion in the U.S.

Characteristics of Members

* Social Class

* Race and Ethnicity

Copyright © Allyn & Bacon 2008   Chapter 18: Religion   31

Religion in the U.S.

Characteristics of Religious Groups

* Diversity

* Pluralism and Freedom

* Competition and Recruitment

* Commitment

Copyright © Allyn & Bacon 2008   Chapter 18: Religion   32

Religion in the U.S.

Characteristics of Religious Groups

* Toleration

* Fundamentalist Revival

* The Electronic Church

* The Internet and Religion

Copyright © Allyn & Bacon 2008   Chapter 18: Religion   33

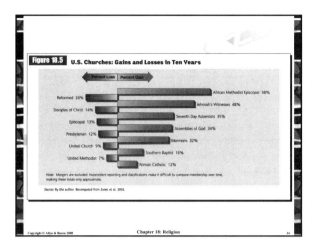

Figure 18.5 U.S. Churches: Gains and Losses in Ten Years

Percent Loss   Percent Gain

Reformed 20%	African Methodist Episcopal 58%
Disciples of Christ 14%	Jehovah's Witnesses 48%
Episcopal 13%	Seventh Day Adventists 35%
Presbyterian 12%	Assemblies of God 34%
United Church 9%	Mormons 32%
United Methodist 7%	Southern Baptist 16%
	Roman Catholic 12%

Note: Mergers are excluded. Inconsistent reporting and classifications make it difficult to compare membership over time, making these totals only approximate.

Source: By the author. Recomputed from Jones et al. 2002.

Copyright © Allyn & Bacon 2008   Chapter 18: Religion   34

Secularization of Religion and Culture

✳ **The Secularization of Religion**

✳ **The Secularization of Culture**

Copyright © Allyn & Bacon 2008   Chapter 18: Religion   35

The Future of Religion

✳ **Religion Thrives**

✳ **People Will Always Ponder Purpose**

✳ **Science Cannot Tell Us About…**

   ✳ The Existence of God

   ✳ The Purpose of Life

   ✳ An Afterlife

   ✳ Morality

Copyright © Allyn & Bacon 2008   Chapter 18: Religion   36

Chapter 18:

Religion

SOCIOLOGY

A Down-to-Earth Approach 9/e

CHAPTER 19
MEDICINE AND HEALTH

CHAPTER SUMMARY

- Sociologists study medicine as a social institution; three of the primary characteristics of medicine as it is practiced in the United States include professionalization, bureaucracy, and the profit motive.

- The symbolic interactionists view health and illness as intimately related to cultural beliefs and practices; definitions of illness vary from one group to the next.

- Components of health include physical, mental, social, and spiritual. The functionalists study the sick role and the ways in which people are excused from normal responsibilities when they assume this role. The conflict perspective stresses that health care is one of the scarce resources over which groups compete. Globally, the best health care is available in the Most Industrialized Nations.

- When medicine in the United States became a profession, it also became a monopoly developing into the U.S.'s largest business enterprise. Due to public outcry, Medicaid and Medicare were established to assist the poor and the elderly.

- Americans are healthier than their ancestors were. Four of the leading causes of death in 1900 don't appear on today's list. However, diabetes and Alzheimer's disease didn't make the top ten in 1900, but they do now.

- The United States has a two-tire system of medical care in which the wealthy receive superior care and the poor inferior medical care.

- One major problem in U.S. health care is defensive medicine. This is when medical procedures are done to protect doctors against possible lawsuits, but they end up adding huge amounts of money to the nation's medical bill. Other problems include depersonalization, medical incompetence, conflict of interest, medical fraud, sexism and racism, medicalization of society, and medically assisted suicide.

- HMOs and diagnosis-related groups are among the measures that have been taken to reduce medical costs. Other solutions include national health insurance, group care, pay-as-you-go programs, and rationing medical care.

- Major threats to health today include HIV/AIDS, obesity and skinniness, alcohol and nicotine, disabling environments, and unethical medical experiments.

- Global travel has increased the risk of diseases occurring worldwide. So far, world health officials have been able to contain these diseases.

- Alternatives to the current health care system include individuals taking more responsibility for their health and a fundamental shift in the medical establishment toward "wellness", alternative and preventive medicine.

LEARNING OBJECTIVES

After reading Chapter 19, you should be able to:

1. Understand the role of sociology in studying medicine. (558)
2. Use the symbolic interactionist perspective to explain how culture influences health and illness. (558)
3. Identify the four components of health. (558)
4. Know what is meant by the sick role and describe the social factors that can affect and/or influence people's claim to it. (559-560)
5. Explain how global stratification adversely affects the quality of medical care in the Least Industrialized Nations and how, for people who live in these nations, this is often a matter of life and death. (560-562)
6. Describe the process and consequences of the development of medicine as a profession and a monopoly in the United States. (562-563)
7. Discuss the changes in physical and mental health patterns in the United States over the past 100 years, and the consequences of those changes. (565)
8. Discuss the controversy in the U.S. over whether medical care is a right or a commodity. (565-566)
9. Identify the social inequalities in the American health care system. (566-567)
10. Describe the current problems in the American health care system including malpractice, medical incompetence, depersonalization, conflicts of interest, medical fraud, sexism and racism, the medicalization of society, and medically assisted suicide. (567-571)
11. Identify the factors that are contributing to the soaring costs of health care in the United States and evaluate the job that that HMOs and diagnosis-related-groups are doing to help reduce those costs. (573)
12. Discuss the pros and cons of national health insurance and rationing medical care. (573-574)
13. Describe the major threats to health in the United States and worldwide: HIV/AIDS; obesity and thinness; alcohol and nicotine; disabling environments; callous experiments; and the globalization of disease. (575-582)
14. Discuss alternatives to the way in which U.S. medicine is usually practiced. (583-584)
15. Examine health characteristics of health care around the world. (584)

KEY TERMS

After studying the chapter, review the definition for each of the following terms.

alternative medicine: medical treatment other than that of standard Western medicine; often refers to practices that originate in Asia, but may also refer to taking vitamins not prescribed by a doctor (584)

defensive medicine: medical practices done not for the patient's benefit but in order to protect a physician from malpractice suits (567)

depersonalization: dealing with people as though they were objects; in the case of medical care, as though patients were merely cases and diseases, not people (569)

disabling environment: an environment that is harmful to health (580)

dumping: the practice of discharging unprofitable patients, or private hospitals sending unprofitable patients to public hospitals (573) y

epidemiology: the study of disease and disability patterns in a population (565)

fee-for-service: payment to a physician to diagnose and treat the patient's medical problems (563)

health: a human condition measured by four components: physical, mental, social, and spiritual (558)

medicalization: the transformation of something into a matter to be treated by physicians (571)

medicine: one of the major social institutions that sociologists study; a society's organized ways of dealing with sickness and injury (558)

professionalization of medicine: the development of medicine into a field in which education becomes rigorous, and in which physicians claim a theoretical understanding of illness, regulate themselves, claim to be doing a service to society (rather than just following self-interest), and take authority over clients (563)

shaman: the healing specialist of a preliterate tribe who attempts to control the spirits thought to cause a disease or injury; commonly called a witch doctor (558)

sick role: a social role that excuses people from normal obligations because they are sick or injured, while at the same time expecting them to seek competent help and cooperate in getting well (560)

two-tier system of medical care: a system in which the wealthy receive superior medical care and the poor inferior medical care (567)

KEY PEOPLE

Review the major theoretical contributions or findings of these people.

Abraham Flexner: He evaluated medical schools in the 1900's. His report led to the professionalization of medicine. (563)

Jack Haas and William Shaffir: These sociologists did a participant observation of medical students and discovered that over the course of medical school their attitudes change from wanting to "treat the whole person" to needing to be efficient in treating the specific ailment. (569)

Talcott Parsons: Parsons was the first sociologist to analyze the sick role, pointing out that it has four elements: (1) not being responsible for your sickness, (2) being exempt from normal responsibilities, (3) not liking the role, and (4) seeking competent help in order to return to daily routines. (560)

PRACTICE TEST

1.   Which of the following is *not* one of the components of health? (558)
     a.   physical
     b.   social
     c.   spiritual
     d.   hereditary

2.   Which did researchers learn about childhood events and later health? (559)
     a.   That children who had been socially isolated had higher blood pressure and cholesterol in adulthood.
     b.   That children who were thinner continued to remain thin through adulthood.
     c.   That children who smoked before age 16 remained smokers throughout adulthood.
     d.   That children who were frequently sick were rarely sick as adults.

3.   How would a sick or injured person who can't fulfill normal role obligations be described? (560)
     a.   a hypochondriac
     b.   in the sick role
     c.   deviant
     d.   all of the above

4.   The individual's claim to the sick role is legitimized primarily by: (560)
     a.   demonstrating to others that he or she is ill.
     b.   a doctor's excuse.
     c.   employers, teachers, and sometimes parents.
     d.   other workers or students who vouch for the fact that the individual is ill.

5.   The country with the highest number of deaths for babies before their first birthday is: (561)
     a.   Greece.
     b.   the Czech Republic.
     c.   Spain.
     d.   the United States.

6.   Physicians defeated midwives by all of the following *except*: (564)
     a.   physicians bribing midwives to sneak into birthing rooms.
     b.   a ruthless campaign portraying midwives as incompetent.
     c.   seeking to control a task done by women.
     d.   convincing the public that birthing is a natural process.

7. The United States government started funding Medicare and Medicaid in: (563)
   a. the 1920s.
   b. the 1940s.
   c. the 1960s.
   d. the 1970s.

8. What is the leading cause of death today? (565)
   a. cancer
   b. heart disease
   c. strokes
   d. diabetes

9. The two-tier system of medical care refers to the: (566)
   a. use of medical students as doctors.
   b. use of nurses to do many duties that are done by doctors.
   c. wealthy receiving superior care while the poor receive inferior care.
   d. placement of patients from mental hospitals into the community.

10. Why do physicians practice defensive medicine? (567)
    a. to make sure that the patient has all of the tests that are needed
    b. to protect themselves from lawsuits
    c. to decrease the cost of medical care
    d. as a form of preventive medicine

11. The practice of referring to people as though they were diseases, not individuals, is: (569)
    a. deinstitutionalization.
    b. defensive medicine.
    c. depersonalization.
    d. objectification.

12. When did Oregon become the only state in which medically assisted suicide is legal? (572)
    a. 1997
    b. 1999
    c. 2003
    d. 2006

13. Sending unprofitable patients to public hospitals is known as: (573)
    a. turfing.
    b. sidewinding.
    c. dumping.
    d. discarding.

14. Which one of the following is a controversial suggestion as to how to reduce medical costs? (574)
   a. creating additional HMO's
   b. classifying illnesses into diagnosis-related-groups (DRG's)
   c. doing group consultation rather than individual consultations
   d. rationing medical care

15. How are circumcision and HIV/AIDS related to one another? (577)
   a. Researchers found that the two factors are unrelated.
   b. About twice as many uncircumcised men came down with HIV.
   c. More circumcised men came down with HIV than uncircumcised men.
   d. Researchers have yet to find a relationship.

16. Which racial and/or ethnic group is at greater risk of contracting AIDS? (577)
   a. Whites
   b. African Americans
   c. Latinos
   d. Asian Americans

17. The most-consumed beverage in the United States is: (579)
   a. beer.
   b. tea.
   c. fruit juice.
   d. bottled water.

18. What drug have full-time college students used the most in the past year? (580)
   a. nicotine from cigarettes
   b. marijuana
   c. ecstasy
   d. alcohol

19. Which of the following statements about smoking is *incorrect*? (580)
   a. Nicotine may be as addictive as heroin.
   b. The rate of cigarette smoking continues to climb, despite warnings about the dangers.
   c. The tobacco industry has a huge advertising budget to encourage people to smoke.
   d. When compared with nonsmokers, smokers are three times as likely to die before age 65.

20. An environment that is harmful to health is referred to as a (n): (581)
   a. disabling environment.
   b. health hazard.
   c. harmful setting.
   d. crippling environment.

21. What threatens to disable the basic environment of the human race? (581)
    a. pollution
    b. globalization
    c. industrialization
    d. glacial melting

22. An example of physicians' and the government's callous disregard of people's health is: (581-582)
    a. the delay in providing open heart surgery for women patients.
    b. the Tuskegee syphilis experiment.
    c. the failure to curb advertising of tobacco products.
    d. all of the above.

23. All of the following are associated with the globalization of disease *except*: (582-583)
    a. isolating people in asylums.
    b. that global travel helps to spread natural immunities against disease.
    c. that diseases mutating into "superbugs" become immune to antibiotics.
    d. the declaration that certain regions of the world are dangerous to visit.

24. *Barefoot doctors* provide much of the health care to the people of which nation? (575)
    a. China
    b. India
    c. Vietnam
    d. Korea

25. Which ordering of countries shows longer to shorter life expectancies? (575)
    a. United States, China, Russia, Sweden
    b. China, Sweden, United States, Russia
    c. United States, Sweden, China, Russia
    d. Sweden, United States, China, Russia

Answer Key

1.   D
2.   A
3.   B
4.   A
5.   D
6.   D
7.   C
8.   B
9.   C
10. B
11. C
12. A
13. C
14. D
15. B
16. B
17. A
18. D
19. B
20. A
21. C
22. B
23. A
24. A
25. D

Chapter 19:
Medicine and Health

SOCIOLOGY

This multimedia product and its contents are protected under copyright law. The following are prohibited by law: any public performance or display, including transmission of any image over a network; preparation of any derivative work, including the extraction, in whole or in part, of any images; any rental, lease, or lending of the program.

Sociology and the Study of Medicine and Health

✳ **Role of Sociology in the Study**

✳ **Study Influence of Self-Regulation, Bureaucracy, and Profit Motive**

✳ **Study How Illness is More than Biology**

Copyright © Allyn & Bacon 2008   Chapter 19: Medicine and Health   2

Symbolic Interactionist Perspective

✳ **Role of Culture in Defining Health and Illness**

✳ **The Components of Health**

Copyright © Allyn & Bacon 2008   Chapter 19: Medicine and Health   3

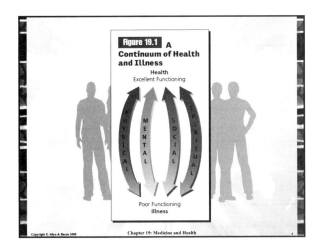

Figure 19.1 A **Continuum of Health and Illness**

Health
Excellent Functioning

PHYSICAL   MENTAL   SOCIAL   SPIRITUAL

Poor Functioning
Illness

Chapter 19: Medicine and Health

The Functionalist Perspective

The Sick Role

✳ **Elements of the Sick Role**

✳ **Ambiguity of the Sick Role**

✳ **Gatekeepers to the Sick Role**

✳ **Gender Differences in the Sick Role**

Chapter 19: Medicine and Health

The Conflict Perspective

✳ **Effects of Global Stratification on Health Care**

Chapter 19: Medicine and Health

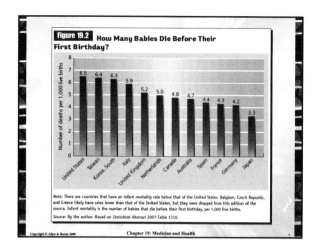

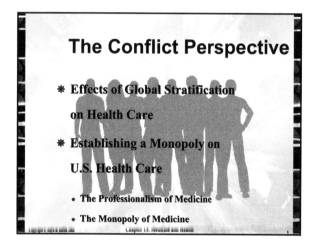

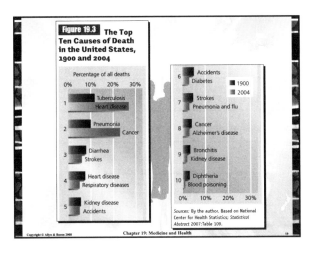

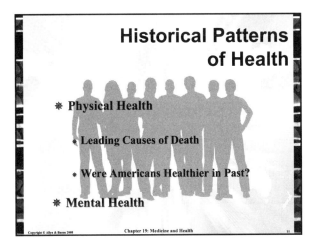

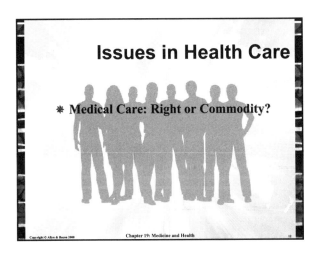

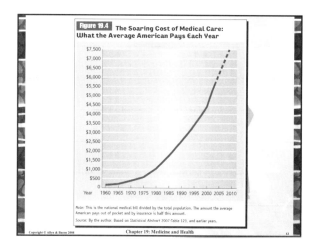

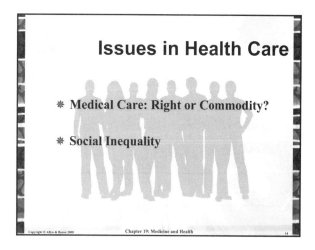

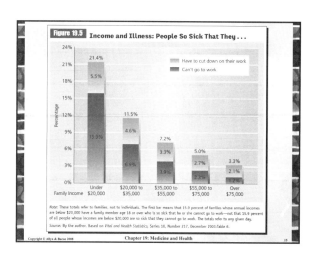

Issues in Health Care

❋ **Medical Care: Right or Commodity?**

❋ **Social Inequality**

❋ **Malpractice Suits and Defensive Medicine**

❋ **Medical Incompetence**

Copyright © Allyn & Bacon 2008   Chapter 19: Medicine and Health   16

Issues in Health Care

❋ **Depersonalization: The**

Medical Cash Machine

❋ **Conflict of Interest**

❋ **Medical Fraud**

Copyright © Allyn & Bacon 2008   Chapter 19: Medicine and Health   17

Issues in Health Care

❋ **Sexism in Medicine**

❋ **The Medicalization of Society**

❋ **Medically Assisted Suicide**

Copyright © Allyn & Bacon 2008   Chapter 19: Medicine and Health   18

Curbing Costs:
From Health Insurance to Rationing Medical Care

* HMOs - Health Maintenance Organizations
* Diagnosis-Related Groups
* National Health Insurance
* Maverick Solutions
* Rationing Medical Care

Copyright © Allyn & Bacon 2008 — Chapter 19: Medicine and Health — 19

Figure 19.6 Who Lacks Medical Insurance?

The percentage of a state's residents who have no medical insurance
- 8.9%–12.0%
- 12.6%–15.7%
- 16.4%–25.0%

Note: The range is broad, from a low of 8.9 percent who lack medical insurance in Minnesota to a high of 25.0 percent in Texas.
Source: By the author. Based on *Statistical Abstract* 2007:Table 145.

Copyright © Allyn & Bacon 2008 — Chapter 19: Medicine and Health — 20

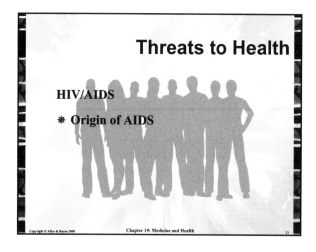

Threats to Health

HIV/AIDS

* Origin of AIDS

Copyright © Allyn & Bacon 2008 — Chapter 19: Medicine and Health — 21

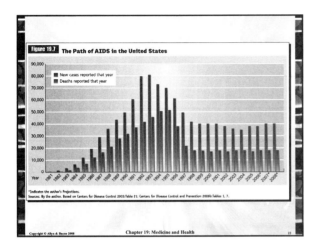

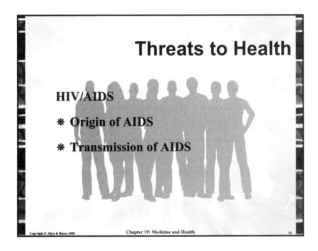

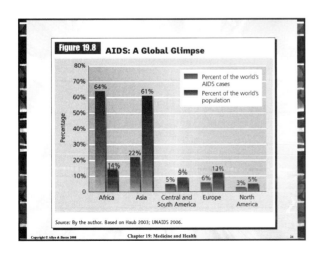

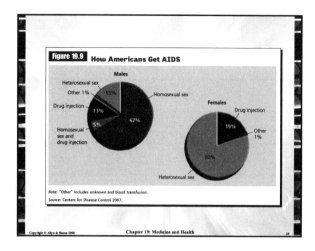

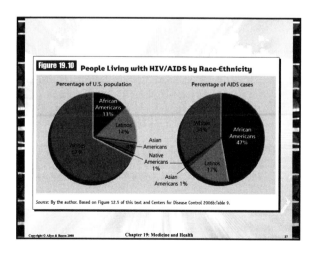

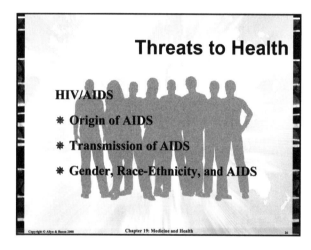

Threats to Health

HIV/AIDS

✳ **Origin of AIDS**

✳ **Transmission of AIDS**

✳ **Gender, Race-Ethnicity, and AIDS**

✳ **The Stigma of AIDS**

✳ **Is there a Cure for AIDS?**

Copyright © Allyn & Bacon 2008   Chapter 19: Medicine and Health   28

Threats to Health

✳ **Weight: Too Much & Too Little**

✳ **Drugs**

   ✳ **Alcohol**

   ✳ **Nicotine**

Copyright © Allyn & Bacon 2008   Chapter 19: Medicine and Health   29

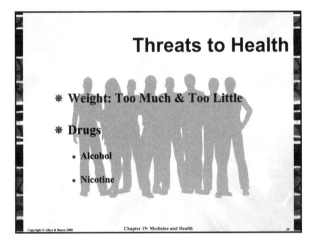

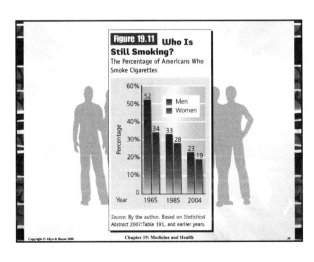

Figure 19.11 Who Is Still Smoking?
The Percentage of Americans Who Smoke Cigarettes

Source: By the author. Based on *Statistical Abstract* 2007:Table 191, and earlier years.

Copyright © Allyn & Bacon 2008   Chapter 19: Medicine and Health   30

Threats to Health

❋ **Obesity and Skinniness**

❋ **Drugs**
  * Alcohol
  * Nicotine

❋ **Disabling Environments**

Copyright © Allyn & Bacon 2008   Chapter 19: Medicine and Health   31

_____

_____

_____

_____

_____

_____

_____

Threats to Health

❋ **Callous and Harmful Medical Experiments**
  * Tuskegee Syphilis Experiment
  * Cold War Experiments
  * Playing God

❋ **Globalization of Disease**

Copyright © Allyn & Bacon 2008   Chapter 19: Medicine and Health   32

_____

_____

_____

_____

_____

_____

_____

The Search for Alternatives

❋ **Treatment or Prevention?**

❋ **Alternative Medicine**

❋ **Heath Care in Global Perspective**

Copyright © Allyn & Bacon 2008   Chapter 19: Medicine and Health   33

_____

_____

_____

_____

_____

_____

_____

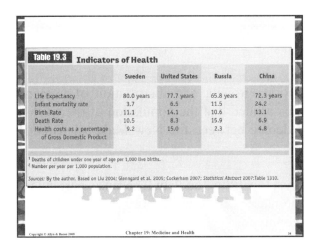

Table 19.3	Indicators of Health			
	Sweden	**United States**	**Russia**	**China**
Life Expectancy	80.0 years	77.7 years	65.8 years	72.3 years
Infant mortality rate	3.7	6.5	11.5	24.2
Birth Rate	11.1	14.1	10.6	13.1
Death Rate	10.5	8.3	15.9	6.9
Health costs as a percentage of Gross Domestic Product	9.2	15.0	2.3	4.8

[1] Deaths of children under one year of age per 1,000 live births.
[2] Number per year per 1,000 population.

Sources: By the author. Based on Liu 2004; Glenngard et al. 2005; Cockerham 2007; *Statistical Abstract* 2007:Table 1310.

Copyright © Allyn & Bacon 2008   Chapter 19: Medicine and Health   34

Chapter 19:

Medicine and Health

SOCIOLOGY

A Down-to-Earth Approach 9/e

CHAPTER SUMMARY

- Demography is the study of the size, composition, growth, and distribution of human populations. Over 200 years ago, Thomas Malthus argued that the population of the world would eventually outstrip its food supply. The debate between the New Malthusians and the anti-Malthusians continues today.

- Starvation occurs not because the earth produces too little food, but because particular places lack food. Droughts and wars are the main reasons for this. Therefore, starvation is due to a misdistribution of food rather than overpopulation.

- People in the Least Industrialized Nations have large families because children are viewed as gifts from God, it costs little to rear them, and they represent parents' social security. To project population trends, demographers use three demographic variables: fertility, mortality, and migration. A nation's growth rate is also affected by unanticipated variables like wars, famines, and changing economic and political conditions.

- Cities can only develop if there is an agricultural surplus; the primary impetus to the development of cities was the invention of the plow about 5,000 or 6,000 years ago. For much of human history cities were small. After the Industrial Revolution cities grew quickly. Urbanization is so extensive today that some cities have become metropolises; in some cases metropolises have merged to form a megalopolis. When a city's population hits 10 it is known as a megacity. Today there are 19 in the world.

- Many urban patters exist. There has been movement from the country to the city, from city to city, between and within cities, from cities to suburbs, and to smaller centers known as micropolises. There has also been a recent trend to retreating to rural areas.

- The primary models that have been proposed to explain how cities expand are the concentric-zone, sector, multiple-nuclei, and peripheral models. These models fail to account for medieval cities, many European cities, and those in the Least Industrialized Nations.

- Some people find a sense of community in cities; others find alienation. Herbert Gans identified five types of city dwellers: cosmopolites, singles, ethnic villagers, the deprived, and the trapped. An essential element in determining whether someone finds community or alienation in the city is that person's social networks. Noninvolvement is generally functional for urbanites, but it impedes giving help in emergencies.

- The decline of U.S. cities is due to forces such as disinvestment, suburbanization, and deindustrialization. Principles to guide future social policy are scale, livability, and social justice.

LEARNING OBJECTIVES

After reading Chapter 20, you should be able to:

1. Discuss what demography is. (590)
2. Know what is meant by the Malthus theorem and state the major points and counterpoints in the debate between the New Malthusians and the Anti-Malthusians. (590-593)
3. Identify the primary causes of famines and starvation. (593-5945)
4. Understand why people in the Least Industrialized Nations have so many children (596)
5. Discuss the implications of different rates of population growth. (597-598)
6. Describe the three demographic variables that are used in estimating population growth (598-600)
7. Explain problems in forecasting population growth. (600-602)
8. Trace the development of cities from ancient times through industrialization and the process of urbanization. (603-606)
9. Identify urban patterns in the United States and the return by some to rural areas. (606-610)
10. Describe and evaluate the four models of urban growth and the return to rural areas. (610-612)
11. Discuss how some people find a sense of community in cities while others become alienated. (612-614)
12. Talk about ways that people who live in cities can create a sense of intimacy. (614)
13. Describe the five types of urban dwellers identified by sociologist Herbert Gans. (615)
14. Explain why many urban dwellers follow a norm of noninvolvement and how this norm, in turn, may contribute to a dysfunctional diffusion of responsibility. (615-616)
15. Identify the primary problems of urban life today and discuss how suburbanization, disinvestment, and deindustrialization contribute to these problems. (617-618)
16. Evaluate current attempts to address urban problems in the United States and discuss the guiding principles for developing future policies to deal with these problems. (618-619)

KEY TERMS
After studying the chapter, review the definition for each of the following terms.

alienation: used in several senses; in this context. It refers to feelings of isolation, that you are not part of something or that no one cares about you (603)

basic demographic equation: growth rate equals births minus deaths plus net migration (600) y

city: a place in which a large number of people are permanently based and do not produce their own food (602)

crude birth rate: the annual number of live births per 1,000 population (599)

crude death rate: the annual number of deaths per 1,000 population (599)

deindustrialization: industries moving out of a country or region (618)

demographic transition: a three-stage historical process of population growth; first, high birth rates and high death rates; second, high birth rates and low death rates; and third, low birth rates and low death rates; a fourth stage has begun to appear in the Most Industrialized Nations, as depicted in Figure 20.3 (592)

demographic variables: the three factors that influence population growth: fertility, mortality, and net migration (598)

demography: the study of the size, composition, growth, and distribution of human populations (590)

disinvestment: the withdrawal of investments by financial institutions, which seals the fate of an urban area (618)

enterprise zone: the use of economic incentives in a designated area with the intention of encouraging investment there (618)

edge city: a large clustering of service facilities and residential areas near highway intersections that provides a sense of place to people who live, shop, and work there (608)

exponential growth curve: a pattern of growth in which numbers double during approximately equal intervals, thus accelerating in the latter stages (590)

fecundity: the number of children that women are capable of bearing (598)

fertility rate: the number of children that the average woman bears (598)

gentrification: middle class people moving into a run-down area of a city, displacing the poor and they buy and restore homes (608)

growth rate: the net change in a population after adding births, subtracting deaths, and either adding or subtracting net migration (600)

human ecology: Robert Park's term for the relationship between people and their environment (such as land and structures); also known as *urban ecology* (610)

invasion-succession cycle: the process by which a group of people displaces a group whose racial-ethnic or social class characteristics differ from their own (611)

Malthus theorem: an observation by Thomas Malthus that although the food supply increases only arithmetically (from 1 to 2 to 3 to 4 and so on), population grows geometrically (from 2 to 4 to 8 to 16 and so forth) (590)

megacity: a city of 10 million or more residents (606)

megalopolis: an urban area consisting of at least two metropolises and their many suburbs (606)

metropolis: a central city surrounded by smaller cities and their suburbs (606)

metropolitan statistical area (MSA): a central city and the urbanized counties adjacent to it (606)

net migration rate: the difference between the number of immigrants and emigrants per 1,000 population (599)

population pyramid: a graphic representation of a population, divided into age and sex (596)

population shrinkage: the process by which a country's population becomes smaller because its birth rate and immigration are too low to replace those who die or emigrate (593)

redlining: the officers of a financial institution deciding not to make loans in a particular area (618)

suburb: a community adjacent to a city (608)

urban renewal: the rehabilitation of a rundown area, which usually results in the displacement of the poor who are living in that area (618)

urbanization: the process by which an increasing proportion of a population live in cities ND cities have a growing influence on the culture (606)

zero population growth: a demographic condition in which women bear only enough children to reproduce the population (602)

KEY PEOPLE
State the major theoretical contributions or findings of these people.

Ernest Burgess: Burgess developed the concentric zone model of urban development. (610-611)

John Darley and Bibb Latané: These social psychologists found that people tend to remain uninvolved when they perceive there are others around who might become involved; they referred to this as the *diffusion of responsibility.* (616)

William Faunce: Writing about the far-reaching implications of exponential growth, this sociologist's views are consistent with the New Malthusians. (590)

William Flanagan: Flanagan has suggested three guiding principles for finding solutions to pressing urban problems: (1) use of regional planning, (2) awareness of human needs, and (3) equalizing the benefits as well as the impact of urban change. (619)

Herbert Gans: Gans studied urban neighborhoods, with the result that he documented the existence of community within cities and identified the several different types of urban dwellers that live there. (614-615)

Chauncey Harris and Edward Ullman: These two geographers developed the multiple-nuclei model of urban growth. Harris later introduced the peripheral model of urban growth to account for more recent developments. (611-612)

Homer Hoyt: Hoyt modified Burgess's model of urban growth with the development of the sector model. (611)

Thomas Malthus: Malthus was an economist who made dire predictions about the future of population growth. (590)

Steven Mosher: This anthropologist did field work in China and wrote about the ruthlessness with which the "one couple, one child" policy is enforced. (600)

Robert Park: Park coined the term "human ecology" to describe how people adapt to their environment. (610)

William Wilson: Wilson observed that the net result of shifting population and resources from central cities to suburbs was the transformation of the cities into ghettos. (617)

Louis Wirth: Wirth wrote a classic essay in which he argued that city life undermines kinship and neighborhood. (614)

PRACTICE TEST

1. What is demography? (590)
    a. the study of the size, composition, growth and distribution of human populations
    b. the study of overpopulation
    c. the study of food supply, distribution and growth
    d. the study of migration

2. What do the New Malthusians believe that the world's population is following?   (590)
    a. a demographic transition.
    b. a unilateral population increase.
    c. an exponential growth curve.
    d. a demographic free-fall.

3. The demographic transition is correctly illustrated by which of the following descriptions? (592)
    a. stage one has high birthrates and low death rates.
    b. stage two has low birthrates and high death rates.
    c. stage one has low birthrates and high death rates.
    d. stage two has high birthrates and low death rates.

4. Which of the following statements is consistent with beliefs of the Anti-Malthusians? (592-593)
    a. people will blindly reproduce until there is no room left on earth.
    b. it is possible to project the world's current population growth into the indefinite future.
    c. most people do not use intelligence and rational planning when it comes to having children.
    d. the demographic transition provides an accurate picture of what the future looks like.

5. The process by which a country's population becomes smaller because its birth rate and immigration are too low to replace those who die and emigrate is: (593)
    a. population transfer.
    b. population annihilation.
    c. population shrinkage.
    d. population depletion.

6. Starvation occurs because: (594)
    a. there is not enough fertile land worldwide on which to grow food.
    b. some parts of the world lack food while other parts of the world produce more than they can consume.
    c. population is growing at a faster rate than the world's ability to produce food.
    d. people do not eat a well-balanced diet.

7. Looking at India's growing population, how long did it take to replace the people who died because of the tsunami? (595)
    a. 8-9 hours.
    b. an 3-4 days.
    c. 1 month.
    d. 2 years.

8. The greatest percentage increase in populations is being seen today in: (595)
    a. Least Developed Nations.
    b. Most Developed Nations.
    c. the United States.
    d. postindustrial nations.

9. Poor people in Least Industrialized Nations need children because: (596)
    a. Gemeinschaft communities do not value children.
    b. children are seen as economic assets.
    c. children counteract the high status of childless couples.
    d. daughters are valued since they can give birth to many children.

10. What is the overall fertility rate for the world? (598)
    a. 1 child.
    b. 1.3 children
    c. 2.7 children
    d. 4 children.

11. Which of the following refers to the number of children that the average women bears? (598)
    a. crude birth rate
    b. fecundity
    c. fertility rate
    d. reproductive rate

12. The number of women that women are capable of bearing is known as the: (598)
    a. reproductive rate.
    b. demographic increase rate.
    c. life expectancy rate.
    d. fecundity rate.

13. Which statement best describes the crude death rate? (599)
    a. the total number of deaths to those over 65 in a year
    b. the total number of deaths per 1000 people in the population in a year
    c. the number of deaths minus the number of births in a year
    d. the number of births per 1000 population minus the number of deaths per 1000 population in a year

14. Around the globe, the flow of migration is generally from: (599)
    a.   most Industrialized Nations to Least Industrialized Nations
    b.   one of the Least Industrialized Nation to another one.
    c.   least Industrialized Nations to Industrializing Nations.
    d.   least Industrialized Nations to Most Industrialized Nations.

15. Which country has the highest number of immigrants to the U.S.? (600)
    a.   China
    b.   Italy
    c.   Spain
    d.   Mexico

16. According to your text, why is it difficult to forecast population growth? (600)
    a.   government programs may encourage or discourage women from having children.
    b.   government bureaus may be dishonest in reporting data.
    c.   there is a lack of computer programs to deal with data adequately.
    d.   births, deaths, and migration are human behaviors and thus impossible to predict.

17. In every country that strongly industrializes, which of the following results? (601)
    a.   children become less expensive.
    b.   the birth rate declincs.
    c.   the growth rate increases.
    d.   children have a shorter period of time of being dependent on their parents.

18. The process by which an increasing proportion of a population lives in cities is: (606)
    a.   suburbanization.
    b.   gentrification.
    c.   megalopolitanism.
    d.   urbanization.

19. What term is used for cities that have grown so large and have so much influence over a region? (606)
    a.   suburb.
    b.   central city.
    c.   megacity.
    d.   metropolis.

20. By what year did half of Americans live in cities? (606)
    a.   1840
    b.   1900
    c.   1920
    d.   1942

21. A "shrinking city" is likely to be found in which state? (608)
    a. New York
    b. Minnesota
    c. Utah
    d. Florida

22. The study of how people adapt to their environment is known as: (610)
    a. human ecology
    b. sociology
    c. biology
    d. psychology

23. When a new group of immigrants enter a city, they tend to settle in low-rent areas. As their numbers increase, those already living in the area begin to move out; their departure creates more low-cost housing for the immigrants. Sociologists refer to this process as: (611)
    a. progressive population replacement.
    b. reverse gentrification.
    c. cycle of assimilation.
    d. invasion-succession cycle.

24. The model that suggests that land use in cities is based on several centers, such as a clustering of restaurants or automobile dealerships is the: (611)
    a. sector model.
    b. concentric-zone model.
    c. multiple-nuclei model.
    d. commerce model.

25. Which category of people is **least** likely to live in an American city by choice? (615)
    a. cosmopolites
    b. the deprived
    c. single people
    d. ethnic villagers

Answer Key

1.   A
2.   C
3.   D
4.   D
5.   C
6.   B
7.   A
8.   A
9.   B
10.   C
11.   C
12.   D
13.   B
14.   D
15.   D
16.   A
17.   B
18.   D
19.   D
20.   C
21.   D
22.   A
23.   D
24.   C
25.   B

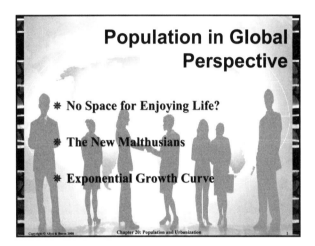

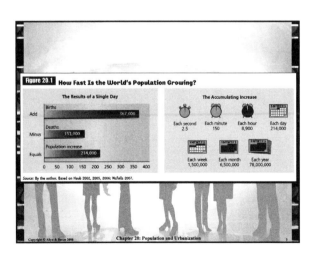

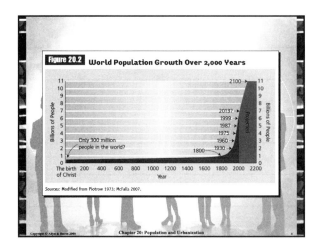

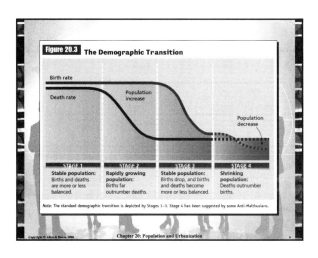

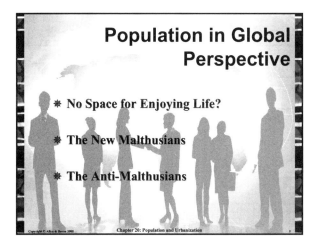

Population in Global Perspective

❋ No Space for Enjoying Life?

❋ The New Malthusians

❋ The Anti-Malthusians

❋ Who is Correct?

Copyright © Allyn & Bacon 2008   Chapter 20: Population and Urbanization   7

_____

_____

_____

_____

_____

_____

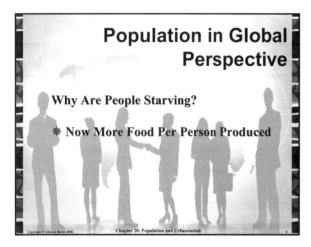

Population in Global Perspective

Why Are People Starving?

❋ Now More Food Per Person Produced

Copyright © Allyn & Bacon 2008   Chapter 20: Population and Urbanization   8

_____

_____

_____

_____

_____

_____

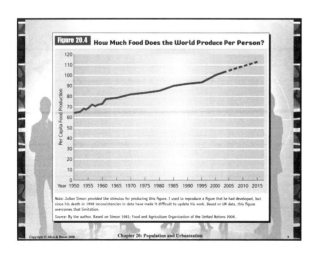

Figure 20.4 How Much Food Does the World Produce Per Person?

Note: Julian Simon provided the stimulus for producing this figure. I used to reproduce a figure that he had developed, but since his death in 1998 inconsistencies in data have made it difficult to update his work. Based on UN data, this figure overcomes that limitation.

Source: By the author. Based on Simon 1981; Food and Agriculture Organization of the United Nations 2006.

Copyright © Allyn & Bacon 2008   Chapter 20: Population and Urbanization   9

_____

_____

_____

_____

_____

_____

Population in Global Perspective

Why Are People Starving?

* ❋ Now More Food Per Person Produced

* ❋ Starvation Occurs in Particular Places

* ❋ Droughts

* ❋ Wars

Copyright © Allyn & Bacon 2008   Chapter 20: Population and Urbanization   10

_____

_____

_____

_____

_____

_____

Population Growth

Why Do Least Industrialized Nations

Have So Many Children?

Copyright © Allyn & Bacon 2008   Chapter 20: Population and Urbanization   11

_____

_____

_____

_____

_____

_____

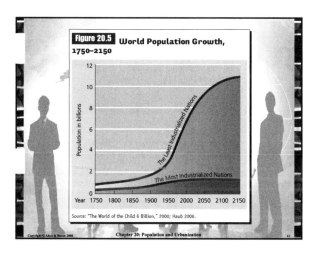

Figure 20.5 World Population Growth, 1750–2150

Population in billions (y-axis: 0, 2, 4, 6, 8, 10, 12)

The Least Industrialized Nations

The Most Industrialized Nations

Year 1750 1800 1850 1900 1950 2000 2050 2100 2150

Source: "The World of the Child 6 Billion," 2000; Haub 2006.

Copyright © Allyn & Bacon 2008   Chapter 20: Population and Urbanization   12

_____

_____

_____

_____

_____

_____

Population Growth

Why Do Least Industrialized Nations Have So Many Children?

❋ Status of Parenthood

❋ Community Support

❋ Reliance on Children in Old Age

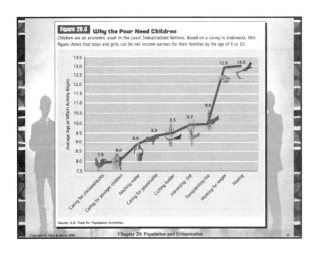

Figure 20.6 **Why the Poor Need Children** Children are an economic asset in the Least Industrialized Nations. Based on a survey in Indonesia, this figure shows that boys and girls can be net income earners for their families by the age of 9 or 10.

Population Growth

Implications of Different Growth Rates

❋ Population Pyramids

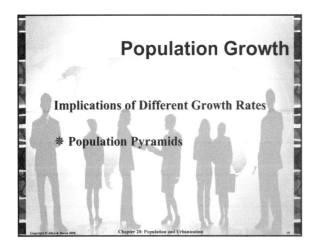

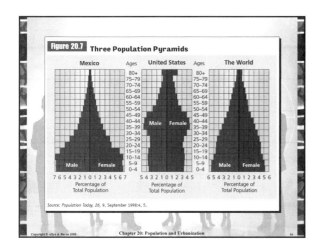

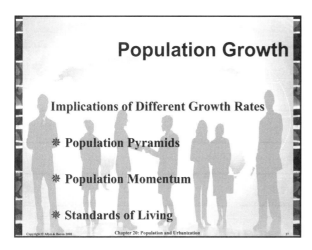

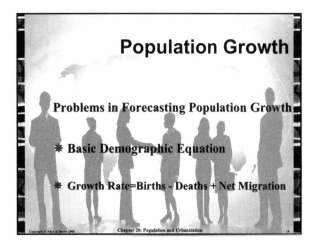

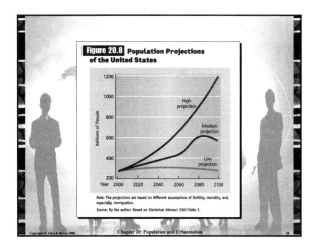

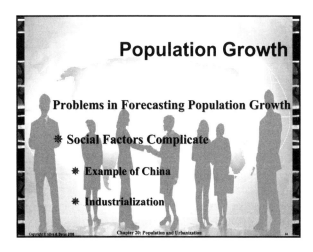

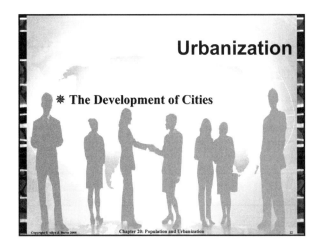

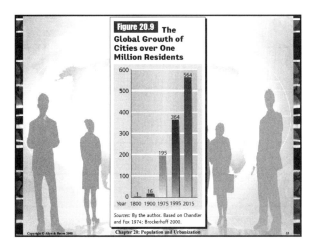

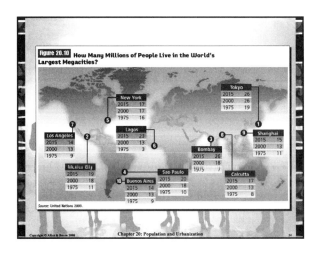

Urbanization

❋ **The Development of Cities**

❋ **The Process of Urbanization**

   ❋ **Metropolises**

   ❋ **Megalopolises**

Chapter 20: Population and Urbanization   25

Urbanization

❋ **U.S. Urban Patterns**

   ❋ **From Country to City**

   ❋ **From City to City**

   ❋ **Between Cities**

   ❋ **Within the City**

   ❋ **From City to Suburb**

   ❋ **Smaller Centers**

❋ **The Rural Rebound**

Chapter 20: Population and Urbanization   26

Figure 20.11 How Urban Is Your State?
The Rural-Urban Makeup of the United States

The most rural states: 38% to 63% urban
Average states: 65% to 78% urban
The most urban states: 80% to 94% urban

Note: The most rural state is Vermont (38% urban). The most urban states are California and New Jersey (94% urban).
Source: By the author. Based on *Statistical Abstract* 2007:Table 33.

Chapter 20: Population and Urbanization   27

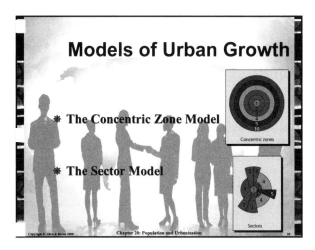

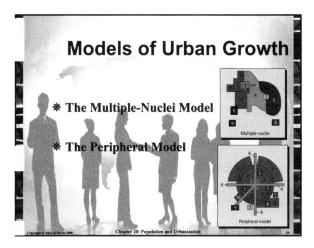

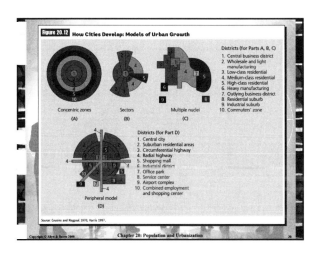

Models of Urban Growth

Critique of the Models

❋ They are Time-Bound

❋ They Do Not Account for
Urban Planning

❋ Fall Short with Cities in Least
Industrialized Nations

Copyright © Allyn & Bacon 2008　　　Chapter 20: Population and Urbanization　　　31

City Life

❋ Alienation in the City

　❋ Impersonality and Self-Interest

　❋ Kitty Genovese

　❋ Cities Undermine Kinship and Neighborhood
　　Relationships

❋ Community in the City

　❋ Gans Research

Copyright © Allyn & Bacon 2008　　　Chapter 20: Population and Urbanization　　　32

City Life

Urban Sentiment: Finding a Familiar World

❋ City Divided into Little Worlds

❋ People Create Intimacy by Personalizing
Shopping

Copyright © Allyn & Bacon 2008　　　Chapter 20: Population and Urbanization　　　33

City Life

Types of Urban Dwellers
- ❋ The Cosmopolites
- ❋ The Singles
- ❋ The Ethnic Villagers
- ❋ The Deprived
- ❋ The Trapped

Copyright © Allyn & Bacon 2008   Chapter 20: Population and Urbanization   34

City Life

- ❋ Norm of Noninvolvement
- ❋ Diffusion of Responsibility

Copyright © Allyn & Bacon 2008   Chapter 20: Population and Urbanization   35

Urban Problems and Social Policy

Suburbanization
- ❋ Movement of People from Cities to Suburbs
- ❋ City Centers Lose in Transition
- ❋ City vs. Suburb

Copyright © Allyn & Bacon 2008   Chapter 20: Population and Urbanization   36

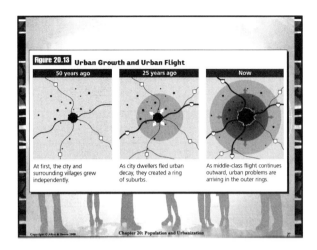

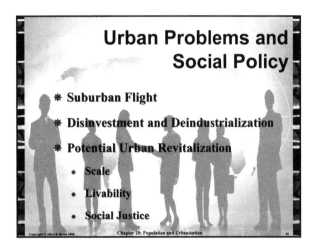

CHAPTER 21
COLLECTIVE BEHAVIOR AND SOCIAL MOVEMENTS

CHAPTER SUMMARY

- Early theorists argued that individuals are transformed by crowds, losing all capacity for rationality. According to Herbert Blumer, crowds go through five stages before they become an acting crowd: social unrest, an exciting event, milling, a common object of attention, and common impulses.

- Contemporary explanations emphasize the rationality of the crowd, the emergence of norms to govern behavior; collective behavior is seen as directed toward a goal, even if it is cruel and destructive behavior.

- Some of the major forms of collective behavior are lynchings, riots, panics, moral panics, mass hysteria, rumors, fads, fashions, and urban legends. Conditions of discontent and uncertainty provide fertile ground for collective behavior.

- Social movements usually involve more people, are more prolonged, are more organized, and focus on social change. Depending on whether their target is individuals or society and the amount of change desired is partial or complete, social movements can be classified as alterative, redemptive, reformative, or transformative. Some social movements have a global orientation and are known as transnational social movements. Metaformative social movements are a rare type of social movement.

- Tactics are chosen on the basis of a group's levels of membership, its publics, and its relationship to authority. Other factors that may be important are friendship, race-ethnicity, and size of town. Because the mass media are the gatekeepers, their favorable or unfavorable coverage greatly affects a social movement's choice of tactics.

- Mass society theory, relative deprivation theory, and ideological commitment theory all attempt to explain why people join social movements. Agent provocateurs are a unique type of participant in social movements.

- Social movements go through distinct stages. Resource mobilization theory accounts for why some social movements never get off the ground while others enjoy great success. To succeed, social movements must focus on broad concerns, which are generally deeply embedded in society and do not lend themselves to easy solutions.

LEARNING OBJECTIVES

After reading Chapter 21, you should be able to:

1. Discuss early explanations of collective behavior, focusing on how the crowd transforms the individual. (624-625)
2. Know the five stages that crowds go through before they become an acting crowd, as identified by Herbert Blumer. (625-626)
3. Understand contemporary views of collective behavior including the minimax strategy and emergent norms. (626)
4. Identify the five kinds of crowd participants, as pointed out by Ralph Turner and Lewis Killian. (627)
5. Discuss and provide examples of collective behavior including riots, rumors, panics and mass hysteria, moral panics, fads and fashions, and urban legends. (627-636)
6. Describe what a social movement is and differentiate between proactive and reactive social movements. (636)
7. Identify and contrast the different types of social movements. (637-638)
8. Discuss the tactics that social movements employ and how and why these tactics are chosen. (638-639)
9. Describe the role that propaganda and the mass media play in helping to determine the effectiveness of social movements. (639-642)
10. Evaluate the different theories that explain why people are attracted to social movements, and the conditions that underlie their attraction. (642-645)
11. Discuss the special role of the agent provocateur in some social movements. (645)
12. Identify the five stages of social movements. (646)
13. Discuss what social movements need to do to succeed and explain why most social movements are unsuccessful. (646-648)

KEY TERMS

After studying the chapter, review the definition for each of the following terms.

acting crowd: an excited group of people who move toward a goal (625)

agent provocateur: someone who joins a group in order to spy on it and to sabotage it by provoking its members to commit illegal acts (645)

alterative social movement: a social movement that seeks to alter only particular aspects of people (637)

cargo cult: a social movement in which South Pacific islanders destroyed their possessions in the anticipation that their ancestors would ship them new goods (637)

circular reaction: Robert Park's term for a back-and-forth communication between the members of a crowd whereby a "collective impulse" is transmitted (625)

collective behavior: extraordinary activities carried out by groups of people; includes lynchings, rumors, panics, urban legends, and fads and fashions (624)

collective mind: Gustave LeBon's term for the tendency of people in a crowd to feel, think, and act in unusual ways (624)

emergent norms: Ralph Turner and Lewis Killian's term for the idea that people develop new norms to cope with a new situation; used to explain crowd behavior (626)

fad: a temporary pattern of behavior that catches people's attention (634)

fashion: a pattern of behavior that catches people's attention and lasts longer than a fad (635)

mass hysteria: an imagined threat that causes physical symptoms among a large number of people (633)

mass society: industrialized, highly bureaucratized, impersonal society (642)

mass society theory: an explanation for why people participate in a social movement based on the assumption that the movement offers them a sense of belonging (642)

metaformative social movement: a social movement that has the goal to change the social order not just of a country or two, but of a civilization, or even the entire world. (638)

millenarian social movement: a social movement based on the prophecy of coming social upheaval (637)

milling: a crowd standing or walking around as they talk excitedly about some event (626)

minimax strategy: Richard Berk's term for the effort people make to minimize their costs and maximize their rewards (626)

moral panic: a fear that grips a large number of people that some evil threatens the well-being of society, followed by hostility, sometimes violence, toward those thought responsible (634)

panic: the condition of being so fearful that one cannot function normally, and may even flee (630)

proactive social movement: a social movement that promotes some social change (636)

propaganda: in its broad sense, the presentation of information in the attempt to influence people; in its narrow sense, one-sided information used to try to influence people (642)

public: in this context, a dispersed group of people relevant to a social movement; the sympathetic and hostile publics have an interest in the issues on which a social movement focuses; there is also an unaware or indifferent public (638)

public opinion: how people think about some issue (639)

reactive social movement: a social movement that resists some social change (636)

redemptive social movement: a social movement that seeks to change people totally, to redeem them (637)

reformative social movement: a social movement that seeks to change only particular aspects of society (637)

relative deprivation theory: in this context, the belief that people join social movements based on their evaluations of what they think they should have compared with what others have (644)

resource mobilization: a theory that social movements succeed or fail based on their ability to mobilize resources such as time, money, and people's skills (646)

riot: violent crowd behavior aimed against people and property (627)

role extension: the incorporation of additional activities into a role (633)

rumor: unfounded information spread among people (629)

social movement: a large group of people who are organized to promote or resist social change (636)

social movement organization: an organization to promote the goals of a social movement (636)

transformative social movement: a social movement that seeks to change society totally, to transform it (637)

transnational social movement: social movements with a new emphasis on some condition in the world, instead of on a condition in a specific country; also known as *new social movements* (637)

urban legend: a story with an ironic twist that sounds realistic but is false (635)

KEY PEOPLE

Review the major theoretical contributions or findings of these people.

William Banbridge: This sociologist found that some people did become frightened after the broadcast of "War of the Worlds" and a few even got into their cars and drove like maniacs, but most of the panic was an invention of the news media. (631)

Richard Berk: Berk developed the minimax strategy to explain collective behavior; people are more likely to act when costs are low and anticipated rewards high. (626)

Herbert Blumer: Blumer identified five stages that precede the emergence of an active crowd. These are tension or unrest, an exciting event, milling, a common object of attention, and common impulses. (625)

Jan Brunvand: This folklorist studied urban legends and suggests that they are modern morality stories. (635)

Hadley Cantril: This psychologist suggests that people panicked after hearing the famous "War of the Worlds" because of widespread anxiety about world conditions. (630)

James Jasper and Dorothy Nelkin: These sociologists argue that many become involved in social movements because of moral issues and an ideological commitment. (644)

Drue Johnston and Norris Johnson: These sociologists studied the behavior of employees during the Beverly Hills Supper Club fire and found that most continued to carry out their roles. (633)

William Kornhauser: Kornhauser proposed mass society theory to explain why people are attracted to social movements. He suggested that these movements fill a void in some people's lives by offering them a sense of belonging. (642)

Gustave LeBon: LeBon argued that a collective mind develops within a crowd, and people are swept away by any suggestion that is made. (624)

Alfred and Elizabeth Lee: These sociologists found that propaganda relies on seven basic techniques, which they labeled "tricks of the trade." (643)

John Lofland: He noted that fashion can also apply to common expressions that change little over time. (635)

Charles Mackay: Mackay was the first to study collective behavior; he suggested that a "herd mentality" takes over and explains the disgraceful things people do when in crowds. (624)

Gary Marx: This sociologist investigated the agent provocateur and found that some are converted to the movement because they share some of the same social characteristics as the movement's members. (645)

Doug McAdam: McAdam challenged the mass society theory on the basis of research findings related to people's decision to become involved in the civil rights struggle. He found they were well integrated into society rather than isolated from it, as mass society theory suggests. (642,644)

John McCarthy and Mayer Zald: They point out that even though people may be upset about a condition in society, without resource mobilization they do not constitute a social movement. (646)

Clark McPhail: This sociologist studied the behavior of crowds, noting that the behavior of crowd participants is cooperative. (626)

Robert Park: Park suggested that social unrest is the result of the circular reaction of people in crowds. (625)

Victor Rodriguez: This sociologist suggests that minorities in the middle class might participate in riots when they feel frustrated with being treated as second-class citizens even when they are employed and living stable lives. (628)

Ellen Scott: Scott studied the movement to stop rape and found that close friendships, race, and even size of town are important in determining tactics. (639)

Alexis de Tocqueville: This 19th century observer of social life noted that people organize collectively to improve their conditions when they are experiencing relative deprivation rather than absolute deprivation. (644)

Ralph Turner and Lewis Killian: These sociologists use the term "emergent norm" to explain the rules that emerge in collective behavior. They note that crowds have at least five kinds of participants: the ego-involved; the concerned; the insecure; the curious spectators; and the exploiters. (626-627)

PRACTICE TEST

1. Lynching is an example of: (624)
    a. collective behavior.
    b. group behavior.
    c. milling.
    d. a directed group.

2. Which of the following correctly sequences the stages for "acting" crowd behavior? (625-626)
    a. social unrest, exciting event, milling behavior, common object
    b. common object, common impulses, milling behavior, exciting event
    c. social unrest, common impulses, milling behavior, common object
    d. exciting event, social unrest, common impulses, common object

3. When people stand or walk around talking about the exciting event this is known as: (626)
    a. a circular reaction.
    b. milling.
    c. an acting crowd.
    d. a collective mind.

4. When people in a crowd get common impulses, these are stimulated by: (626)
    a. an aggressive leader.
    b. those who have started the unrest.
    c. those who are most passive.
    d. a sense of excitement passed from one person to another.

5. Richard Berk used the term "minimax strategy" to describe the tendency for: (626)
    a. crowds to operate with a minimum of strategy.
    b. for humans to minimize costs and maximize rewards.
    c. those in authority to maximize the costs of an action in order to minimize rewards.
    d. society to respond to even the most minimum of social movements.

6. The development of new norms to cope with a new situation is: (626)
    a. emergent norms.
    b. developmental norms.
    c. surfacing norms.
    d. none of the above.

7.   According to Turner and Killian, which crowd participant's role is most   important? (627)
      a.   the ego-involved
      b.   the concerned
      c.   the curious spectators
      d.   the exploiters

8.   Sociological research on riot behavior has shown that: (627)
      a.   only the deprived participate in riots.
      b.   the usual background conditions of riots are a low degree of frustration, but a high degree of anger.
      c.   precipitating events can bring collective violence to the surface.
      d.   riots usually never stem from a precipitating event.

9.   Information passed from one person to another about subliminal message in Disney movies is an example of: (629)
      a.   hearsay.
      b.   scuttlebutt.
      c.   a rumor.
      d.   gossip.

10.   People believe in rumors for all of the following reasons EXCEPT that: (629)
      a.   rumors deal with a subject that is important to the individual.
      b.   rumors give power to the person communicating the rumor.
      c.   rumors replace ambiguity with some form of certainty.
      d.   rumors are attributed to a credible source.

11.   Research has found that when panic occurs in a threatening situation: (631)
      a.   primary group bonds break down.
      b.   not everyone panics.
      c.   gender roles break down.
      d.   work roles break down.

12.   An imagined threat that causes physical symptoms among a large number of people is: (633)
      a.   collective mind.
      b.   panic.
      c.   mass hysteria.
      d.   circular reaction.

13.   Which statement about moral panics is *incorrect*? (634)
      a.   moral panics occur when people are concerned about something viewed as immoral.
      b.   moral panics are generally based on an event that has been verified as true.
      c.   moral panics thrive on uncertainty and anxiety.
      d.   moral panics are fueled by the mass media.

14. "Tickle Me Elmo" and Beanie Babies were: (634)
    a.   fashions
    b.   fads
    c.   styles
    d.   trends

15. Which of the following would be an example of a fashion? (635)
    a.   the bungalow house
    b.   mini skirts
    c.   the use of the word "cool"
    d.   all of the above.

16. A social movement that promotes social change is a: (636)
    a.   reactive social movement.
    b.   proactive social movement.
    c.   redemptive social movement.
    d.   reformative social movement.

17. When the Women's Christian Temperance Union tried to get people to stop drinking alcohol, what type of social movement was this? (637)
    a.   redemptive social movement.
    b.   reformative social movement.
    c.   alterative social movement.
    d.   nihilistic movement.

18. Research shows that when social movements become institutionalized: (639)
    a.   violence will not be directed against authorities.
    b.   leaders of social movements no longer pay attention to "publics."
    c.   "publics" become a focused group of people with a common interest.
    d.   violence is not used against the opposition.

19. Propaganda is best defined as: (642)
    a.   the presentation of untrue information in an attempt to influence people.
    b.   the presentation of information in an attempt to influence people.
    c.   unfair coercion.
    d.   illegal forms of persuasion.

20. The mass media: (642)
    a.   is the gatekeepers to social movements.
    b.   engage in biased reporting, controlled by people who have an agenda to get across.
    c.   is sympathetic to some social movements, while ignoring others; it all depends on their individual biases.
    d.   all of the above

21. Which of the following is not one of the seven basic techniques of propaganda?   (643)
    a.   tricks of the trade.
    b.   name calling.
    c.   card stacking.
    d.   testimonials.

22. We will miss the basic reason for people's involvement in social movements if we overlook: (644)
    a.   the sense of belonging.
    b.   deprivation issues.
    c.   the moral issue.
    d.   people's identity needs.

23. Research on *agent provocateurs* shows that such agents: (645)
    a   work their way into the center of the group.
    b.   seldom share common group characteristics such as social class or age.
    c.   promote activities of the group at the expense of succeeding as agents.
    d.   never allow themselves to provoke illegal activities.

24. At which stage of a movement do social leaders emerge? (646)
    a.   initial unrest and agitation
    b.   institutionalization
    c.   resource mobilization
    d.   organization

25. The crucial stage for social movements to continue beyond the initial stage is: (646)
    a.   initial agitation and unrest.
    b.   institutionalization and unrest.
    c.   resource mobilization.
    d.   organization.

Answer Key

1.   A
2.   A
3.   B
4.   D
5.   B
6.   A
7.   A
8.   C
9.   C
10.   B
11.   B
12.   C
13.   B
14.   B
15.   C
16.   B
17.   C
18.   A
19.   B
20.   D
21.   A
22.   C
23.   A
24.   A
25.   C

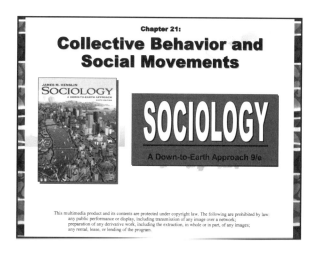

Chapter 21:
Collective Behavior and Social Movements

SOCIOLOGY

A Down-to-Earth Approach 9/e

This multimedia product and its contents are protected under copyright law. The following are prohibited by law: any public performance or display, including transmission of any image over a network; preparation of any derivative work, including the extraction, in whole or in part, of any images; any rental, lease, or lending of the program.

Collective Behavior: Early Explanations

The Transformation of the Individual

✳ How the Crowd Transforms the Individual

✳ Charles Mackay

• Herd Mentality

Copyright © Allyn & Bacon 2008   Chapter 21: Collective Behavior and Social Movements   2

Collective Behavior: Early Explanations

The Transformation of the Individual

✳ How the Crowd Transforms the Individual

✳ Gustave LeBon

• Collective Mind

Copyright © Allyn & Bacon 2008   Chapter 21: Collective Behavior and Social Movements   3

Collective Behavior: Early Explanations

The Transformation of the Individual

✳ How the Crowd Transforms the Individual

✳ Robert Park

  ✳ Circular Reaction

Copyright © Allyn & Bacon 2008   Chapter 21: Collective Behavior and Social Movements   4

Collective Behavior

The Acting Crowd - Five Stages

✳ Tension or Unrest

✳ Exciting Event

✳ Milling Behavior

✳ Common Object

✳ Common Impulses

Copyright © Allyn & Bacon 2008   Chapter 21: Collective Behavior and Social Movements   5

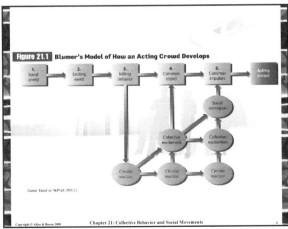

Figure 21.1 Blumer's Model of How an Acting Crowd Develops

Source: Based on McPhail 1991:11.

Copyright © Allyn & Bacon 2008   Chapter 21: Collective Behavior and Social Movements   6

Contemporary View: The Rationality of the Crowd

❋ **The Minimax Strategy**

❋ **Emergent Norms—Five Kinds of Participants**

  • **The Ego-Involved**

  • **The Concerned**

  • **The Insecure**

  • **The Curious Spectators**

  • **The Exploiters**

Copyright © Allyn & Bacon 2008   Chapter 21: Collective Behavior and Social Movements   7

Forms of Collective Behavior

Riots

❋ **Background Conditions**

❋ **Precipitating Event**

❋ **General Context**

Copyright © Allyn & Bacon 2008   Chapter 21: Collective Behavior and Social Movements   8

Forms of Collective Behavior

Rumors

❋ **Short-Lived**

❋ **Replace Ambiguity or Uncertainty**

❋ **Of Little Consequence**

❋ **Pass from Person to Person**

Copyright © Allyn & Bacon 2008   Chapter 21: Collective Behavior and Social Movements   9

Forms of Collective Behavior

Panics and Mass Hysteria

❋ **The Classic Panic**

❋ **The Occurrence of Panics**

❋ **Not Everyone Panics**

Chapter 21: Collective Behavior and Social Movements

Forms of Collective Behavior

❋ **Moral Panics**

❋ **Fads and Fashions**

❋ **Urban Legends**

Chapter 21: Collective Behavior and Social Movements

Social Movements

❋ **Proactive Social Movements**

❋ **Reactive Social Movements**

❋ **Social Movement Organizations**

Chapter 21: Collective Behavior and Social Movements

Types of Social Movements

❋ **Alternative Social Movements**

❋ **Redemptive Social Movements**

❋ **Reformative Social Movements**

Copyright © Allyn & Bacon 2008   Chapter 21: Collective Behavior and Social Movements   13

Types of Social Movements

❋ **Transformative Social Movements**

❋ **Millenarian Social Movements**

❋ **Transnational Social Movements**

❋ **Metaformative Social Movements**

Copyright © Allyn & Bacon 2008   Chapter 21: Collective Behavior and Social Movements   14

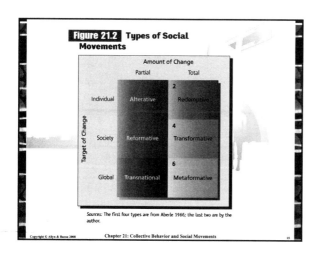

Figure 21.2 Types of Social Movements

	Amount of Change	
Target of Change	Partial	Total
Individual	Alterative	2 Redemptive
Society	Reformative	4 Transformative
Global	Transnational	6 Metaformative

Sources: The first four types are from Aberle 1966; the last two are by the author.

Copyright © Allyn & Bacon 2008   Chapter 21: Collective Behavior and Social Movements   15

Tactics of Social Movements

Levels of Membership

✻ The Inner Core

✻ The Committed

✻ The Less Committed

Copyright © Allyn & Bacon 2008 — Chapter 21: Collective Behavior and Social Movements — 16

Tactics of Social Movements

The Publics

✻ Sympathetic Public

✻ Hostile Public

✻ Disinterested Public

Copyright © Allyn & Bacon 2008 — Chapter 21: Collective Behavior and Social Movements — 17

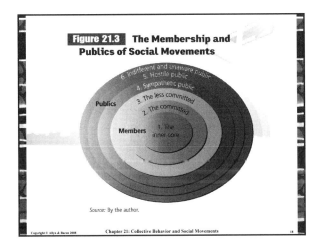

Figure 21.3 The Membership and Publics of Social Movements

6. Indifferent and unaware public
5. Hostile public
4. Sympathetic public
3. The less committed
2. The committed
1. The inner core

Publics

Members

Source: By the author.

Copyright © Allyn & Bacon 2008 — Chapter 21: Collective Behavior and Social Movements — 18

Tactics of Social Movements

❋ Relationship to Authorities

❋ Other Factors

Copyright © Allyn & Bacon 2008   Chapter 21: Collective Behavior and Social Movements   19

Propaganda and the Mass Media

❋ Name-Calling

❋ Glittering Generality

❋ Transfer

❋ Testimonials

Copyright © Allyn & Bacon 2008   Chapter 21: Collective Behavior and Social Movements   20

Propaganda and the Mass Media

❋ Plain Folks

❋ Card Stacking

❋ Bandwagon

Copyright © Allyn & Bacon 2008   Chapter 21: Collective Behavior and Social Movements   21

Why People Join Social Movements

✳ Mass Society Theory

✳ Deprivation Theory

Copyright © Allyn & Bacon 2008   Chapter 21: Collective Behavior and Social Movements   22

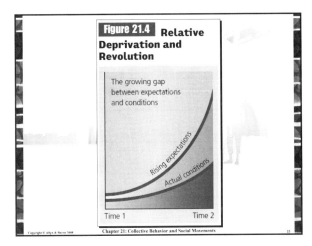

Figure 21.4 Relative Deprivation and Revolution

The growing gap between expectations and conditions

Rising expectations

Actual conditions

Time 1   Time 2

Copyright © Allyn & Bacon 2008   Chapter 21: Collective Behavior and Social Movements   23

Why People Join Social Movements

✳ Mass Society Theory

✳ Deprivation Theory

✳ Moral Issues and Ideological Commitment

✳ Agent Provocateur

Copyright © Allyn & Bacon 2008   Chapter 21: Collective Behavior and Social Movements   24

Success and Failure of Social Movements
Five Stages

❋ Initial Unrest and Agitation

❋ Resource Mobilization

❋ Organization

❋ Institutionalization

❋ Organizational Decline and

Possible Resurgence

Copyright © Allyn & Bacon 2008   Chapter 21: Collective Behavior and Social Movements   25

_____

_____

_____

_____

_____

_____

_____

Success and Failure of Social Movements

❋ Rocky Road to Success

❋ Social Movements Rarely

Solve Social Problems

❋ Many Social Movements

Affect Society

Copyright © Allyn & Bacon 2008   Chapter 21: Collective Behavior and Social Movements   26

_____

_____

_____

_____

_____

_____

_____

Chapter 21:
Collective Behavior and Social Movements

SOCIOLOGY

A Down-to-Earth Approach 9/e

_____

_____

_____

_____

_____

_____

CHAPTER 22
SOCIAL CHANGE AND THE ENVIRONMENT

CHAPTER SUMMARY

- Social change, the alteration of culture and society over time, is a vital part of social life. Social change has included four social revolutions: domestication, agriculture, industrialization, and information; the change from *Gemeinschaft* to *Gesellschaft* societies; capitalism and industrialization; modernization; and global stratification.

- One of the most significant changes has been the shifting arrangement of power among nations. This includes a change from G-7 to G-9, dividing up the world's markets, threats to G-8, connections with Africa, and advances in information technology.

- Theories of social change include evolutionary theories; cyclical theories; and conflict theories. William Ogburn identified technology as the basis cause of social change. The processes of social change are invention, discovery, and diffusion.

- Technology is a driving force in social change, and it can shape an entire society by changing existing technology, social organization, ideology, values, and social relationships. This is evident when examining the impact of the automobile and the computer. It is possibly that the changes in technology could perpetuate present inequalities nationally. It is possible that it will do the same on a global level.

- Social change has often had a negative impact on the natural environment. Today we face problems such as acid rain, global warming, and the greenhouse effect. Environmental problems are worldwide, brought about by industrial production and urbanization, the pressures of population growth, and inadequate environmental regulation. The world today is facing a basic conflict between the lust for profits through the exploitation of the world's resources and the need to produce a sustainable environment.

- A worldwide environmental movement has emerged, which seeks solutions in education, legislation, and political activism. Green parties are political parties which have emerged that focus on environmental concerns.

- Environmental sociology is the study of the relationship between human societies and the environment. Its goal is not to stop pollution or nuclear power, but rather to study the affects of human on the physical environment and its affects on humans.

- If we are to survive, we must seek harmony between technology and the environment. It is essential that we reduce or eliminate the harm that technology does to the environment.

LEARNING OBJECTIVES
After reading Chapter 22, you should be able:

1. Describe the social transformation of society in terms of the four major social revolutions; the shift from *Gemeinschaft* to *Gesellschaft* societies; and the development of capitalism, industrialization and modernization. (652-653)
2. Discuss conflict, power, and global politics among nations. (654-656)
3. Identify and evaluate the different theories of social change, including cultural evolution, natural cycles, conflict theory, and William Ogburn's processes of invention, discovery, and diffusion. (656-658)
4. Define cultural lag and provide examples of it along with an evaluation of Ogburn's theory (658-659)
5. Discuss the various ways that technological innovations are able to change society including changes in social organization, ideology, conspicuous consumption, and social relationships. (660-661)
6. Discuss the far reaching impact of the automobile on cities, farm life and villages, architecture, courtship and sexual norms, and women's roles. (661-663)
7. Discuss the far reaching impact that the computer has had on education, the workplace, business and finance, and national and global stratification. (664-666)
8. Describe how the globalization of capitalism contributes to environmental decay. (667-668)
9. Identify and compare the environmental problems of the Most Industrialized Nations, the Industrializing Nations, and the Least Industrialized Nations. (668-671)
10. Discuss the goals and activities of the environmental movement. (671)
11. Identify the main assumptions of environmental sociology. (672-674)
12. Suggest ways to achieve harmony between technology and the environment. (674)

KEY TERMS
After studying the chapter, review the definition of each of the following terms.

acid rain: rain containing sulfuric and nitric acid (burning fossil fuels releases sulfur dioxide and nitrogen oxide which become sulfuric and nitric acids when they react with moisture in the air) (668)

alienation: Marx's term for workers' lack of connection to the product of their labor; caused by their being assigned repetitive tasks on a small part of a product—this leads to a sense of powerlessness and normlessness; others use the term in the general sense of not feeling a part of something (660)

corporate welfare: the gifts or financial incentives (tax breaks, subsidies, and even land and stadiums) given to corporations in order to attract them to an area or induce them to remain (669)

cultural lag: Ogburn's term for human behavior lagging behind technological innovation (658)

dialectical process: (of history) each arrangement, or thesis, contains contradictions, or antitheses, which must be resolved; the new arrangement, or synthesis, contains its own contradictions, and so on (657)

diffusion: the spread of invention or discovery from one area to another; identified by William Ogburn as one of three processes of social change (658)

discovery: a new way of seeing reality; identified by William Ogburn as one of three processes of social change (658)

ecosabotage: actions taken to sabotage the efforts of people thought to be legally harming the environment (671)

environmental injustice: refers to the pollution of our environment affecting minorities and the poor the most (670)

environmental sociology: a specialty within sociology where the focus is the relationship between human societies and the environment (672)

global warming: an increase in the earth's temperature due to the greenhouse effect (669)

greenhouse effect: the buildup of carbon dioxide in the earth's atmosphere that allows light to enter but inhibits the release of heat; believed to cause global warming (668)

invention: the combination of existing elements and materials to form new ones; identified by William Ogburn as the first of three processes of social change (658)

modernization: the transformation of traditional societies into industrial societies (653)

postmodern society: another term for postindustrial society; its chief characteristic is the use of tools that extend the human abilities to gather and analyze information, to communicate, and to travel (660)

social change: the alteration of culture and societies over time (652)

sustainable environment: a world system that takes into account the limits of the environment, produces enough material goods for everyone's needs, and leaves a heritage of a sound environment for the next generation (668)

KEY PEOPLE

Review the major theoretical contributions or findings of these people.

James Flink: A historian that noted that the automobile changed women "from producers of food and clothing onto consumer of prepared foods and ready-made clothes." (663)

Karl Marx: He noted that capitalism set in motion an antagonistic relationship between capitalists and workers that remain today. Marx developed the theory of dialectical materialism. (652, 657, 660-661)

Lewis Henry Morgan: Morgan's theory of social development once dominated Western thought. He suggested that societies pass through three stages: savagery, barbarism, and civilization. (656)

William Ogburn: Ogburn identified three processes of social change: invention, discovery, and diffusion. He also coined the term "cultural lag" to describe a situation in which some elements of culture adapt to an invention or discovery more rapidly than others. (657-659) y

Oswald Spengler: Spengler wrote *The Decline of the West* in which he proposed that Western civilization was declining. (656-657)

Arnold Toynbee: This historian suggested that each time a civilization successfully meets a challenge, oppositional forces are set up. Eventually, the oppositional forces are set loose, and the fabric of society is ripped apart. (657)

Max Weber: Weber argued that capitalism grew out of the Protestant Reformation. (653)

PRACTICE TEST

1.   The first social revolution refers to: (652)
    a.   the development of horticultural and pastoral societies.
    b.   the invention of the printing press.
    c.   the invention of the plow.
    d.   the invention of the steam engine.

2.   What did Karl Marx see as the cause of societies changing from *Gemeinschaft* to *Gesellschaft*? (652)
    a.   stagnation and population growth
    b.   capitalism
    c.   advances in technology
    d.   economic surplus

3.   Which sociologist felt that the rise of capitalism was linked with the Protestant reformation in Europe? (653)
    a.   Emile Durkheim
    b.   Karl Marx
    c.   Edwin Sutherland
    d.   Max Weber

4.   All of the following are correct pairings of Weber's ideal type of traditional societies versus modern societies EXCEPT: (654)
    a.   absolute versus relativistic.
    b.   more ascribed versus more achieved.
    c.   nuclear versus extended.
    d.   simple versus complex.

5.   Which country will soon be included to be G-9? (655)
    a.   China.
    b.   Peru.
    c.   Nigeria.
    d.   Australia.

6.   Which country threatened to aim its missiles at Europe for retaliation for the U.S. plan to put missiles in Poland? (655)
    a.   China
    b.   Russia
    c.   Egypt
    d.   Mexico

7.   Cultural evolution: (656)
    a.   includes only unilinear theories.
    b.   assumes that unilinear theories are superior to multilinear theories.
    c.   assumes that all societies proceed through the same sequence of stages towards industrialization.
    d.   assumes cultural progress.

8.   What is the primary focus of cyclical theories of societal development? (656)
    a.   how both technology and agriculture influence a society's development
    b.   how societies evolve according to a set pattern of stages
    c.   how societies evolve along different patterns
    d.   how entire civilizations rise and fall

9.   Marx's notion of power in terms of its effect on society: (657)
    a.   assumes that a synthesis of power can never occur.
    b.   assumes that the dialectic process underlies the dynamics of history.
    c.   mandates that antithesis is not a fundamental process of change in power.
    d.   could never be applied to the dynamics of power exemplified by the G-8.

10.   A new way of seeing reality as a second process of change is known as: (658)
    a.   diffusion
    b.   discovery
    c.   invention
    d.   cultural lag

11.   Ogburn's analysis has been criticized because: (658)
    a.   it is too narrow in focus, not suitable for explaining the transformation of industrial into postindustrial societies.
    b.   it does not recognize the importance of technology for social change.
    c.   it places too great an emphasis on technology as the source for almost all social change.
    d.   it predicts that material culture will change in response to symbolic culture, when in fact it is symbolic culture that changes in response to material culture.

12.   Luddites are: (659)
    a.   a native Brazilian tribe.
    b.   an endangered species of tree.
    c.   people who oppose new technology.
    d.   members of a social movement opposing corporate welfare.

13.   The effect of technology on society is such that: (660)
    a.   technology can affect changes in social organization but not in ideology.
    b.   technology produces alienation, which leads to dissatisfaction and unrest.
    c.   technology affects social organization only during its initial introduction.
    d.   technology can never really reshape society in general.

14. Technology refers to: (660)
    a.   the tools needed to accomplish tasks
    b.   tools that alienate workers
    c.   diffusion of goods and services
    d.   none of the above

15. The fact that as men were drawn out of their homes to work in factories, family relationships changed is an example of: (661)
    a.   changes in social organizations produced by technology.
    b.   changes in social relationships produced by technology.
    c.   changes in ideologies produced by technology.
    d.   none of the above.

16. Which of the following is *not* one of the ways that computers are transforming education? (665)
    a.   they are making new areas of study available to students on-line.
    b.   they are changing the way that students learn.
    c.   they are increasing the opportunities for teachers and administrators to carry out surveillance on students.
    d.   they are expanding the gap in educational opportunities between wealthy school districts and poor school districts.

17. Which of the following will become a part of mainstream education. (665)
    a.   telecommunication
    b.   distance learning
    c.   teletransportation
    d.   all of the above

18. One concern about the expansion of the information superhighway is: (666)
    a.   interest in accessing it will outstrip capacity to carry so many users.
    b.   social inequalities will become greater, both on a national and global basis.
    c.   people will tie up the services with nonessential activities.
    d.   people will become even more alienated as they relate more and more through their computers and less and less face to face.

19. Which of the following is true about Star Wars? (667)
    a.   the Pentagon is building its own Internet.
    b.   robots are being used in Iraq.
    c.   the Defense Department is planning to "weaponize space."
    d.   all of the above.

20.   What is the name of the new space program from the Air Force? (667)
    a.   "Rods from God"
    b.   "Sticks from Mars"
    c.   "View from God"
    d.   "Space command"

21.   The consequence of burning fossil fuels is: (668)
    a.   acid rain.
    b.   the greenhouse effect.
    c.   global warming.
    d.   all of the above.

22.   Pollution of the natural environment is such that: (668)
    a.   it actually had its strongest impact on our species before the Industrial Revolution occurred.
    b.   the major polluters of the Earth are the Most Industrialized Nations.
    c.   Least Industrialized Nations produce more pollution than Most Industrialized Nations.
    d.   industrial growth added very little to existing pollution levels.

23.   What portion of a state is called "cancer alley"? (669)
    a.   Texas
    b.   New York
    c.   Louisiana
    d.   California.

24.   Pollution of the environment that affects minorities and the poor is knows as: (670)
    a.   environmental discrimination.
    b.   tactical discrimination
    c.   environmental injustice.
    d.   disabling discrimination.

25.   A sociological implication of the destruction of the Amazon rain forests is that: (671)
    a.   from early on, Western societies realized that tribal knowledge had great worth since it was not exclusively based on superstitious ideas.
    b.   Amazonian Indian tribes did not lose their ethnic identity or composition.
    c.   it destroyed certain plant species that are sources of healing medicines.
    d.   ethnocentrism is unrelated to the process of the destruction of rain forests.

Answer Key

1.   A
2.   B
3.   D
4.   C
5.   A
6.   B
7.   D
8.   D
9.   B
10.   B
11.   C
12.   C
13.   B
14.   A
15.   B
16.   D
17.   B
18.   B
19.   D
20.   A
21.   A
22.   B
23.   C
24.   C
25.   C

How Social Change Transforms Social Life

❋ **Four Social Revolutions**

❋ **From *Gemeinschaft* to *Gesellschaft***

❋ **Capitalism, Modernization, and**

Industrialization

Copyright © Allyn & Bacon 2008   Chapter 22: Social Change and the Environment   2

How Social Change Transforms Social Life

❋ **Social Movements**

❋ **Conflict, Power, and Global Politics**

   * From G-7 to (Almost) G-9

   * Dividing up the Worls

   * Two Threats to the G-8

   * Africa Connections

   * Information Technology

Copyright © Allyn & Bacon 2008   Chapter 22: Social Change and the Environment   3

Theories and Processes of Social Change

* **Cultural Evolution**
  * Unilinear
  * Multilinear
  * Cultural Progress
* **Natural Cycles**
* **Conflict Over Power**

Copyright © Allyn & Bacon 2008   Chapter 22: Social Change and the Environment

How Social Change Transforms Social Life

Marx's Model - Conflict Over Power

* **Thesis (Current Arrangement of Power)**
* **Antithesis (Contradiction)**
* **Synthesis (New Arrangement of Power)**
* **Classless State**

Copyright © Allyn & Bacon 2008   Chapter 22: Social Change and the Environment

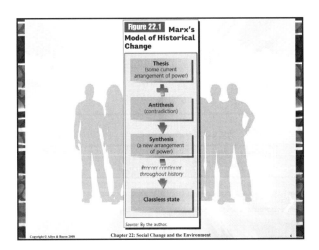

Figure 22.1 Marx's Model of Historical Change

Thesis (some current arrangement of power)

Antithesis (contradiction)

Synthesis (a new arrangement of power)

Process continues throughout history

Classless state

Source: By the author.

Copyright © Allyn & Bacon 2008   Chapter 22: Social Change and the Environment

Theories and Processes of Social Change

Ogburn's Theory

* Invention

* Discovery

* Diffusion

* Cultural Lag

Theories and Processes of Social Change

Evaluation of Ogburn's Theory

* Too Unidirectional

* The Way People Adapt to Technology Only Part of the Story

* However, He Never Said Technology was the Only Force for Social Change

How Technology Changes Society

* Technology is Tools and Skills

* Postmodern Societies Possess Technology that Greatly Extend Human Ability

The Social Significance of Technology

❋ **Changes in Social Organization**

❋ **Changes in Ideology**

❋ **Changes in Ostentatious Consumption**

❋ **Changes in Social Relationships**

Copyright © Allyn & Bacon 2008   Chapter 22: Social Change and the Environment   10

The Impact of the Automobile

❋ **Displacement of Existing Technology**

❋ **Effects on Cities**

❋ **Effects on Farm Life and Villages**

❋ **Changes in Architecture**

❋ **Changed Courtship and Sexual Norms**

❋ **Effects on Women's Roles**

Copyright © Allyn & Bacon 2008   Chapter 22: Social Change and the Environment   11

The Cutting Edge of Change

❋ **Computers in Education**

❋ **Computers in the Workplace**

❋ **Computers in Business and Finance**

❋ **Changes in the War**

Copyright © Allyn & Bacon 2008   Chapter 22: Social Change and the Environment   12

Cyberspace and Social Inequality

✳ **Access to Libraries of Information**

✳ **World Linked by Almost Instantaneous Communication**

✳ **National and Global Stratification**

Represents a Digital Divide

Copyright © Allyn & Bacon 2008   Chapter 22: Social Change and the Environment   13

_____

_____

_____

_____

_____

_____

_____

The Growth Machine vs. The Earth

✳ **Environmental Problems in the Most Industrialized Nations**

✳ **Industrial Growth at the Cost of Natural Environment**

✳ **Major Polluters in Most Industrialized Nations**

Copyright © Allyn & Bacon 2008   Chapter 22: Social Change and the Environment   14

_____

_____

_____

_____

_____

_____

Figure 22.2 The Worst Hazardous Waste Sites

Note: These are the waste sites so outstandingly threatening to public health that they made the national priority list. New Jersey is in a class by itself. This small state has 18 more hazardous waste sites than its nearest competition Pennsylvania, with 96.

Source: By the author. Based on Statistical Abstract of the United States 2007:Table 368.

Copyright © Allyn & Bacon 2008   Chapter 22: Social Change and the Environment   15

_____

_____

_____

_____

_____

_____

The Growth Machine vs. The Earth

❋ **Fossil Fuels and the Environment**

❋ Ozone Depletion

❋ Greenhouse Effect

❋ Global Warming

Chapter 22: Social Change and the Environment 16

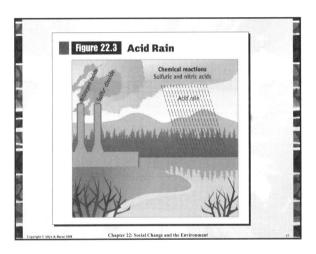

Figure 22.3 Acid Rain

Chapter 22: Social Change and the Environment 17

The Growth Machine vs. The Earth

❋ Fossil Fuels and the Environment

❋ The Energy Shortage and Multinational Corporations

❋ Environmental Injustice

Chapter 22: Social Change and the Environment 18

Environmental Problems in Industrializing and Least Industrialized Nations

* Exported Pollution from Industrialized Nations

* Destruction of Habitat

* Disappearance of Rain Forests

Copyright © Allyn & Bacon 2008   Chapter 22: Social Change and the Environment   19

_____

_____

_____

_____

_____

_____

_____

The Environmental Movement

* Green Political Parties

* Activists Seek Solutions in…

  * Politics

  * Education

  * Legislation

Copyright © Allyn & Bacon 2008   Chapter 22: Social Change and the Environment   20

_____

_____

_____

_____

_____

_____

_____

Environmental Sociology

Main Assumptions:

* Physical Environment a Significant Variable

* Human Beings Depend on Natural Environment

* Human Actions Have Unintended Consequences

* The World is Finite; Limits to Economic Growth

Copyright © Allyn & Bacon 2008   Chapter 22: Social Change and the Environment   21

_____

_____

_____

_____

_____

_____

_____

Environmental Sociology

Main Assumptions:

* **Economic Expansion Requires Extraction of Resources from Environment**
* **Increased Extractions Lead to Ecological Problems**
* **Ecological Problems Restrict Economic Expansion**
* **Governments Create Environmental Problems**

Copyright © Allyn & Bacon 2008   Chapter 22: Social Change and the Environment   22

Environmental Sociology

* **Technology and the Environment: The Goal of Harmony**

* **Abuse of Environment Not Inevitable**

* **Must Discover Ways to Reduce or Eliminate Harm to the Environment**

Copyright © Allyn & Bacon 2008   Chapter 22: Social Change and the Environment   23

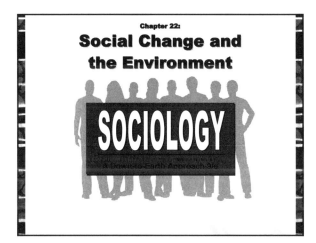

Chapter 22:
Social Change and the Environment

SOCIOLOGY

A Down-to-Earth Approach 9/e

NOTES

NOTES

NOTES

NOTES

NOTES

NOTES

NOTES

NOTES

NOTES

NOTES

NOTES

NOTES

NOTES

NOTES

NOTES

NOTES

NOTES